CW01455093

Linguistic Coping Strategies

Studies in Interpretation

Melanie Metzger and Earl Fleetwood, General Editors

Linguistic Coping Strategies in Sign Language Interpreting

Jemina Napier

GALLAUDET UNIVERSITY PRESS

Washington, DC

Studies in Interpretation
A Series Edited by Melanie Metzger and Earl Fleetwood

Gallaudet University Press
Washington, DC 20002
http://gupress.gallaudet.edu

© 2016 by Gallaudet University
All rights reserved. Published 2016
Printed in the United States of America

ISBN 978-156368-658-0
ISSN 1545-7613

♾ This paper meets the requirements of ANSI/NISO Z39.48-1992 (Permanence of Paper).

Contents

Acknowledgments

In addition to those people I specifically mention here, I would like to thank all my colleagues and friends for expressing an interest in my work and for encouraging me to apply my interpreting experience in an academic field.

In particular I would like to thank Mary Brennan, David Brien, Judith Collins, Margo Currie, Peter Llewellyn Jones, Liz Scott Gibson, and Maureen Reed, who lectured on my master's degree course and inspired me to want to conduct further research on interpreting. Additionally, thanks go to Graham H. Turner and Kyra Pollit for engaging with me in many a conversation about interpreting, both linguistic and otherwise, and for their encouragement of my academic pursuits.

Special thanks go to Robert Adam for helping me settle into a new country and for being my friend and colleague. Robert introduced me to Renwick College at the Royal NSW Institute for Deaf and Blind Children, where I was provided with an office. Therefore, I would also like to thank Greg Leigh and all other staff members at Renwick College for making me feel welcome, and I would like to thank Rod Beattie for helping me out with applications for funding and development of a survey instrument.

Further thanks go to Roz Barker and Trevor Johnston for their patience, diligence, and unfailing support as supervisors. Cynthia Roy became my mentor, and I thank her for her support and encouragement and for making me feel like I had something to offer.

For their financial support, I would particularly like to acknowledge the Australian Federal Government Department of Education, Training and Youth Affairs for the Commonwealth Scholarship that enabled me to move to Australia to study; the Victorian Services for Deaf Children for the grant that meant I could meet the expenses of my data collection and analysis; and the Macquarie University Postgraduate Research Fund and the Macquarie University Linguistics Department Postgraduate Research Fund for supporting my trip to the Conference of Interpreter Trainers (CIT) convention in 2000, where I was able to present my research

These acknowledgments are from the original 2002 book.

findings and get feedback. In addition, thanks to Renwick College and the Australian Sign Language Interpreters' Association (NSW) for their sponsorship of my attendance at the CIT (2002) convention to report the complete research findings.

I would like to thank all those people who were specifically involved in the research itself, namely, all the interpreters who responded to my survey; the ten interpreters who were involved in the analytical study; Colin Allen for being my research assistant; Adam Schembri and Della Goswell for doing reliability checks; Adam Schembri, Dani Fried, and Andy Carmichael for piloting the interpreting tasks; Caroline Conlon, Leonie Jackson, Trevor Maggs, and Darlene Thornton for being involved in the discussion panel; Michelle Maguire for interpreting the discussion panel; Peter Bonser and Viona Woodroffe for clarifying issues with regards to Auslan interpreters and interpreting; plus coordinators at all the Australian Deaf Society interpreting services, for helping me track down as many Auslan interpreters as possible.

I would like to give particular thanks to Adam Schembri, who gave me the idea for my research topic during one of our many discussions on linguistics and interpreting. He has been an excellent friend and colleague.

I would also like to thank all my family and friends for supporting me throughout the PhD research and adaptation of the book, including Melinda and Brian, Mark, Zoe, Karl, Bow, Cecy, Dylan, Adam and Joe, Amanda, Caroline, Colin, Della, Evie and Fabio, Peter and Michael, Robert, and Trevor, to name but a few.

Last, but by no means least, thanks to Andy Carmichael for making me believe in myself. I'd like to think that I could have done it anyway, but I really don't think that I could. Without you being there to share with, it wouldn't have been half as rewarding.

Prologue

> When you know a language, you can speak to and be understood by others who know that language. This means you have the capacity to produce sounds that signify certain meanings and to understand or interpret the sounds produced by others. . . . Deaf persons produce and understand sign languages just as hearing persons produce and understand spoken languages (Fromkin, Rodman, Collins, & Blair, 1990, pp. 3–4).

Speculations over the number of languages used throughout the world have varied from 3,000 to 10,000, with the most regular evaluations citing numbers of 4,000 or 5,000 (Crystal, 1987). In addition to this, it has been estimated that half of the world's population can speak more than one language (Grosjean, 1982). The other half of the world's population, however, is monolingual. Typically it is these people who would rely on translators and interpreters for any formal contact and dialogue with persons from different languages and cultures. Yet, although a large proportion of people in the world may have the ability to use more than one language, very few of them will have the competence to effectively translate between two languages (Grosjean, 1997).

TRANSLATING AND INTERPRETING

> Translation is often used as a generic term to refer to the transfer of thoughts and ideas from one language (source) to another language (target) regardless of the form of either language (written, spoken, or signed). When the form of the source language is either spoken or signed, the transfer process is referred to as interpretation (Brislin, 1976; cited in Cokely, 1992a, p. 1).

It can be seen from the above quote that the term *language* is pivotal in understanding what is meant by the translating and interpreting process. This is a supposition that anybody can make, and it is consistently referred to in the literature related to the field of translation and interpretation. Accompanying the initial supposition is an additional assumption that any translator or interpreter must be equally fluent in the languages they work with. In order to transfer thoughts and ideas from one language to another, however, it is not enough to just have bilingual fluency.

Bilingualism

Several writers have considered the difference between bilingual competence and translational competence (see Baetens Beardsmore, 1986; Hoffman, 1991; Isham & Lane, 1994; Romaine, 1995). Grosjean (1997) studied bilingual individuals and stated that few bilinguals are proficient translators and interpreters. He listed certain factors that can influence a person's ability to perform as an interpreter. These factors may include unequal fluency in both languages; an accent in the second language; late acquisition or learning of the second language; lack of stylistic varieties in each language; undeveloped transfer skills; or lack of pragmatic competence and cultural knowledge about the two distinct groups. Grosjean made the distinction between a *regular bilingual* and a *distinct* or *interpreter bilingual*, by clearly stating that "interpreter bilinguals, unlike regular bilinguals, will have to learn to use their languages (and the underlying skills that they have in them) for similar purposes, in similar domains of life, with similar people. This is something that regular bilinguals do not often need to do" (p. 168). It can be seen, therefore, that although balanced fluency in at least two languages is essential, translators and interpreters are required to have a wide range of knowledge and skills in order to effectively transfer messages between two different languages.

Interpreting Skills

According to Frishberg (1990), the art of interpretation requires "an understanding of the dynamics of human interaction . . . an appreciation of social and cultural differences, the ability to concentrate and maintain one's attention, a good deal of tact, judgment, stamina, and above all a sense of humor" (p. 3), as well as competence in at least two languages. The knowledge and skills listed above are only a few from the gamut of those that translators and interpreters are expected to develop prior to, and maintain throughout, their career in order to effectively transfer a message from one language and culture to another. Other desired components of an interpreter's repertoire include the following, derived from various sources on translating and interpreting: interpersonal skills; public speaking skills; advocacy skills; "listening" skills; effective short- and long-term memory; cognitive information processing skills; analytical skills; contextual knowledge; world knowledge; specialist knowledge; professionalism; flexibility; objectivity; self-discipline; responsibility; acting skills; independence; motivation; willingness to learn; self-confidence; ability to deal with situations encountered while interpreting; awareness of one's own limitations; and ability to provide peer support (Frishberg, 1990; Napier, 1998a; Neumann Solow, 1981, 2000; Schein & Delk, 1974; Seleskovitch, 1978). After reading this extensive catalog of interpreter skills requirements, it is possible to discern why Grosjean (1997) and others have determined that bilingualism alone is insufficient to guarantee effective interpreting skills.

TERMINOLOGY

In order to facilitate any discussion on interpreting, it is important to clarify terms that are familiar to those working in the field and that are consistently referred to throughout this book. These include key terms that are widely recognized by interpreters, interpreter researchers, and interpreter educators. The following paragraphs present the most common terms compiled from several sources (Frishberg, 1990; Neumann Solow, 1981, 2000; Seleskovitch, 1978; Simon, 1994).

It is important to recognize the fact that interpreters work between two languages. Any research on interpreting needs to specify the difference between the language from which the message originates (*source language*) and the language into which the message is rendered (*target language*). The term *translation* can refer either to the process of changing a written text in one language to a written text in another language, or to the process of translation and interpretation between source and target languages. The term *interpretation*, however, refers specifically to the process of changing a message produced in one language into another language, regardless of whether the two languages are spoken or signed (e.g., English to Spanish, Spanish to Spanish Sign Language, Spanish Sign Language to Australian

Sign Language[1]). With regard to the person who provides an interpretation, the term *interpreter* is used generically throughout this book since it is the most common referent for people working with two or more languages.

The interpretation process can occur consecutively or simultaneously. *Consecutive interpretation* involves the interpreter providing the interpretation after the speaker or signer has finished the presentation of their message, which may occur after a phrase, a concept, or an entire speech. Alternatively, *simultaneous interpretation* is a process whereby the interpreter renders the message at almost the same time it is conveyed by the speaker or signer. There is often a short delay, called *decalage* or *lag time*, since the interpreter needs time to hear or see the original utterance before being able to process it.

Various studies of interpreting provide discussion from a psycholinguistic or sociolinguistic perspective, yet it seems that these terms are sometimes used differently in interpreter research literature. Interpreting literature tends to regard psycholinguistic and sociolinguistic analysis of interpreting as distinct processes, rather than just labels for subdisciplines in linguistics that are not necessarily mutually exclusive. *Psycholinguistic analysis* of interpreting refers to the cognitive processes involved in interpreting and the language processing that takes place (Ingram, 1985; Lörscher, 1996; Tweney, 1978). *Sociolinguistic analysis*, however, refers to the consideration given to linguistic and cultural factors that may influence interpreters in the language choices they make (Cokely, 1985, 1992a; Pergnier, 1978; Roy, 1989a, 1992, 1996, 2000a). Although this book touches occasionally on psycholinguistic issues related to interpreting, it is essentially reporting a sociolinguistic study of sign language interpreters.

Interpreters who work between a spoken and signed language tend not to engage in the task of written translation because signed languages are visual-gestural languages with no standard written orthography.[2] Sign language interpreters usually work simultaneously as there is no conflict between two languages being vocalized one over top of the other, and they cannot realistically take notes in order to interpret large consecutive chunks of information because they use their hands to interpret.

---

1. Hereafter referred to as Auslan.

2. In 2016 this concept has been updated due to video capabilities to record and preserve, sign language translations. See Warm (2014).

As interpreters work between two languages, any discussion of interpreters and interpreting should typically refer to both the languages being used (for example, an Auslan/ English interpreter). This book incorporates discussion of interpretation between different sign languages, predominantly American Sign Language (ASL) and British Sign Language (BSL), and spoken English, as well as referring to interpreters of other spoken languages. For the purposes of expediency, however, references in this book will be to interpreters by the sign language, or language other than English, that they use. For example, Auslan/English interpreters will be referred to as Auslan interpreters, ASL/English or BSL/English interpreters as ASL or BSL interpreters, and French/English or Russian/ English interpreters as French or Russian interpreters.

Another convention that is used is in relation to gender reference. It is widely recognized that interpreters can be either male or female. The majority of sign language interpreters, however, are women (Atwood & Gray, 1985; Stewart, Schein, & Cartwright, 1998). Therefore, again for expediency, in any discussion of interpreters throughout this book, if the gender of an interpreter is irrelevant, the pronoun *she* will be used.

SIGN LANGUAGE INTERPRETING: AN EMERGING PROFESSION

Sign language interpreting has often been referred to as an "emerging profession" (Fenton, 1993; Scott Gibson, 1992). There is a dearth of research in this area and little status afforded to those who choose to work in the field. To date, North America has been at the forefront of professional development, with formal recognition of sign language interpreting as a profession in 1964 (Quigley, 1965), followed by the establishment of the Registry of Interpreters for the Deaf (RID), the provision of specific training courses for sign language interpreters, and professional development for the trainers of interpreters under the umbrella of the Conference of Interpreter Trainers (CIT), which was established in 1979 (Simon, 1994).

As a result of the professionalization of sign language interpreting in North America, research studies of ASL interpreting first began to appear in the mid-1970s (Carter & Lauritsen, 1974; Dicker, 1976; Domingue & Ingram, 1978; Nowell & Stuckless, 1974; Sternberg, Tipton & Schein, 1973). The North Americans were closely followed by British researchers, writing about sign language interpreting as a unique language process (Hough, 1981; Kyle & Woll, 1985; Llewellyn Jones, 1981a, 1981b). Several writings on sign language interpreting emerged from other countries, such as Belgium (Demanez, 1987), Germany (Donath, 1987), Scandinavia (Hansen, 1991; Hassinen & Lehtomaki, 1986), and Japan (Kamata et al, 1989), to name but a few. Literature on sign language interpreting only began to appear in Australia, however, in the mid- to late-1990s (Bremner & Housden, 1996; Madden 2001; Ozolins & Bridge, 1999). Since the recognition of sign language interpreting as a profession, many researchers have carried out studies on various aspects of interpreting between signed and spoken languages, yet there is still a dearth of literature in the area.

AN INNOVATIVE STUDY OF SIGN LANGUAGE INTERPRETERS

This book discusses the findings of an innovative study of interpreters working between English and Auslan, and explores how the findings can be equally applied among sign language interpreters working with other sign languages, and possibly to spoken language interpreters. The study focused on Auslan interpreters working in a university lecture. Through informal discussion with members of the Australian Sign Language Interpreters Association (ASLIA), it was noted that many Auslan inter- preters have not completed a university education or undergone any interpreter training, yet they regularly work in universities. Observations of, and discussions with, counterparts in the sign language interpreting professions in other countries such as the UK and the US also revealed similar circumstances. This situation obviously raises many questions in relation to language fluency (both comprehension and production), ser- vice provision, ethical practice, the impact upon the educational experi- ences of Deaf people,[3] and the implications for the education and training

---

3. Any discussion involving Deaf people concentrates specifically on those peo- ple who use sign language as their first or preferred language and who perceive themselves as members of a linguistic and cultural minority group, as opposed to persons with a hearing loss. This follows the convention first proposed by Woodward (1972) and later developed by Padden (1980) of using the uppercase D

of sign language interpreters. Two key issues to consider are the types of linguistic coping strategies used by sign language interpreters while interpreting for university lectures and the impact the interpreters' formal educational background might have on their use of such strategies.

Coping strategies can be defined as those methods or techniques adopted by interpreters to ensure that they are best equipped to cope with the variety of different factors that may impact their interpreting. There are various sources of demand on interpreters that arise from linguistic factors associated with the languages being used and nonlinguistic factors, such as environmental, interpersonal, and intrapersonal demands (Dean & Pollard, 2001). In general, coping strategies can be considered as those strategies used by interpreters to deal with the demands placed upon them by nonlinguistic factors such as working in teams and preparation techniques. Linguistic coping strategies, however, are those strategies that specifically deal with the linguistic factors that influence an interpretation. Examples of linguistic coping strategies used by interpreters would include the application of linguistic and cultural knowledge, communication management, translation style, the use of linguistic transference, and the use of additions, substitutions, and omissions within an interpretation.

This book reports on sign language interpreters' translation style and omission production as linguistic coping strategies while interpreting a university lecture, and the extent to which educational background influenced translation style and the number and types of omissions produced.

ORGANIZATION OF THE BOOK

In order to place this study within the wider scene of linguistic and interpreting research, it is worthwhile to examine and discuss theoretical and empirical literature that focuses on sociolinguistic issues relevant to interpreting, especially those specifically pertinent to sign language

---

to signify a Deaf identity. Whenever "hearing" people are mentioned, this refers to the majority of people in society who do not have any kind of hearing loss and who are not necessarily familiar with the Deaf community, its culture, and the concept of a Deaf identity.

interpreting. Chapter one concentrates on sociolinguistic and sociocultural contexts of interpreting, thus providing a wider context for those significant influences on a sign language interpreter's ability to interpret a university lecture effectively. The beginning of the chapter introduces a framework for interpreting, providing an overview of information that is fundamental to understanding the study, with a focus on the interpreting process, models of interpreting, and interpreting techniques. Comparisons are then made between spoken and signed language interpreters in relation to bilingualism and the bimodality of sign language interpreting. Finally, chapter one discusses the discourse environment factors to consider, including the university lecture as a discourse genre, situational variance of language register, typical language features of university lecture text, and the challenges faced by sign language interpreters when interpreting this kind of text.

Chapter two goes on to discuss the notion of coping strategies used by interpreters, reviewing relevant research studies and thus defining linguistic coping strategies, the use of translation style and omissions as linguistic coping strategies, and the concept of metalinguistic awareness. Chapter three provides an overview of discourse-specific studies on interpreting relevant to the study, namely conference and educational interpreting. Chapter four details the analysis of linguistic coping strategies by describing the methodology of the study. A technique for defining lexical density of language is introduced, and an "omission taxonomy" used to analyze the participants' interpretations is outlined.

Chapter five discusses the findings of the study using transcribed extracts from the videotaped interpreting task. Finally, chapter six provides a discussion of the issues to consider as a consequence of the research findings in relation to the linguistic coping strategies of interpreters working in a university lecture, and it presents the perspective of Deaf university students and their expectations as consumers of interpreting services. Chapter six also discusses the implications of this research in relation to sign language interpreter training and education, followed by discussion of the wider implications of this study regarding interpreting in different contexts. The chapter concludes with suggestions for future research.

Introduction to the Second Edition

Linguistic Coping Strategies:

Fifteen Years Later

In 2002, Douglas McLean published a revised version of my PhD dissertation as *Sign Language Interpreting: Linguistic Coping Strategies*. This text is now widely used in interpreter training programs all over the world. I have received feedback from interpreter educators, practitioners, and students alike telling me how much they value the book; they have even called it a practitioner's "bible."

The book and other publications drawing from the research have been widely cited by researchers in signed language interpreting (e.g., Goswell, 2012; Leeson, 2005; Roy & Metzger, 2014; Stone, 2009; Wang, 2013), and also by researchers in spoken language interpreting (e.g., Bartłomiejczyk, 2006; Pöchhacker, 2004). Metzger (2006, p. 283) states that the study has "significant implications regarding interpreter practice, the training of interpreters, and raise[s] questions for further research." Thus, when Douglas McLean released the rights to the book, I thought it worthwhile to keep it in print. However, since the research is now 15 years old, it is important to contextualize my work with an update of other research conducted since 2001 that may have built upon or complemented this original piece of research.

In studying the linguistic coping strategies sign language interpreters employed during a university lecture in Australia, I focused on four main areas.

1. An analysis of the *translation style* used by the interpreters and the relationship between their familiarity with university discourse and the translation style that they chose (see also Napier, 2002a, 2002c, 2005a);
2. An analysis of the *interpreting omissions* produced with respect to the lexical density of the text and the use of academic English and subject-specific terminology (see also Napier, 2003, 2004);

3. An analysis of the interpreters' reflections on their decision-making strategies (their *metalinguistic awareness*), which informed the types of omissions they produced (see also Napier & Barker, 2004b);
4. An exploration of Deaf university students' perceptions and preferences of interpreters' linguistic choices and use of translation style when interpreting university lectures (see also Napier & Barker, 2004a).

My study was similar to Locker's (1990) research in the United States (US), where she also elicited the perceptions of Deaf college students. But Locker focused on comparing the perceived differences between transliteration and interpretation, terms that were previously defined in the US as being distinct and separate practices (e.g., Livingston, Singer, & Abrahamson, 1994; Siple, 1995, 1996; Sofinski, 2003; Sofinski, Yesback, Gerhold, & Bach-Hansen, 2001; Winston, 1989; Winston & Monikowski, 2003).[1] But these distinct terms are used less in the literature now. Metzger (1995, 1999) had previously discussed notions of free and literal interpretation in her study of interpreters' footing shifts in mediating medical consultations. My study presents the first evidence of how interpreters can blend free and literal translation approaches, how each translation style operates on a continuum, and how interpreters may deliberately move between the different styles.

In building on Newmark's (1987, 1991) discussion of free and literal translation with respect to spoken/written languages, I adopted a functionalist approach to translation and interpreting that draws on systemic functional linguistics (Halliday, 1985, 1993, 1994), and I suggested that interpreters can have a dominant or extremely dominant translation style. I also borrowed from the sociolinguistic concept of language contact that has been used to discuss the features of sign language when a spoken and a signed language (or two signed languages) come into contact (see Adam, 2012; Lucas & Valli, 1989, 1990). Thus this study complements Davis's examination of how interpreters work in a language contact situation and his discussion of *cross-linguistic strategies* used by interpreters and when they adopt language contact strategies and borrow from

---

1. In fact the Registry of Interpreters for the Deaf (RID) in the US previously provided certifications in either Interpretation or Transliteration.

English into American Sign Language as a deliberate interpreting strategy (Davis, 1990a, 1990b 2003, 2005).

Furthermore, I described a form of *translational contact* where interpreters can move between the different translation styles within the same piece of interpretation and make deliberate linguistic choices according to their knowledge and understanding of the *context of situation* (Halliday & Hasan, 1985). Essentially, this means that interpreters make decisions based on who they know is in the audience, their assumptions about the needs of the audience, and the clues they receive from the audience. This aligns with other theoretical frameworks that have been applied in studies of interpreting, such as *audience design* (Mason, 2000) and *relevance theory* (Sperber & Wilson, 1986).[2] Relevance theory, in particular, has been used as a framework for analyzing spoken/written translation and interpreting (Blakemore & Gallai, 2014; Gutt, 2000) and also sign language interpreting (Stone, 2009), in relation to interpreters' decisions about meeting audience needs.

My original research also opened up a new discussion in the sign language interpreting sector with respect to how omissions may not necessarily be erroneous. When Franz Pöchhacker asked me in 2013 to contribute an entry on *omissions* to the new *Routledge Encyclopedia of Interpreting Studies* (Pöchhacker, 2015), I queried whether someone else who had conducted more recent research might be better placed to write the entry. Pöchhacker responded that my study was still the most advanced work on the subject (Pöchhacker, personal communication, 13 May 2013). So it would appear, that although this study is 15 years old, it is still a reference point for spoken and signed language interpreting research and the consideration of interpreting omissions.

The key to my discussion of omissions is the proposal that interpreters can reflect on, and potentially decide strategically, how and why to omit information. This idea was not necessarily new. Spoken language interpreting researchers had already suggested definitions for omissions that are produced deliberately and strategically as part of an interpreter's cognitive decision-making process. Barik (1975) studied the number and type of omissions in relation to text type and directionality, and he proposed

---

2. Relevance theory was first developed by Sperber and Wilson with respect to direct communication in the same language.

a taxonomy that distinguished between four types of omissions: *skipping* (of a single lexical item); *comprehension* (omission of a larger unit of meaning, as a result of an inability to comprehend the source language message); *delay* (omission of a larger unit of meaning, due to lagging too far behind the speaker); and *compounding* (conjoining elements from different clauses or sentences). These omissions have also been referred to as *condensing strategies* (Sunnari, 1995), *selective reductions* (Hatim & Mason, 1990), and *compression strategies* (Chernov, 2004). But it was a new idea in sign language interpreting studies.

Cokely (1992a, 1992b) extended Barik's work to sign language interpreter output and only recently have sign language interpreter researchers begun to study directionality (Nicodemus & Emmorey, 2015; Wang & Napier, 2016). Cokely developed a *miscue taxonomy*, in which he defined morphological, lexical, and cohesive omissions as miscue types. He then applied his miscue taxonomy to a study of the effects of lag time on interpreter errors (1992b). He found that lexical omissions were the most prevalent, followed by cohesive omissions and a much smaller number of morphological omissions. The interpreters who had a shorter lag time made more omissions than those with a longer lag time, with over twice as many total miscues.

What was particularly new from my study was the idea that every interpretation contains *omission potential*. I borrowed from Halliday's (1978) term *meaning potential* (which has been discussed by Hatim & Mason [1990] with respect to interpreters) to explain that interpreters can ignore the form of the message and focus entirely on the meaning, that interpreters can explore a range of semantic choices in order to achieve meaning, and that every message has a potentially different meaning depending on the context of the situation. In the same way, I suggested that interpreters can consider the omission potential of any text, in that the omissions produced by interpreters may change depending on the context of the situation, and that interpreting students can be taught specifically to examine the types of conscious omissions they produce and to identify the omission potential of texts (Napier, 2005b).

Whereas all the studies reported here analyze monologic interpretations in one language direction, Wadensjö's (1998) work gives an account of omissions in interpreter-mediated communication in dialogic contexts. While incorporating similar components to those of Barik and Cokely, she uses alternative terminology with more positive connotations. In her taxonomy, she defines three types of *rendition* that could be considered as omissions: *reduced renditions* (information expressed less explicitly than in the original), *summarized renditions* (text corresponding to two or more prior originals), and *zero renditions* (an original utterance that is not translated). Wadensjö stresses that the interpreter's renditions must be considered within the whole context of the dialogic interaction, as interpreters aim to produce contextually, linguistically, and culturally appropriate utterances that meet the communicative goals of the original speakers.[3]

More recently, various authors suggest that omissions can be considered from a pragmatic perspective, whereby they are treated as conscious decisions made by the interpreter rather than mistakes resulting from miscomprehension. Bartłomiejczyk (2006) examines strategic omissions in relation to directionality, and Pym (2008) suggests that omissions can be considered low risk or high risk, depending on their potential detrimental impact.

My third focus area was the *metalinguistic awareness* that interpreters have with respect to their interpreting decisions. This topic has been further explored by other sign language interpreter researchers and practitioners (e.g., Lakner & Turner, 2015). During retrospective interviews, I tapped into the metalinguistic awareness of my study participants by asking them to reflect on and self-analyze their interpreting output, translation styles, and production of omissions. The results revealed that the interpreter participants had a high level of metalinguistic awareness about their own work. This approach has also been adopted by other researchers in the form of *think aloud protocols* (Russell & Winston, 2014; Stone, 2009), and educators have acknowledged that it is important for practitioners to engage in *reflection* (Ganz Horwitz, 2014; Goswell, 2012), and *reflective practice* (Dean & Pollard, 2013; Hetherington, 2012).

The final study area examines the perspectives of Deaf university students with respect to the nature of sign language interpreting in university lectures. In my study, four Deaf people participated in a panel (focus group) discussion where they commented on their interpreting preferences after viewing two videotaped segments of university lecture interpretation, one demonstrating a predominantly free approach and the other a predominantly literal approach. I explored the Deaf students'

---

3. See Major and Napier (2012) for the application of Wadensjö's rendition categories to the analysis of sign language interpreting in healthcare dialogues.

expectations in relation to the educational backgrounds and qualifications of university interpreters; and the students' level of comprehension of interpretations.

I have explored the perspectives of Deaf consumers on interpreters and interpreting in relation to access to healthcare information (Major, Napier, Ferrara, & Johnston, 2012; Napier & Kidd, 2013; Napier, Major, Ferrara, & Johnston, 2014; Napier & Sabolcec, 2014), with respect to video remote interpreting (Napier 2012; Napier & Leneham, 2011; Skinner, Turner, Napier, & Wheatley, submitted for publication), in educational interpreting (Carty, Leigh, Goswell, & Napier, submitted for publication), and in my other research more generally (Napier, 2011; Napier & Rohan, 2007). The perspective of Deaf consumers has been further examined by sign language interpreter researchers in other countries, including Canada (Stratiy, 2005), the Netherlands (De Wit & Sluis, 2014), and the United States (Forestal, 2005; Kurz & Langer, 2004).

Aspects of my study have been, or are now being, replicated in sign language interpreting studies by graduate students (e.g., De Wit, 2010; Heyerick, 2014; Kauling, 2015). It is my hope that by keeping this book in print, the study will continue to inform interpreting students, educators, practitioners, and researchers of spoken and signed language interpreting.

ACKNOWLEDGMENTS

I am grateful to Melanie Metzger and Earl Fleetwood, the co-editors of the Studies in Interpretation series, for choosing to include this book in that series. I would like to thank Doug McLean for releasing the copyright of the book to me so that I could work with Gallaudet University Press to ensure that the book could remain in print.

REFERENCES

Adam, R. (2012). Language contact and borrowing. In R. Pfau, M. Steinbach, & B. Woll (Eds.), *Sign language: An international handbook* (pp. 841–861). Berlin, Germany: De Gruyter Mouton.

Barik, H. A. (1975). Simultaneous interpretation: Qualitative and linguistic data. *Language and Speech, 18,* 272–297.

Bartłomiejczyk, M. (2006) Strategies of simultaneous interpreting and direction-ality. *Interpreting, 8*(2), 149–174.

Blakemore, D., & Gallai, F. (2014). Discourse markers in free indirect style and interpreting. *Journal of Pragmatics 60*, 106–120.

Carty, B., Leigh, G., Goswell, D., & Napier, J. (2015). *Teachers' interactions with deaf students in sign language interpreted classrooms: Use of questions.* Manuscript submitted for publication.

Chernov, G. V. (2004). *Inference and anticipation in simultaneous interpreting: A probability-prediction model.* Amsterdam, Netherlands: John Benjamins.

Cokely, D. (1992a). Effects of lag time on interpreter errors. In D. Cokely (Ed.), *Sign language interpreters and interpreting* (pp. 39–69). Burtonsville, MD: Linstok Press.

Cokely, D. (1992b). *Interpretation: A sociolinguistic model.* Burtonsville, MD: Linstok Press.

Davis, J. (1990a). *Interpreting in a language contact situation: The case of English-to-ASL interpretation* (Unpublished doctoral dissertation). University of New Mexico, Albuquerque.

Davis, J. (1990b). Linguistic transference and interference: Interpreting between English and ASL. In C. Lucas (Ed., *Sign language research: Theoretical issues* (pp. 308–321). Washington, DC: Gallaudet University Press.

Davis, J. (2003). Cross-linguistic strategies used by interpreters. *Journal of Interpretation*, 95–128.

Davis, J. (2005). Code choices and consequences: Implications for educational interpreting. In M. Marschark, R. Peterson, & E. A. Winston (Eds.), *Interpreting and interpreter education: Directions for research and practice* (pp. 112–141). New York, NY: Oxford University Press.

Dean, R. K., & Pollard, R. Q. (2013). *The demand control schema: Interpreting as a practice profession.* North Charleston, SC: CreateSpace.

De Wit, M. (2010). *Linguistic coping strategies from International Sign to English* (Unpublished master's research essay). Heriot-Watt University, Edinburgh, Scotland.

De Wit, M., & Sluis, I. (2014). Sign language interpreter quality: The perspective of deaf sign language users in the Netherlands. *The Interpreter's Newsletter, 19*, 63–85.

Forestal, L. (2005). Attitudes of deaf leaders toward signed language interpreters and interpreting. In M. Metzger & E. Fleetwood (Eds.), *Attitudes, innuendo, and regulators: Challenges of interpretation* (pp. 71–91). Washington, DC: Gallaudet University Press.

Ganz Horwitz, M. (2014). Demands and strategies of interpreting a theatrical performance into American Sign Language. *Journal of Interpretation, 23*(1), Article 4. Retrieved from http://digitalcommons.unf.edu/joi/vol23/iss1/4

Goswell, D. (2012). Do you see what I see? Using ELAN for self-analysis and reflection. *International Journal of Interpreter Education, 4*(1), 73–82.

Gutt, E. (2000). *Translation and relevance: Cognition and context.* Manchester, United Kingdom: St. Jerome.

Halliday, M. A. K. (1985). *Spoken and written language.* Burwood, Victoria, Australia: Deakin University Press.

Halliday, M. A. K. (1993). *Language in a changing world.* Burwood, Victoria, Australia: Applied Linguistics Association of Australia, Deakin University.

Halliday, M. A. K. (1994). *An introduction to functional grammar.* London, United Kingdom: Edward Arnold.

Halliday, M. A. K., & Hasan, R. (1985). *Language, context and text: Aspects of language in a social semiotic perspective.* Burwood, Victoria, Australia: Deakin University Press.

Hatim, B., & Mason, I. (1990). *Discourse and the translator.* London, United Kingdom: Longman.

Hetherington, A. (2012). Supervision and the interpreting profession: Support and accountability through reflective practice. *International Journal of Interpreter Education, 4*(1), 46–57.

Heyerick, I. (2014). *Linguistic interpreting strategies: Designing a research methodology* (Unpublished master's dissertation). KU Leuven, Belgium.

Kauling, E. (2015). *From omission to mission: The influence of preparation and background knowledge on omissions in the sign language interpretation of a university lecture* (Unpublished master's dissertation). Heriot-Watt University, Edinburgh, Scotland.

Kurz, K. B., & Langer, E. C. (2004). Student perspectives on educational interpreting: Twenty deaf and hard of hearing students offer insights and suggestions. In E. Winston (Ed.), *Educational interpreting: How it can succeed* (pp. 9–47). Washington, DC: Gallaudet University Press.

Lakner, K., & Turner, G. H. (2015). Connecting research and practice to create digital resources for sign language interpreters: Professional development through knowledge exchange. In S. Ehrlich, & J. Napier (Eds.), *Interpreter education in the digital age: Innovation, access, and change* (pp. 209–227). Washington, DC: Gallaudet University Press.

Leeson, L. (2005). Making the effort in simultaneous interpreting: Some considerations for signed language interpreters. In T. Janzen (Ed.), *Topics in signed language interpreting* (pp. 51–68). Amsterdam, Netherlands: John Benjamins.

Livingston, S., Singer, B., & Abramson, T. (1994). Effectiveness compared: ASL interpretation versus transliteration. *Sign Language Studies, 82,* 1–54.

Locker, R. (1990). Lexical equivalence in transliterating for deaf students in the university classroom: Two perspectives. *Issues in Applied Linguistics, 1*(2), 167–195.

Lucas, C., & Valli, C. (1989). Language contact in the American Deaf community. In C. Lucas (Ed.), *The sociolinguistics of the Deaf community* (pp. 11–40). San Diego, CA: Academic Press.

Lucas, C., & Valli, C. (1990). ASL, English, and contact signing. In C. Lucas (Ed.), *Sign language research: Theoretical issues* (pp. 288–307). Washington, DC: Gallaudet University Press.

Major, G., & Napier, J. (2012). Interpreting and knowledge mediation in the healthcare setting: What do we really mean by "accuracy"? In V. Montalt & M. Shuttleworth (Eds.), *Linguistica Antiverpiesa Series: No. 11. Translation and knowledge mediation in medical and health settings* (pp. 207–226). Antwerp, Belgium: Artesius University College.

Major, G., Napier, J., Ferrara, L., & Johnston, T. (2012). Exploring lexical gaps in Australian Sign Language for the purposes of health communication. *Communication & Medicine, 9*(1), 37–47.

Mason, I. (2000). Audience design in translating. *The Translator, 6*(1), 1–22.

Metzger, M. (1995). *The paradox of neutrality: A comparison of interpreters' goals with the reality of interactive discourse* (Unpublished doctoral dissertation). Georgetown University, Washington, DC.

Metzger, M. (1999). *Sign language interpreting: Deconstructing the myth of neutrality.* Washington, DC: Gallaudet University Press.

Metzger, M. (2006). Salient studies of signed language interpreting in the context of community interpreting scholarship. In E. Hertog & B. van der Veer (Eds.), *Linguistica Antiverpiensia Series: No. 5. Taking stock: Research and methodology in community interpreting* (pp. 263–291). Antwerp, Belgium: Hogeschool Antwerpen, Hoger Instituut voor Vertalers en Tolken.

Napier, J. (2001). *Linguistic coping strategies of sign language interpreters* (Unpublished doctoral dissertation). Macquarie University, Sydney, Australia.

Napier, J. (2002a). *Sign language interpreting: Linguistic coping strategies.* Coleford, United Kingdom Douglas McLean.

Napier, J. (2002b). Linguistic coping strategies of interpreters: An exploration. *Journal of Interpretation,* 63–92.

Napier, J. (2002c). University interpreting: Linguistic issues for consideration. *Journal of Deaf Studies and Deaf Education, 7*(4), 281–301.

Napier, J. (2003). A sociolinguistic analysis of the occurrence and types of omissions produced by Australian Sign Language/English interpreters. In M. Metzger, S. Collins, V. Dively, & R. Shaw (Eds.), *From topic boundaries to omission: Research on interpretation* (pp. 99–153). Washington, DC: Gallaudet University Press.

Napier, J. (2004) Interpreting omissions: A new perspective. *Interpreting 6*(2), 117–142.

Napier, J. (2005a). Linguistic features and strategies of interpreting: From research to education to practice. In M. Marschark, R. Peterson, & E. A. Winston (Eds.), *Interpreting and interpreter education: Directions for research and practice* (pp. 84–111). New York, NY: Oxford University Press.

Napier, J. (2005b). Teaching interpreters to identify omission potential. In C. Roy (Ed.), *Advances in teaching sign language interpreters* (pp. 123–137). Washington, DC: Gallaudet University Press.

Napier, J. (2011). "It's not what they say but the way they say it." A content analysis of interpreter and consumer perceptions of signed language interpreting in Australia. *International Journal of the Sociology of Language, 207*, 59–87.

Napier, J. (2012). Exploring themes in stakeholder perspectives of video remote interpreting in court. In C. J. Kellett (Ed.), *Interpreting across genres: Multiple research perspectives* (pp. 219–254). Trieste, Italy: EUT Edizioni Universtà di Trieste.

Napier, J. (2015). Omissions. In F. Pöchhacker (Ed.), *Routledge Encyclopedia of Interpreting Studies* (pp. 289–291). London, United Kingdom: Routledge.

Napier, J., & Barker, R. (2004a). Accessing university education: Perceptions, preferences, and expectations for interpreting by deaf students. *Journal of Deaf Studies and Deaf Education, 9*(2), 228–238.

Napier, J., & Barker, R. (2004b). Sign language interpreting: The relationship between metalinguistic awareness and the production of interpreting omissions. *Sign Language Studies, 4*(4), 369–393.

Napier, J., & Kidd, M. (2013). English literacy as a barrier to healthcare information for deaf people who use Auslan. *Australian Family Physician, 42*(12), 896–899.

Napier, J., & Leneham, M. (2011). "It was difficult to manage the communication": Testing the feasibility of video remote signed language interpreting in courts in NSW, Australia. *Journal of Interpretation, 21*, 53–62.

Napier, J., Major, G., Ferrara, L., & Johnston, T. (2014). Medical Signbank as a model for sign language planning? A review of community engagement. *Current Issues in Language Planning, 15*, 279–295. doi: 10.1080/14664208.2014.972536

Napier, J., & Rohan, M. (2007). An invitation to dance: Deaf consumers' perceptions of signed language interpreters and interpreting. In M. Metzger & E. Fleetwood (Eds.), *Translation, sociolinguistic, and consumer issues in interpreting* (pp. 159–203). Washington, DC: Gallaudet University Press.

Napier, J., & Sabolcec, J. (2014). Direct, translated, or interpreter-mediated? A qualitative study of access to preventative and on-going healthcare information for Australian Deaf people. In B. Nicodemus & M. Metzger (Eds.), *Investigations in healthcare interpreting* (pp. 51–89). Washington, DC: Gallaudet University Press.

Newmark, P. (1987). *A textbook of translation*. London, United Kingdom: Longman.

Newmark, P. (1991). *About translation*. Clevedon, United Kingdom: Multilingual Matters.

Nicodemus, B., & Emmorey, K. (2015). Directionality in ASL–English interpreting: Accuracy and articulation quality in L1 and L2. *Interpreting, 17*(2), 145–166.

Nord, C. (1997). *Translating as a purposeful activity: Functionalist approaches explained*. Manchester, United Kingdom: St. Jerome Publishing.

Pöchhacker, F. (2004). *Introducing interpreting studies*. London, United Kingdom: Routledge.

Pöchhacker, F. (Ed.). (2015). *Routledge Encyclopedia of Interpreting Studies*. London, United Kingdom: Routledge.

Pym, A. (2008). On omission in simultaneous interpreting: Risk analysis of a hidden effort. In G. Hansen, A. Chesterman, & H. Gerzymisch-Arbogast (Eds.), *Efforts and models in interpreting and translation research: A tribute to Daniel Gile* (pp. 83–105). Amsterdam, Netherlands: John Benjamins.

Roy, C., & Metzger, M. (2014). Researching signed language interpreting research through a sociolinguistic lens. *International Journal of Translation & Interpreting Research, 6*(1), 158–176.

Russell, D., & Winston, E. (2014). Tapping into the interpreting process: Using participant reports to inform the interpreting process in educational settings. *International Journal of Translation & Interpreting Research, 6*(1), 102–127. doi: ti.106201.2014.a07

Siple, L. (1995). *The use of additions in sign language transliteration* (Unpublished doctoral dissertation). State University of New York, Buffalo.

Siple, L. (1996). The use of additions in sign language transliteration. In D. M. Jones (Ed.), *Assessing our work: Assessing our worth. Proceedings of the 11th National Convention of the Conference of Interpreter Trainers* (pp. 29–45). Northridge, CA: CIT.

Skinner, R., Turner, G. H., Napier, J., & Wheatley, M. (Jemina—what year?). *Democracy, telecommunications and deaf citizenship*. Manuscript submitted for publication.

Sofinski, B. A. (2003). Adverbials, constructed dialogue, and use of space: Oh my! Nonmanual elements used in signed language transliteration. In M. Metzger, S. Collins, V. Dively, & R. Shaw (Eds.), *From topic boundaries to omission: New research on interpretation* (pp. 154–186). Washington, DC: Gallaudet University Press.

Sofinski, B. A., Yesbeck, N. A., Gerhold, S. C., & Bach-Hansen, M. C. (2001). Features of voice-to-sign transliteration by educational interpreters. *Journal of Interpretation*, 47–68.

Sperber, D., & Wilson, D. (1986). *Relevance: Communication and cognition.* Oxford, United Kingdom: Blackwell.

Stone, C. (2005). *Towards a Deaf translation norm* (Unpublished doctoral dissertation). University of Bristol, United Kingdom.

Stone, C. (2009). *Toward a Deaf translation norm.* Washington, DC: Gallaudet University Press.

Stratiy A. (2005). Best practices in interpreting: A deaf community perspective. In T. Janzen (Ed.), *Topics in signed language interpreting* (pp. 231–250). Amsterdam, Netherlands: John Benjamins.

Sunnari, M. (1995) Processing strategies in simultaneous interpreting: "Saying it all" versus synthesis. In J. Tommola (Ed.), *Topics in interpreting* (pp. 109–119). Turku, Finland: University of Turku, Centre for Translation & Interpreting.

Wadensjö, C. (1998). *Interpreting as interaction.* London, United Kingdom: Longman.

Wang, J. (2013). *Working memory and signed language interpreting* (Unpublished doctoral dissertation). Macquarie University, Sydney, Australia.

Wang, J., & Napier, J. (2016). Directionality in signed language interpreting. *Meta.*

Winston, E. (1989). Transliteration: What's the message? In C. Lucas (Ed.), *The sociolinguistics of the Deaf community* (pp.147–164). San Diego, CA: Academic Press.

Winston, E., & Monikowski, C. (2003). Marking topic boundaries in signed interpretation and transliteration. In M. Metzger, S. Collins, V. Dively, & R. Shaw (Eds.), *From topic boundaries to omission: New research on interpretation* (pp. 187–227). Washington, DC: Gallaudet University Press.

Linguistic Coping Strategies

Chapter 1

Sociolinguistic and Sociocultural

Contexts of Interpreting

In order to establish a context for the work of sign language interpreters, it is necessary to explore sociolinguistic and sociocultural factors that may influence that work. In understanding a framework for interpreting in general, it is possible to identify the unique nature of sign language interpreting in comparison with spoken language interpreting. Other sociolinguistic and sociocultural factors to consider include those relevant to the discourse environment and the challenges for interpreters when dealing with particular linguistic features of source texts.

A FRAMEWORK FOR INTERPRETING

In order to effectively explore the linguistic coping strategies of sign language interpreters, it is necessary to establish a framework for the way in which interpreters work. By exploring the generic nature of an interpreter's work, it is possible to establish a context for the study. As a route to understanding the complexities involved in interpreting, it is essential to discuss not only the linguistic processes involved, but also the behavioral aspects of an interpreter's role.

The fundamental nature of interpreting as a process for transferring ideas from one language into another was introduced in the prologue. The process involved in the transference of concepts between two languages is not, however, as straightforward as it would seem, hence the need for interpreters to maintain a multilayered skills base. Cokely (1995) neatly defines the various layers of the interpreting process as follows:

> [the] competent and coherent use of one naturally evolved lan
> guage to express the meanings and intentions conveyed in another

I

naturally evolved language for the purpose of negotiating an opportunity for a successful communicative interaction in real time within a triad involving two principal groups who are incapable of using, or who prefer not to use, the language of the other individual or group (p. 1).

As indicated by the above definition, interpreting is a highly complex linguistic process involving "intriguing mechanisms by which the brain is able to process two languages simultaneously" (Ingram, 1978, p. 113). Particular writings have presented a psycholinguistic perspective of the cognitive information processes involved in interpreting (Flores d'Arcais, 1978; Ford, 1981; Goldman-Gisler, 1978; Goldman-Gisler & Cohen, 1974; Ingram, 1974, 1985; Isham, 1994; Isham & Lane, 1993; Le Ny, 1978; Lörscher, 1996; Massaro, 1978; Moser, 1978; Seleskovitch, 1976; Tweney, 1978). A psycholinguistic approach often emphasizes a linear process of interpreting, whereby the information from the source language is decoded, analyzed, and re-encoded into the target language, with an emphasis on memory. However, this approach has limitations as it implies that the transfer process only takes place between two languages rather than between languages, communities, and cultures.

Other authors (Cokely, 1985, 1992a; Frishberg, 2000; Metzger, 1995, 1999; Neumann Solow, 2000; Pergnier, 1978; Roy, 1989a, 1992, 1996, 2000a) have stated that any study of interpretation should apply a framework of sociolinguistic parameters, as interpreters can be seen to mediate not only between two individual languages, but also between communities and cultures. Any interpretation therefore needs to be based on a linguistic and cultural understanding of the participants within an interaction, and their differing norms and values. Scott Gibson (1992) asserted that interpretation is more than just comprehension of a message. She stated that any interpretation should re-express the thoughts of one language into another, incorporating the same intent and style as would be used by a native speaker of the second language. Additionally, Scott Gibson emphasized that interpreters must be both bilingual and bicultural, "for accurate transmission of information may take place only if based on a deep knowledge of both languages, both cultures, and the cultural differences involved" (p. 255).

By adopting a sociolinguistic/sociocultural approach to interpreting, the focus is not on the decoding and re-encoding of information in different languages, but rather on the message that is delivered and the meaning it conveys. A sociolinguistic perspective emphasizes that the crux of any interpretation is to achieve "dynamic equivalence" (Hatim & Mason, 1990); that is, to get the message right by ensuring that the target language audience derives the same meaning from a message as is intended by the source language presenter. Therefore, rather than the interpreting process being about language transmission and change, it is about the message within a sociolinguistic and sociocultural context (Pergnier, 1978).

In the sign language interpreting world, the focus on whether to "reformulate language" or "convey the message" has been greatly influenced by the various models of interpreting mooted over the last twenty years. Perspectives on the role of an interpreter have been defined in several ways, such as "service models" (Witter-Merithew, 1987, 1988), "images of the interpreter" (Frishberg, 1990), "philosophical frames" (Humphrey & Alcorn, 1996), and "models of interpreting" (Stewart, Schein & Cartwright, 1998). Lee (1997) stated that the interpreter's role is influenced by a multitude of different factors, yet there are established models that have been developed and improved upon as more research has been conducted in the field. Lee commented that "while we define our role to persons outside the field . . . we talk amongst ourselves, as professionals, about the model of interpreting that we work under" (p. 41).

An interpreting model is considered as "a hypothetical representation of a process or object; it serves to display, verbally or graphically, an event, object, or series of events" (Stewart et al., 1998, p. 33). Early models gave little recognition for the sociolinguistic or sociocultural factors that may affect an interpreter's work, or the fact that interpreters will inevitably influence any communicative interaction with their presence. Proposed models included the *cognitive model*, (Stewart et al., 1998), the *conduit model* (Neumann Solow, 1981), and the *facilitator of communication model* (Frishberg, 1990; Neumann Solow, 1981). Several writers recognized, however, that a metaphorical description of the interpreter as a conduit that does not have an impact on communication cannot account for human dynamics and the need for interpreters to be flexible (Humphrey & Alcorn, 1996; McIntire & Sanderson, 1993; Metzger, 1999; Roy, 1993).

A model of interpreting based on sociolinguistic paradigms is the best way to represent the complete dynamic of interpreting, whereby interpreters engage in a complex linguistic and cultural process of transferring information between languages, with the recognition that they may contribute to, rather than hinder, any communicative interaction. The central focus of a *sociolinguistic model* is the human interaction between participants, whereby the various sociolinguistic factors that may influence an interpreter's work are acknowledged, and the effect that an interpreter can have on any interaction is also recognized. Rather than being "invisible" and relying on understanding of language alone, a sociolinguistic or *bilingual-bicultural model* (McIntire & Sanderson, 1993) requires the interpreter to identify and consider the setting, the participants, the purpose(s), and the message within any interaction (Stewart et al., 1998). Interpreters have been recognized as being members of a "third culture" (Atwood & Gray, 1986; Bienvenu, 1987; Napier, 2002; Sherwood, 1987). This notion stems from the fact that interpreters are often the only people present within an interaction who can identify issues for representatives of the two cultures coming together and, therefore, use their understanding of those cultures to make appropriate language adjustments (Roy, 1993).

Cokely (1985, 1992a) has been one of the major advocates of a sociolinguistic model of the interpreting process. He defined a sociolinguistic approach to interpreting as being multifaceted through parallel, rather than linear, processing. In his proposed *sociolinguistically sensitive process model*, he posited seven key stages to the interpreting process. The pictorial depiction of the model implies that processing occurs sequentially, however, Cokely clarified this point by stating that "it is more helpful to think of the process as one in which there is multiple nesting of stages" (1992a, p. 128). In this way the key processes and sub-processes can be described, but it is acknowledged that the major stages are not necessarily discrete entities and may overlap.

The seven major processes outlined by Cokely are (1) message reception, (2) preliminary processing, (3) short-term message retention, (4) semantic intent realization, (5) semantic equivalence determination, (6) syntactic message formulation, and (7) message production. Additionally, he hypothesized that a range of subprocesses and factors can influence the overall interpreting process. These include cross-linguistic and cultural awareness, linguistic and syntactic competence, physical and psychological factors, and semantic, syntactic, and contextual knowledge.

Hence, rather than seeing the interpreter as an entity who does not have an effect on interaction, the interpreter is recognized as a human being who can influence and is influenced by the participants, languages, cultures, and social norms of any interaction. Baker-Shenk (1986) has stated that it is impossible for sign language interpreters to be completely neutral as they are members of the hearing majority and, therefore, members of the society that has historically oppressed Deaf people. A sociolinguistic, bilingual-bicultural approach to interpreting provides the opportunity for interpreters to use their knowledge of both Deaf and hearing cultures to address power imbalance and provide the opportunity for meaningful interaction (Page, 1993). The interpreter can be regarded as an "ally" of the Deaf community (McIntire & Sanderson, 1993) who takes on the role of linguistic and cultural mediator to empower Deaf people to gain equal access to information.

Taking Cokely's (1992a) model one step further, Stewart et al. (1998) suggested an *interactive model* of interpreting, which gives consideration to extralinguistic, as well as sociolinguistic and sociocultural factors that can affect the interpreting process. The components that affect the interpreting process are grouped into categories: *Participants, Message,* and *Environment.* The category of "participants" refers to the initiator of any interaction (also known as the source language presenter), the receiver of the message (also known as the target language group/individual), and the interpreter, who processes the message. The "message" category refers to the information being expressed by the primary participants. The "environment" category incorporates "the physical and psychological context in which an interpreted discourse occurs. . . [which subsumes] the social context of an interpreted discourse." (p. 34). The success of the model is dependent on the interactions that take place between each category, which implies the "multiple nesting of stages" as suggested by Cokely (1992a).

This model incorporates all sociolinguistic factors as outlined by Cokely, but also explicitly considers the nature of communicative interaction. The interpreting process is defined not just as a process of translating information between languages but also between cultures and communities. The central focus is the fact that all language exchange takes place within an interaction and, that in order to effectively interpret between languages and cultures, the interpreter has to be considered as part of the interaction. As opposed to preceding models, the interactive model acknowledges that an interpreter brings something to any interaction and can personally contribute to effective understanding between interlocutors using different languages by conveying the meaning of a message so that it is culturally appropriate.

Other writers, such as Metzger (1995, 1999), Roy (1989a, 1992, 1996, 2000a), and Wadensjö (1998), have also maintained that an interactive approach is the only feasible way to adequately describe the interpreting process. An interactive model of interpreting, therefore, should be considered as the ideal framework for interpreting. By looking at the interpreting process from an interactional perspective, it is possible to determine the extent of, and reasons for, linguistically and culturally effective interpretations. Nonetheless, an interactive model can only be applied successfully when interpreters adopt a sociolinguistic and sociocultural approach to their work and concede that every individual interpretation will vary according to the context of a situation.

Interpretation: A Sociolinguistic/Sociocultural Approach

Texts often depend on prior textual experiences in order to evoke significant meanings (intertextuality). When recipients of the discourse have not had experience with language and thus, the relevant prior texts, it becomes the responsibility of the translator to provide a translation that allows the recipients to infer the ideological stances intended in the source (Metzger, 1995, p. 28).

In order for the interpreter to be able to provide discourse participants with a sociocultural framework in which to make inferences about "ideological stances," it is necessary for the interpreter to be bilingual and bicultural. Being bicultural and bilingual is not enough, however; interpreters need to have the tools to determine what something means to their target audience and the best way for a message to be interpreted in a meaningful way, in order for it to make sense with regards to the audience's cultural norms and values. Therefore, not only do interpreters need to understand the sociolinguistic and sociocultural contexts of their audiences' world view, but they also need to utilize appropriate interpretation methods to ensure that they have the facility to convey the meaning of a message within a sociocultural framework.

According to the kind of experiences people have had throughout their life and the culture to which they feel they belong, they will develop a set of assumptions about the world and the people with whom they interact. *Frame theory* is one explanation for how people categorize their knowledge based on their experiences with similar situations, and thus may use lexical, grammatical, and experiential knowledge, consciously or unconsciously, to make judgments about a discourse situation and its participants.

Several writers, including Goffman (1974), Gumperz (1982), Hatim and Mason (1990), Metzger (1995, 1999), Roy (2000d), Schiffrin (1993), Tannen (1979, 1993), and Wilcox and Wilcox (1985), have referred to "frame" or "schema" theory in relation to discourse. Wilcox and Wilcox defined schema theory as "a theory about knowledge" that offers an explanation of how comprehension takes place and how it is influenced by prior knowledge and contextual influences. Schema or "frame" theory claims that the meaning of a message is not decoded, as described in cognitive models of language, but rather it is constructed.

Essentially, frame theory describes "frames" of concepts, which people use to "hang" information on, and it is upon these frames that people base their assumptions about objects, people, and places. The "frames" are constructed of different values, which will vary from person to person depending on their life experience. When put together, the values give rise to a concept. In the same way that individuals make assumptions about people, objects, and places, they do the same for "unwritten" rules of behavior in the form of "scripts." Schank and Abelson (1977) defined scripts as a "standard event sequence" (p. 38), whereas Hatim and Mason (1990) referred to scripts as "stabilized plans with pre-established routines" (p. 160). These scripts are used to guide a person through particular forms of social intercourse according to certain expectations of behavior within any particular environment, which again will depend on the types of social interactions that one has been exposed to while growing up.

New information is given based on an assumption of what is already known, and bridging inferences are made between frames and scripts to make further assumptions about information that is being received. Interpreters, therefore, when entering into an interpreting assignment will come with their own frames and scripts about the people, the subject, and the event. All other participants, whether Deaf or hearing, will also have their own assumptions that may influence the interaction. As a consequence, the assumptions held by the interpreter will inevitably have some kind of influence over the interpretation itself, meaning that when considering models of the interpreting process, this must be a central factor.

As cited earlier, the interactive model, by adopting a sociolinguistic approach, has the capacity to incorporate the interpreter as participant into the interpretation process and, therefore, to acknowledge that the interpreter, as well as primary interlocutors, will have an influence on any interaction that takes place. By using their contextual knowledge of both communities, their languages and cultures, and subsequently making assumptions and judgments about what their audiences mutually understand, interpreters can ensure they make any interpretation linguistically and culturally effective for all participants. Interpreters will make specific language choices according to their frames of reference, what certain concepts mean to them, and inferences they make about what concepts will mean to their source and target language audiences from a cultural perspective (Napier, 1998b, 1998c, 2000, 2001). Interpreters will therefore construct the meaning of a message according to the perspective of the listener/receiver (Frishberg, 2000).

In order for interpreters to ensure that their audiences are making the same inferences about the message they are receiving, they need to search for linguistic and cultural equivalents. It is not sufficient to search for directly translatable words in each language because sociocultural contexts may alter the way certain expressions are understood. Hatim and Mason (1990) stated that the interpretation process is "an evolving entity, a process whereby producers and receivers cooperate and communicate by making assumptions about a shared cognitive environment" (p. 100). To best deal with the sociolinguistic and sociocultural contexts of interpreting, interpreters need to recognize their linguistic abilities, cultural knowledge, and the fact that their interpretations can be enhanced by using their knowledge. In this way, interpreters can be seen to positively contribute to any communicative interaction. It is posited here that *free interpretation* is the most appropriate and dynamic interpretation method to utilize in order to apply the fundamentals of frame theory and perform effectively as a linguistic and cultural mediator.

Interpreting Techniques

The principle of free interpretation centers on the concept of the interpreter being more than just a conduit. It is not enough for an interpreter to be extremely fluent in both languages; she must have a deep understanding of the potentially opposing cultural norms and values and should make judgments about her interpretation accordingly. Although linguists would assume that fluency implies cultural awareness, the application of this concept to interpreting is a comparatively recent phenomenon. Much of interpreting literature states that an interpreter must use not only her cultural knowledge and understanding of the participants involved, but also her metalinguistic awareness to judge the effectiveness of any interpretation.

According to McKee (1996), one of the biggest difficulties faced by interpreters of any language is the fact that interaction participants who do not share the same language may also not share any experiences, knowledge, or familiarity with a particular situation. She stated that interpreters will often accompany individuals into situations where they are acquiring new information that is not culturally relevant, or will be working in situations where participants know nothing about each other's community, language, or cultural values. Therefore, "we may feel that in our interpretation we have not made something clear, but more often than not, the participants simply don't share the same set of knowledge or assumptions, or ways of going about things" (p. 22).

Thus it can be argued that the interpreter has to be prepared for the different assumptions held by the different cultures. Every interpreter will take one piece of information and interpret it differently, according to what that piece of information means to them; but what they also have to consider is what it will mean to the participants using the target language once the message has been translated.

In relation to free interpretation, the key is in the assumptions brought to, and the inferences made during, any interpreting assignment. In order to make assumptions about the target audience, the interpreter needs to be bicultural as well as bilingual. Familiarity with the community and its culture will expose the interpreter to knowledge such as the standard of education that people have received, the kind of information that community members have been exposed to, and the nature of language use alongside cultural norms and values. The interpreter can make considered choices throughout the translation by making inferences about the audience members' cultural and linguistic understanding of the topic being discussed and can then transpose cultural meaning appropriately (Hatim & Mason, 1990). Tajfel (1969) described how "enculturation acts as a reference point against which all else is measured and interpreted"; therefore, interpreters need to be aware of differing cultural perspectives and how cues may be acted upon or ignored (cited in Cavell & Wells, 1986, p. 99). Too often, interpreters focus too closely on a syntactical, lexical interpretation, relying on the form of the language. The ability to paraphrase the meaning of an utterance to impart cultural significance can be more important than the ability to translate "word-for-word" by concentrating on the form of the message. Free interpretation, therefore, can be regarded as a method of interpretation whereby "the linguistic structure of the source language is ignored, and an equivalent is found based on the meaning it conveys" (Crystal, 1987, p. 344); as opposed to a *literal interpretation*, where "the linguistic structure of the source text is followed, but is normalized according to the rules of the target language" (p. 344). For example, if interpreting from English into Auslan, the literal delivery of Auslan would incorporate English word order or lip-patterns while also using Auslan features. Much of sign language interpreting literature refers to literal interpretation as *transliteration* (Cerney, 2000).

The crux of any interpretation is to get the message right and to ensure that the target audience is receiving the same message as those listening to or watching the source language presenter. Thus interpretation has to be more than mere word-for-word translation from one language to another. The search should be for equivalent meaning rather than equivalent lexical items (Seleskovitch, 1978). The word *equivalence* is central to the concept of free interpretation. During any assignment, an interpreter will bring her own frames about the situation; she will have her own assumed knowledge about participants involved, and she will make inferences according to those assumptions. By being both bilingual and bicultural, the interpreter should be able to find equivalents between two languages by understanding, and making inferences about, what something means to a particular audience. Hatim and Mason (1990) reinforced this point by stating that every lexical item has several equivalents in another language, depending on the *denotative meaning* (primary lexical meaning) and the *connotative meaning* (additional meaning beyond the primary meaning) that is imparted in different contexts. It is not enough, therefore, to know substitutable lexical equivalents in two languages; rather interpreters must be able to find terms that "will express 'the same thing' regardless of the words used in the original statement" (Baker (1992, p. 87). That produces the "sense" of any message (Seleskovitch, 1992).

On this premise, everything that is said in one language can be expressed in another, provided that the two languages belong to societies that have attained comparable levels of development. Seleskovitch (1978) postulated that the only reason particular words are deemed untranslatable is because different languages express concepts in different ways, whereby exact lexical equivalents will not necessarily exist. Different communities will, however, have similar frames of reference, and the "words, i.e., the concepts they represent are 'untranslatable' only when their referent does not yet exist in the society using the target language" (p. 88).

Seleskovitch noted that a necessary part of the translation process might involve introducing a new concept into an existing cultural framework before formalizing it in the target language by giving it a name. Subsequently, during any assignment, an interpreter will use her language skills and cultural knowledge to make decisions about whether a concept is new to the audience, and she will express the idea accordingly. The search for linguistic and cultural equivalence is fundamental to any interpreting process to ensure that all participants in any interaction leave having received the same message. This equivalence presents a challenge when certain words or concepts may hold positive connotations for one audience, yet negative associations for another (Frishberg, 1990; Lane, Hoffmeister, & Bahan, 1996), meaning that interpreters have to consider the "culturally rich realities" of the interaction participants (Cokely, 2001).

The connotations of any concept must be reflected in the language choices that are made; it is not enough to interpret sign-for-word, or word-for-sign, without paying heed to the cultural values inherently embedded in certain signs or words. A skilled interpreter, adopting the role of linguistic and cultural mediator within an interactive model, should use free interpretation as a matter of course, as she should regard this as the only feasible way of translating between two languages and cultures. In recognizing the influence of additional sociolinguistic factors, Crystal (1987) stated that in addition to being bilingual and bicultural, interpreters need a thorough understanding of the discourse being used in the interpreting context and, thus, any social, cultural, or emotional connotations that may influence the intended effect of the message.

The concept of free interpretation is often alluded to in different writings, but it has only been discussed specifically by Metzger (1999) and Napier (2001), who defined free interpretation as "the process by which concepts and meanings are translated from one language into another by incorporating cultural norms and values; assumed knowledge about these values; and the search for linguistic and cultural equivalents" (Napier, 2001, p. 31).

One other issue to recognize, however, is the appropriateness of using a more literal interpreting technique as a translation style in particular discourse environments, due to the formality of the environment and the needs of the target audience. This issue will be explored further in chapter 3.

SIGN LANGUAGE INTERPRETERS AND SPOKEN LANGUAGE INTERPRETERS: A COMPARISON

Discussion thus far has highlighted that interpreters work with people who cannot, or choose not to, use the same language. It has also been suggested that interpreters work as mediators between individuals who have different cultural experiences. Many interpreters will work with linguistic minority groups and, therefore, will be working with communities who are not of equal status in society (Gentile, Ozolins, & Vasilakakos, 1996). Interestingly, Gentile et al. observe that "the interpreter is likely to belong to the same ethnic group as the client speaking the 'lower status' language," and that "these dynamics impinge directly on the interpreter" (p. 21).

Although the essential processes of interpretation are the same regardless of the languages used (Roberts, 1987), and because sign language interpreters similarly work between communities of incomparable status there are many issues that confront sign language interpreters that are different from those faced by spoken language interpreters. For instance, if Deaf people are considered members of an ethnic group, it is impossible for sign language interpreters to truly belong to the same group by virtue of the fact that they can hear. This situation means that sign language interpreters are confronted with various linguistic issues in terms of their use of sign language, in relation to their membership in the Deaf community, and their bilingual status.

The Deaf Community and Its Language Use

Many writers (Brennan, 1992. Brien, 1991; Higgins, 1980; Ladd, 2002; Lane et al., 1996) have discussed the concept of the Deaf community and have defined Deaf people as a linguistic and cultural minority group who identify with one another based on shared language, identity, social, and educational experiences. Baker and Cokely (1980) defined four "avenues" of membership to the Deaf community: audiological, political, linguistic, and social. People who satisfy all four avenues are considered "core" members of the community, whereas other people are considered "peripheral" members. For example, Padden (1980) stated that the inability to hear is not a requisite of being a member of the Deaf community: "A deaf community may include persons who are not themselves Deaf, but who actively support the goals of the community and work with people to achieve them' (p. 41). Therefore, this definition can include interpreters and nondeaf family members, but only as peripheral members of the community. Thus, although people who can hear may be accepted by the community, they will never be considered as true members of the "ethnic group."

The Deaf community is often considered to be a disenfranchised group in society that has experienced oppression at the hands of the nondeaf majority. Several writers (such as Baker-Shenk, 1986; Lane, 1993) refer to Deaf people as an "oppressed group" whose lives have historically been dictated and controlled by "hearing" people. Deaf people have experienced the denigration of their language and cultural values and have been stigmatized as "abnormal" (Higgins, 1980). Being members of a stigmatized group has had obvious implications on the social and cultural identity of Deaf people. They have been denied the right to use their language and have had their culture, traditions, and beliefs devalued in a power struggle with the dominant members of society (that is, those that can hear) (Humphrey & Alcorn, 1996).

According to Rawlings and Jensema (1977), only 5 to 10% of Deaf children in deaf schools have Deaf parents (cited in Meadow-Orlans, 1990). For the majority of Deaf people, therefore, their first opportunity to identify themselves with other Deaf people and develop a personal notion of deafness as a social identity is when they enter the education system. Lane (1993) cited residential schools as being one of the most salient of Deaf cultural values.

Paradoxically, the education system seems to have been one of the most oppressive institutions in the experience of Deaf people. As a result of the 1880 Congress on Education of the Deaf in Milan, the use of sign language was banned in schools, and the vast majority of Deaf children received their education through an oral approach, where they were encouraged to use whatever residual hearing they had, lipread, and develop their speech skills, rather than use sign language (Erting, 1994; Lane et al., 1996). Deaf cultural values continued to develop almost in spite of the education system, as Deaf people relied on the residential schools to bring them together at an early age and give them a sense of shared experience.

Over the years the education system has changed, with many residential schools being closed down and Deaf children being placed either in self-contained units within local schools or fully integrated into schools with nondeaf children. Thus, due to the diverse educational experiences of Deaf people and the language or mode of their education, their use of sign language may vary (Kannapell, 1989). Other factors that can influence Deaf persons' sign language proficiency include whether they used sign language in the home as children (regardless of whether their parents were Deaf or hearing), whether they have a Deaf signing partner, and whether they work in a Deaf or hearing environment. Although a person may use some form of signed communication, he or she may not necessarily be a fluent user of a naturally occurring sign language.

Humphrey and Alcorn (1996), among others, have described a "sign communication spectrum" that may be encountered when interacting with members of the Deaf community. The continuum includes manual communication forms such as Signed English,[1] contact varieties of signed and spoken languages, and natural sign languages.

---

1. Signed English is the word-for-word manual representation of English. Several methods for manually representing English have been used over the years—"Some use just twenty-six hand configurations to represent the letters of the alphabet, others use a combination of signs used by the deaf and fingerspelling, others use a combination of deaf signs, fingerspelling and contrived signs. They all have in common the aim of manually representing English, word for word, if not morpheme by morpheme" (Johnston, 1989, p. 473).

With the more recent introduction of bilingual education programs for Deaf children, however, Deaf people may be just as comfortable using a written form of spoken language as they are with a manual form of sign language. Even for those Deaf individuals whose first or preferred language is a naturally occurring sign language, the sign system that they choose to use or receive may vary according to the context of the situation they are in.

Aside from implications of language use for interpreters, in that they have to consider the background and educational experiences of each Deaf client they meet, as well as the communication method they may prefer, there is one other factor to consider. As a consequence of being oppressed by the dominant members of society who can hear, there are obvious ramifications for the working relationship between Deaf people and sign language interpreters, as interpreters are members of the majority group.

Although Padden (1980) has delineated how nondeaf people may be members of the Deaf community, it seems that there are limits to how far Deaf people will go to welcome hearing people into the fold. In order for interpreters to adequately enculturate themselves and become proficiently bilingual, it is necessary for them to be accepted into the Deaf community.

Traditionally, hearing people have taken on paternalistic roles within the Deaf community. Corfmat (1990) and Scott Gibson (1992), among others, have described how interpreting for Deaf people was once considered an inherent part of the role of welfare workers for the Deaf, and how the majority of the time it was relatives of Deaf individuals who would fulfill these roles. Regardless of being able to hear, these people would have almost automatic entry to membership in the Deaf community, would be native or near-native in their sign language fluency, and, therefore, could be considered as bilingual.

The role of sign language interpreters was professionalized in an attempt "to liberate Deaf people from the yoke of paternalism and care" (Pollitt, 1997, p. 21). Along with more research into the linguistic status of sign languages, more hearing people have become involved with the Deaf community through their interest in the language, rather than a sense of duty to help. The process of professionalization seemed to meet the demands of the Deaf community, yet Scott Gibson (1994) described "the cult of professional expertise" as one of the most fundamental difficulties experienced by sign language interpreters, due to the divergent needs of interpreters and the Deaf community. Phillip (1994) discussed a lack of reciprocation from hearing interpreters for Deaf people allowing them to become members of the community. Due to improved societal attitudes towards sign languages (Burns, Matthews, & Nolan-Conroy, 2001), there has been a surge of interest in learning a sign language as a second language (some would even argue that it is "trendy"), meaning there are far more hearing people choosing to train as sign language interpreters.

In highlighting the issues of sign language interpreting, language use, and the education of Deaf people, Corker (1997) expressed anxiety at the power struggle enforced on Deaf people and interpreters by the fact that interpreters are often better educated about the Deaf community and its language and culture, and they are often more proficient in sign language than a lot of Deaf people themselves. As a consequence of this dichotomy, Corker stated that interpreters are often "more sophisticated in their ability to manufacture discourses using the rules of the dominant culture" (p. 19).

Much of the literature that discusses the nature of the relationship between Deaf people and hearing interpreters implies a fractious interdependence (Napier, 2001). Interpreters rely on the trust and generosity of Deaf people to let them into the community so that they can become bilingual and bicultural, and Deaf individuals rely on interpreters to be bilingual and bicultural in order to mediate between themselves and the wider majority. The literature indicates that Deaf people do not want to be helped by hearing individuals, yet they are wary of anyone who has a genuine interest in working with the Deaf community if they have not grown up in that community themselves. Pollitt (1997) attributed the current state of mistrust to the fact that interpreters have adopted the professional values of the nondeaf majority and, as a consequence, have been "seen to eschew the precious cultural values of the Deaf community, who in their own terms were not clients, but teachers, mentors, family members and friends" (pp. 21–22).

Interestingly, Pollitt noted that the professional values on which sign language interpreters chose to model their own were those of spoken language interpreters. This seems like common sense as ultimately interpreters perform the same function regardless of their working languages. Yet it can be seen from the descriptions of the Deaf community, its language, culture, and status in society, that the role of the sign language interpreter is multifaceted. Although the essential process of interpretation is the same regardless of the languages used, signed and spoken language interpreting does not necessarily precipitate the same working conditions, roles, and boundaries. It can be argued that many of the required traits are similar, yet some issues for sign language interpreters are unique.

Bilingual and Bimodal Interpreting

Some of the issues that sign language interpreters face in working with the Deaf community have already been reflected upon, including the skeptical views of Deaf people as to what hearing individuals can offer them and the diverse forms of communication used in the Deaf community. The issue of language variation has implications for the training of interpreters, as the only way that they can become native-like in their use of sign language is to enculturate themselves. Unfortunately, sign language interpreters cannot follow the path of spoken language interpreters and go and live in the country from which their second language is derived. There is no "Deafland" where they can travel to immerse themselves in the language. Their enculturation depends upon their ability to interact with members of the Deaf community, which has inherent difficulties as already outlined.

While spoken language interpreters often come from the ethnic group for whom they are interpreting, this is obviously not the case for sign language interpreters. This fact has wider implications for their language use, and it highlights yet another issue that differs from spoken language interpreters. Generally, spoken language interpreters will work into their "mother tongue" or "A" language (Baker, 1992; Bowen, 1980), from their second into their first, native language. This pattern follows the assumption that people will always use their first language more competently, coherently, and accurately. For sign language interpreters, however, this is often not the case (Frishberg, 1990). Unless an interpreter has been exposed to sign language from a very young age through parents or siblings, it is unlikely that she will acquire a sign language as her first language. Yet sign language interpreters are more likely to work consistently from, for example, English into Auslan or BSL, meaning that they are invariably working from their "A" language into their "B" language. Due to the power imbalance between Deaf and hearing people, interpreters are usually present at communication events where Deaf people are relying on nondeaf individuals for information, which means that the interpreting process often conveys messages one way.

Another language issue that affects the working practices of sign language interpreters is that of modality. Spoken language interpreters work between two linear languages, whereby one word is produced after another, and the message is built up sequentially. Sign languages, however, are visual-spatial languages that can convey meaning by creating a picture using space, location, referents, and other descriptive elements. Therefore sign language interpreters are constantly transferring information between two alternate modalities, which requires the representation of information in very different ways. This process is commonly referred to as *bimodal interpreting*.

It has already been noted that interpreters work at the interface of bilingual, bicultural interaction, yet consideration needs to be given to the bimodality of sign language interpreting and the impact this can have on communicative interactions between Deaf and hearing individuals. Brennan and Brown (1997) devoted much discussion to interactional effects of bimodal interpreting in courtroom settings, but the issues are pertinent to all situations where sign language interpreters work. They suggested that the realities of bimodal interpreting "inevitably change the dynamics of live interactions" (p. 125), due to the visual nature of sign languages. Brennan and Brown listed certain elements for consideration. First, the issue of eye contact was highlighted. In order to receive the message, Deaf individuals need to maintain eye contact with the interpreter, whereas in the norms of hearing interaction, participants engaging in the interaction would maintain eye contact with each other. Therefore Deaf participants may miss out on visual cues given by their hearing counterparts. Similarly, hearing individuals may focus their attention on the interpreter (as this is where the "voice" is coming from) and miss out on visual-gestural cues given by the Deaf person. Second, the vulnerability of sign language interpreters was raised in that they are always visible to all participants in any situation, and so they may attract a great deal of attention (see also Siple, 1993).

Brennan and Brown (1997) also stated that because Deaf and hearing people use gesture in very different ways, it would be easy for someone to misconstrue the meanings and intentions of another person by referring to their own frames of reference for how gesture should be used.

Certain facial expressions that are intrinsic to the grammatical use of sign languages may be misinterpreted by hearing people. When receiving information, for example, Deaf people often nod their head to indicate that they are understanding the signs they see, in the same way that non-deaf English-speaking people might use "mmm, hmm" or "uh-huh" to affirm they understand what they are hearing. The head nod, however, may be misconstrued, as typically a head nod is a gesture for agreement in wider Western society. Although a Deaf person might be nodding, it does not necessarily mean that he or she agrees with the information being received.

As sign languages express information in a visual-spatial dimension, Brennan and Brown postulated that they encode visual information as a matter of course, as the "real-world" visual information pervades the grammatical features of the language. This element of sign language use therefore places certain demands on sign language interpreters, which may not be appreciated by spoken language interpreters. When hearing certain abstract concepts or generic descriptions, it is necessary for sign language interpreters to receive detailed visual information that needs to be implicitly encoded visually into any interpretation. Brennan and Brown cited an example in BSL of the sentence "X broke the window," indicating that the interpreter ideally needs to know what type of window it is and how it was broken, in order to accurately represent visually the window and how it was broken. Similarly if someone is "murdered," is it done with a knife, gun, by strangulation, or suffocation? All of these concepts require visual representation in sign language in order to make sense to the Deaf receiver.

Thus when interpreting for Deaf clients, sign language interpreters face the challenge of constantly having to visualize what they hear in a linear form, or create sequential meaning from a visual picture. This factor adds an extra dimension to the interpreting process, as the interpreters have to transfer meaning not only between two languages and cultures, but also between opposing modalities of language production.

The use of language also affects signed and spoken language inter-preters differently in another way. In the long term, the demand for sign language interpreters will never cease. In comparison with spoken lan-guage interpreters, whose clients have the option to learn the majority language and, therefore, desist with their use of interpreters, the clients of sign language interpreters do not have that option. Deaf people will always be unable to hear and will always rely on interpreters for access to information (Ozolins & Bridge, 1999). As Davis (1989, 1990a, 1990b) pointed out, Deaf people use interpreters because they cannot hear, not necessarily because they cannot understand or use the source language.

Thus far, interpreting in the context of the Deaf community has been discussed in order to give a clearer picture of the particular issues faced by sign language interpreters. By identifying general sociolinguistic and sociocultural issues in working with this consumer group, it is possible to focus on the specific context of this study. When considering issues faced by Auslan interpreters in their everyday work in relation to managing communication, other issues can be highlighted in relation to interpreting for university lectures. The skills employed by interpreters have to be adapted to allow for conditions specific to the university discourse environment. Interpreting, therefore, can be considered as a *discourse process* (Roy, 2000a).

DISCOURSE ENVIRONMENT: FACTORS TO CONSIDER

In order to adequately conduct any research on interpreting, it is necessary to recognize and establish the sociolinguistic and sociocultural contexts of any situation that may influence the language that is used. Language variation obviously has an impact on interpreting as a discourse process, as interpreters will need to adapt to the source language they are receiving, as well as modulate their target language production accordingly.

The Context of Situation

The functional grammar approach to linguistics focuses on the purpose and use of language, and it examines spoken and written languages within the contexts of their usage. The relationship between words used and meanings derived is not regarded as arbitrary. Rather, language is determined as being functional, whereby meaning is created through the choice of words and the syntactic structure through which the words are produced (Gerot & Wignell, 1995).

Thus, the study of language from a functional perspective and, therefore, the study of interpretation of language cannot be separated from the situations where language use takes place (Hatim & Mason, 1990). Halliday and Hasan (1985) described context and text of language (whether written, spoken, or signed) as being aspects of the same process, whereby the context acts as a "bridge between the text and the situation in which texts actually occur" (p. 5). Many writers have discussed the relationship between language, communicative interaction, and context (Brown & Fraser, 1979; Crystal, 1984; Halliday, 1978, 1993; Hymes, 1967, 1972; Ryan & Giles, 1982; Sinclair & Coulthard, 1975), propounding the notion that all languages function within contexts of situations and, therefore, are relatable to those contexts. With this in mind, Halliday (1978) stated that the purpose of defining the context is not to question idiosyncratic use of vocabulary, grammar, or pronunciation; but rather to identify "*which* kinds of situational factor determine *which* kinds of selection in the linguistic system" (p. 32).

Crystal and Davey (1969), Halliday (1978), and Hymes (1967) have proposed sets of concepts for describing the context of a situation. Hymes outlined factors for consideration when analyzing language in context of situation: the form and content of the message; the setting; the participants; the intent and effect of the communication; the key points; the medium and genre; and the norms of interaction within that particular setting.

In further extending these factors, Halliday (1978) summarized general concepts for describing how linguistic features of communication may be affected by the context of a situation, under three headings: "field of discourse," "tenor of discourse," and "mode of discourse." The "field" refers to the institutional setting where language use occurs, the subject matter, the participatory activity as a whole and the degree of emphasis placed on the language itself. The "tenor" defines the relationship and interpersonal dynamics between participants; whereas the "mode" describes the channel of communication adopted (i.e., spoken, written, signed), the "speech" genre, and the spontaneity of the utterance. He stated that the impact of context of situation on language leads to a systematic relationship emerging between language and environment, with linguistic features being assigned to different components of the semantic system—features from the "field" being assigned to the ideational component, the "tenor" to the interpersonal component, and the "mode" features to the textual component.

Crystal and Davey (1969) also suggested that contextual factors influence language use by describing three categories of linguistic features. These include "province," "status," and "modality." The first category focuses on the utterance that takes place and the extralinguistic factors that influence its use; the second category refers to the participants of an interaction and their social standing; and the third category considers the purpose of the utterance. According to Crystal and Davey, these linguistic features combine to cause speakers to follow expected conventions for particular types of discourse setting.

All of the conceptual breakdowns discussed thus far serve to illustrate the point that consideration of context of situation is paramount in describing language use. If the context of situation influences language use and the linguistic choices that interlocutors make, the same context will inevitably influence the linguistic choices made by interpreters. According to Cokely (1992a), interpreters are engaged in a process of constantly assessing the components influencing the interaction participants and the source language they produce, in order to accurately account for these components within the target language production. He stated that by examining the components affecting communicative behavior, it is possible for interpreters to "identify components that pertain to the context within which the interaction occurs and components that pertain to the nature of the communicative message itself" (p. 19).

Drawing on the work of Halliday (1978) and Hymes (1972), and writing specifically on interpretation, Cokely (1992a) identified components that affect communicative behavior as "interaction factors" and "message factors." The interaction factors that may influence the context of situation and, therefore, the work of interpreters, were defined within a taxonomy devised to include setting, purpose, and participants. The setting takes into account a range of environmental or extralinguistic factors that may influence interactive outcomes; whereas the purpose considers the activities, participant goals, and subject matter that occur within an interaction. The "activity" component accounts for the range of purposes in which participants might be involved in an activity. The "participant" component refers to characteristics of individuals, or characteristics of actual or perceived relationships between individuals, that may affect the communicative interaction. In referring to the work of Hymes (1972),

Cokely also highlighted the importance for interpreters to recognize how "message factors" may affect an interaction. The message form and content is obviously a crucial component to consider, along with the message key, its channel and language form, the interaction norms and interpretation norms, and the discourse genre.

It can be seen, therefore, that by defining the nature of a communicative interaction and establishing the context of situation, it is possible to predict what should be expected of interpreters when placed in those situations. In discussing the context of situation, it has been acknowledged that language use varies according to the situation a person is in and the context of any interactional involvement they have. The language variation that arises as a consequence of contextual and situational diversity is the biggest consideration for working interpreters, as they must be prepared to adapt their language use accordingly.

Situational Language Variation

Situational variables are observable where the same person speaks differently in different environments. Studying language from this angle often means thinking about the role or function which language is playing in a situation. This in turn means that you can gauge the status and mutual familiarity of speakers, and their reason for needing to communicate, from the style or **register** which they use. (Wray, Trott, & Bloomer, 1998, p. 93).

In discussing language variety and situations of use, Finegan, Besnier, Blair, and Collins (1992) used the term *linguistic repertoire* to describe language varieties exhibited in the speaking and writing patterns of a speech community. Others refer to *diatypic variation* when classifying language according to its use in social situations (Wray, et al., 1998). According to Zimmer (1989), register, or style variation, involves differential language use that is sensitive to situational factors. Wardhaugh (1992) and Fromkin et al. (1990), however, made a clear distinction between style and register.

Wardhaugh (1992) described *styles* as different ways of speaking either formally or informally, depending on the circumstances. He defined *register*, however, as "sets of vocabulary items associated with discrete occupational or social groups" (p. 49). Fromkin et al. (1990) described styles as "situation dialects" that range between two extremes of informal and formal language use and are influenced by the speaker's attitude towards the receiver, the subject matter, or the purpose of the communication. *Register* is defined as language variety that is determined entirely by subject matter. Fromkin et al. asserted that style or register variation includes not only changes in vocabulary but also an adaptation of grammatical rules. For example, "in an informal style, the rules of contraction are used more often, the syntactic rules of negation and agreement may be altered, and many words are used that do not occur in the formal style" (p. 266). Different subject matters such as legal prose or cooking recipes are given as examples of different register variation, with the former using longer sentences, more archaic words, longer adverbial elements, and explicit repetition; whereas the latter uses short simple sentences, verbs in the imperative mood, and prepositional phrases. In summarizing their concept of the linguistic repertoire of a monolingual community, Finegan et al. (1992) stated that language register is determined by a set of linguistic features, combined with characteristic patterns of how the language is used in different situations, yet with all varieties of the language relying on essentially the same grammatical system. In addition, they asserted that rules governing register variations accompany nonlinguistic behavior such as standing, sitting, physical proximity and face-to-face positioning.

Many of these various definitions have developed as a consequence of an established model of register devised by Joos (1967), which postulated five different styles of communication, ranging through different levels of formality. Halliday (1978) has criticized this particular model by questioning the notion of "formality" and what it means. It should be acknowledged that by concentrating on finite styles, this type of model can be limiting because language is a living entity and is therefore difficult to compartmentalize. Nonetheless, for the purpose of analyzing language production and the impact that this can have on interpreters, it is worth exploring the definitions put forward by Joos (1967), as they provide categories that can be generalized for discussion of language and interpretation.

Joos proposed five distinct registers or styles of language use: frozen, formal, consultative, informal, and intimate. Each register has specific characteristics and unwritten rules that determine interactional norms, syntactical and sentence complexity, lexical choices, "volume" of speech production, rate of speech production, and appropriate subject matter for discussion. The characteristics of each register are now briefly introduced.

The frozen register incorporates texts that are the same each time they are used and are usually ritualistic in their use. For example, recitation of the Lord's Prayer or singing of the national anthem. In these instances, the meaning and intent is derived more from the purpose of the frozen text, rather than what the text itself actually says. That is, the ritual of people coming together in church to recite the Lord's Prayer would give more meaning than listening to the words of the prayer itself.

The formal register refers to situations where invariably there is one dominant speaker and a group of listeners, with virtually no turn-taking between the speaker and audience. Examples of situations where formal register is used would include a keynote address at a conference, a university lecture, or a presidential address. These types of settings are often distinguishable by physical and psychological separation between speaker and audience, whereby physical positioning and lighting psychologically emphasize the boundaries between speaker and audience. Certain characteristics of language use in a formal register would include no turn-taking, less colloquialisms in lexical choices, more convoluted and complex sentence structure, slower and more deliberate rate of speech production, and amplified volume of speech production.

Consultative register is used during interactions when one interlocutor has "expert" knowledge, and their advice or guidance is being sought. The difference between this and formal register is that interaction occurs between speaker and audience to ensure that communication is happening. Common examples include meetings between teacher and student, doctor and patient, or lawyer and client. There are certain unwritten rules for turn-taking and interaction that are expected to be adhered to, such as a student raising his or her hand in the classroom before addressing the teacher or a patient not interrupting when a doctor is giving a diagnosis. Language characteristics include the use of complete, compound sentence structures and specialized or technical vocabulary pertinent to the subject matter being discussed. Individuals will change their role according to the knowledge being sought and their ability to provide that knowledge. Humphrey and Alcorn (1996) give an example of an interaction between a lawyer and a plumber. Depending on whether it is legal advice or a quote for plumbing that is required, this will dictate whether it is the lawyer or the plumber who takes on the role of "expert" in that particular interaction.

The use of informal register tends to imply the equal status of the interaction participants. Turn-taking is more fluid, and acceptable levels of interruptions are allowed. Sentences tend to be shorter, which therefore leads to a faster rate of delivery. Use of colloquialisms, slang, and less punctilious use of grammar are often observed in informal discourse. Common examples of this register of language use would be interactions between neighbors, students, or work colleagues.

Intimate register is used by individuals when interacting with others with whom they share one or more common experiences. Due to assumed knowledge, the communication dynamics change in that information does not necessarily need to be clearly presented. This register would most often be used between friends, parents and children, siblings, and couples; it is identifiable by rapid turn-taking, the use of incomplete sentences, and lack of specialized vocabulary or terminology.

Although Joos (1967) presented these registers as discrete entities, observation of language use demonstrates that overlap does occur. For example, speakers at formal functions may incorporate consultative or informal register norms into their presentations in order to create more of a rapport between themselves and their audiences. Similarly, teachers may use a more formal style and discourage interaction, even when they are in the consultative setting of a classroom (Humphrey & Alcorn, 1996). Therefore, although it is useful to refer to the work of Joos as a basis for describing language, the context of situation also needs to be taken into account, adopting more descriptive techniques as suggested by Halliday (1978).

The concept of language registers and styles presents a challenge for interpreters in that they need to be familiar with the norms of interaction and language use for different situations, and they must adapt their interpretations accordingly. In searching for linguistic and cultural equivalents, interpreters need to be aware of appropriateness of language use in relation to context of situation. For instance, a perfect equivalent may be found, but its use would only be appropriate for informal conversation, not for a formal lecture presentation.

The concept of register variation or "diglossia" in signed languages has been debated, and there is general agreement within the literature that it does exist (Davis, 1989; Deuchar, 1979, 1984; Fontana, 1999;

Lee, 1982; Llewellyn Jones, Kyle, & Woll, 1979; Lucas & Valli, 1989, 1990; Stokoe, 1969; Woodward, 1973; Zimmer, 1989). There has been some disagreement, however, about the salient characteristics of a sign language register. Zimmer stated that register "is an abstract notion that is not easily definable, and any given speech event may be difficult to categorize as a variant" (1989, p. 257).

The main issues for sign language researchers have been the "continuum" of sign language varieties that can exist simultaneously within one Deaf community and whether one form of signed communication should be considered as more "formal" than another. It is widely accepted that sociolinguistic variation exists in signed languages across age, social class, gender, ethnic group, religious affiliation, educational background, and geographical location in the form of accents and dialects (Lucas, Bayley, Valli, Rose, & Wulf, 2001; Sutton-Spence & Woll, 1998), but the notion of variation according to language use within particular situations has given rise to different theories.

Earlier notions of diglossia in signed languages were discussed by Stokoe (1969) and Deuchar (1979), who distinguished between a "high" variety of sign language used at formal functions, and a "low" variety used informally. Deuchar stated that the high variety she observed in BSL was actually a form of Signed English, with the low variety being a purer form of BSL with no English interference. This theory does not deserve much credence, however, due to the perjorative undertones of superior versus inferior language use, especially as in a later publication, Deuchar (1984) commented that the Signed English she had previously observed tended to be the variety of sign language used by hearing people involved with the Deaf community, rather than that of Deaf people themselves. More appropriately, Woodward (1973) suggested a diglossic continuum rather than two distinct varieties. Llewellyn Jones et al. (1979) accepted the notion of two varieties of sign language (that is, BSL and Signed English), but suggested that Signed English is not commonly used among members of the Deaf community, but rather is a form of communicating with hearing people. Thus Llewellyn Jones et al. perceived that members of the British deaf community were not diglossic in their language use because those who used the high variety were marginal to the community or part of its elite, and, therefore, they had privileged access to a more formal variety of language that was inaccessible to the majority of the community.

Lawson (1981) stated that Deaf people had not yet become adjusted to the idea of using BSL as the language of formal meetings, hence the reliance on Signed English. Llewellyn Jones (1981a) demonstrated, however, that a formal register exists in BSL by videotaping Deaf sign language users in different environments, including formal meetings. In retrospect, it is possible that the use of Signed English observed by Deuchar (1979, 1984) and Llewellyn Jones (1981a) was in fact a contact variety of BSL used in formal situations.

Thus it can be seen that it is feasible to consider sign languages as having their own form of situational language variation. Examples of situations where more formal registers of signed languages are used are academic lectures, business meetings, banquets, and church (Baker & Cokely, 1980; Lee, 1982).

Zimmer (1989) presented findings of a study that demonstrated that situational language variance does exist within ASL. Although this is only one study, and it is not necessarily conclusive that all sign languages demonstrate situational variance, it is worth considering as an overview of the linguistic characteristics of a signed language register. In Zimmer's study, a Deaf native signer was videotaped in three different situations: a lecture, an informal talk, and an interview; and his sign language output was analyzed for phonological, lexical, morphological, and syntactical differences.

Zimmer stated that there was a phonological distinction in the use of space between the three situations. In the lecture, the Deaf person used a much larger signing space (volume), whereas in the other two he used a more neutral space. Body movements were also more pronounced when lecturing, with more switching of signs between the dominant and non-dominant hand. In the lecture, there was no overt evidence of assimilation of signs (whereby signs assimilate features of other signs immediately preceding or following each other), and no use of anticipation (whereby the base handshape is in place before the dominant handshape begins to make the sign). Also there was infrequent use of perseveration (whereby a nondominant base handshape stays in place after the dominant hand has moved onto making the next sign).

Lexical and morphological differences noted included the use of particular signs used in the lecture that were not used in the informal talk or interview, plus the use of colloquial signs in direct speech but not in the body of the lecture. A certain type of morphological inflection was noticeable in the lecture presentation, where Zimmer suggested the exaggerated movement of a sign was used instead of some nonmanual features.

Syntactically, the lecture made extensive use of rhetorical questions, made more use of metaphorical signs and metaphorical description, less topicalization, and more boundary marking with use of the lexical item *now*. Although this data was only collected from one Deaf signer, it is sufficient to illustrate that sign languages incorporate marked differences in the production of the language according to the context of situation. Sign language interpreters, therefore, are faced with the same challenge as spoken language interpreters in dealing with the variety of language registers they may come across in different interpreting situations. Zimmer (1989) noted that knowledge of language register variation is critical for interpreters to be able to effectively reproduce an equivalent message, as an interpretation can be accurate content-wise, but lacking if an inappropriate register is used.

From my own observations of Deaf people using Auslan and BSL in different contexts, it would seem that situational variance does occur. As a working interpreter, I have interpreted in a variety of different situations, from meetings, to conferences, to performances, and have noted a difference in sign language output of Deaf participants, depending on the formality of the situation. It is my opinion, therefore, that characteristics of language contact between signed and spoken languages are prevalent in formal discourse environments, such as university lectures. As this comment is not based on any empirical research, the statement should be regarded merely as an anecdotal observation.[2]

Nonetheless, the issue of language contact has been recognized in the sign language research field, and it merits consideration. Lucas and Valli (1989) stated that "one of the major sociolinguistic issues in the deaf community concerns the outcome of language contact" (p. 11), in the fact that a specific kind of signing exists as a result of contact between signed and spoken languages. The majority of studies of language contact in the Deaf community have taken place in the US; however, one recent study of the situation in Italy observed that similar phenomena are present in other Deaf communities (Fontana, 1999).

---

2. I have since conducted research comparing language contact features used by deaf presenters and interpreters in academic lectures (see Napier, 2006).

Woodward (1973) claimed that this contact variety is a pidgin—a result of interaction between Deaf and hearing people. Cokely (1983b), Lucas and Valli (1989, 1990), and Davis (1989), however, refuted this claim. Cokely (1983b) referred to criteria normally required as pre-conditions for the development of a pidgin language (asymmetrical spread of the dominant language, relatively closed network of interaction, and attitude of a significant number of users that the emerging variety is a separate entity), to illustrate that language contact between ASL and English has not necessarily led to the emergence of a pidgin. Instead, he argued that the dynamics of "foreigner talk,"[3] judgments of proficiency, and learners' attempts to master the target language result in a continuum of language varieties within ASL.

Lucas and Valli (1989, 1990) described the characteristics of language contact between ASL and English as code-switching and code-mixing, whereby English words are mouthed on the lips or manually coded (finger-spelled) while the signer is still using linguistic features of ASL. They also noted that contact signing yields "idiosyncratic syntactic constructions . . . that fit neither the ASL nor the English grammatical system" (p. 30).

Lucas and Valli (1989, 1990) and Fontana (1999) suggested a variety of sociolinguistic factors that influence the use of code-switching and mixing between a signed and a spoken language, including lack of familiarity between participants, and more importantly for the purposes of this study, associated with the formality of a situation. According to Lucas and Valli (1989, 1990), more English "interference" occurs in more formal situations, when technical or specialized terms are used, and thus are incorporated into ASL in the form of mouth patterns or fingerspelling.

Davis (1989, 1990a, 1990b) adopted the same perspective on language contact as Lucas and Valli (1989, 1990), and he referred to code-switching and code-mixing between ASL and English as "interlingual transference." He explored the use of these language contact phenomena in interpretations of English into ASL and found that the mouthing of English words

---

3. "Foreigner talk" is the simplified register often identified as being appropriate for addressing foreigners or 'outsiders' (Fontana, 1999). Certain features that characterize foreigner talk include: short sentences; lack of function words; avoidance of colloquialisms; repetition of lexical items; slow and exaggerated enunciation; and less use of inflections (Ferguson & DeBose, 1977; cited in Cokely, 1983b).

and the use of fingerspelling is patterned. Typically, he found that "English mouthing marks fingerspelled words, most lexicalized fingerspelling is used for emphasis, lists, numbers, and question words" (1989, p. 101); and all of these features were identified as being appropriate to ASL. In relation to fingerspelling, Davis stated that an English word might be fingerspelled because an equivalent ASL sign does not exist. Alternatively he observed that a "multi-meaning" ASL sign can be prefaced, or tagged, with a finger-spelled word. In such cases, Davis noted that "the fingerspelled words are flagged in very specific ways, for example, mouthing, eye-gaze, indexing, labelling, quotation markers, and palm orientation" (p. 102).

Davis's (1989, 1990a, 1990b) study showed that interpreters used contact varieties of sign language appropriate to the situation they were interpreting in, which was a lecture. These findings thus agree with the conclusions of Lucas and Valli (1989, 1990) that the formality of a situa-tion influences the use of language contact phenomena in sign language. Davis (1989, 1990a, 1990b) also demonstrated that the sign language interpreters in his study reflected the typical language use of Deaf people in this type of situation. Napier and Adam (2002), in a linguistic comparison of BSL and Auslan interpreters, drew similar conclusions. After comparing the sign language output of five BSL and five Auslan interpreters interpreting for the same formal presentation, they found that the interpreters' use of language reflected the language use of the Deaf communities for whom they were interpreting. For example, in rela-tion to fingerspelling, "Auslan exhibits a greater degree of fingerspelling use than does BSL . . . and this is reflected in the use of fingerspelling in the five Auslan interpreted texts" (p. 28). When considering the notion of language contact and sign language variation, the discussion highlights the need for interpreters to appropriately reflect the language used by Deaf people when participating in formal interactions and to observe the "rules" of the discourse genres in which they are interpreting.

Discourse Genres

Discourse analysis can be applied to any form of communicative inter-action in an attempt to identify various discourse genres. Studies of alter-native discourses have included genres such as narratives (Chafe, 1980), jokes (Sacks, 1974), and conversations (Schegloff, 1972; Tannen, 1984b). Discourse analysis is relevant to the study of both monologue and dialogue (Longacre, 1983); therefore, lectures, as typical monologues, can be considered as a distinct discourse genre. Cokely (1992a) noted, however, that very few descriptive studies have focused on the particular monologic discourse of lectures. Instead, general observations have been made about the characteristics of lectures. Before going on to discuss these characteristics, it is necessary to define what is meant by *a lecture.*

> A lecture is an institutionalized extended holding of the floor in which one speaker imparts his views on a subject, these thoughts comprising what can be called his "text." The style is typically serious and slightly impersonal, the controlling intent being to generate calmly considered understanding, not mere entertainment, emotional impact, or immediate action. (Goffman, 1981, p. 165)

Lakoff (1982) defined lectures in a similar way to that of Goffman (1981), whereby one participant in the interactive discourse is in control, selects the subject matter, and decides when the discourse should start and finish (cited in Cokely, 1992a). Therefore it can be seen that lectures can be characterized as nonreciprocal monologues, or "expository monologues" (Cokely, 1992a, p. 27).

In drawing on the work of Longacre (1983) and applying discourse analysis to expository monologues in general, certain characteristics can be identified as being distinct from those of narratives. A typical expository monologue relies on topical or logical linkage, as opposed to the inherent chronological nexus often observed in narratives. The focus of expository monologues tends to be on a theme or set of related themes, rather than on participants (such as in narratives). Plus, more tension—struggle or polarization—can be found in an expository monologue than in a narrative. Longacre noted that effective expository discourse should inherently incorporate an effort to ensure clarity of information, especially when people receiving the discourse may not have the necessary background knowledge.

In focusing on characteristics of a lecture, and the language production within this discourse genre, Goffman (1981) highlighted three different modes of speech production that establish presenters on a different "footing"[4] with their audience. These modes are memorization, reading

---

4. "A change in footing implies a change in the alignment we take up to ourselves and the others present as expressed in the way we manage the production

aloud, and fresh talk. He stated that lecturers often choose to read aloud from prepared texts, which influences the reception and responsiveness of an audience. According to Goffman, people may choose to read out printed text rather than spontaneously provide fresh talk due to the different dynamics of written and spoken texts, which implies that written language has more status.

> Consider the effect of "high style," even if issuing from a patently read address. Elegance of language—turns of phrase, metaphor, parallel structures, aphoristic formulations—can be taken as evidence not only of the speaker's intelligence...but also of his giving his mind and ability over to the job he is now performing. (p. 189)

Goffman asserted that the register of language used in a lecture is important in defining the relationship between speaker and audience. Therefore, although perceptions of "good writing" and "good speaking" are systematically different, people will often choose to read aloud previously prepared texts when delivering a lecture, as printed text tends to be more coherent than spontaneously produced spoken text.

This finding has implications for interpreters who are working in university lectures. Halliday (1978) suggested that academics often deliver lectures using a written language structure of speech production. He argued that academics are so influenced by their environment and the assumption of literate intelligence of university students that they produce lexically dense spoken text when lecturing. Lexically dense spoken text is characterized by its conformity to typical written language structure, with a higher number of lexical words than grammatical words.

Before discussion of lexical density can take place, however, it is necessary to consider characteristics of a lecture provided in a signed language rather than a spoken language, and whether there are any marked differences. Sign language interpreters working in lectures would need to consider the expectations of spoken and sign language users attending a lecture and the language use they would expect to receive.

---

or reception of an utterance. A change in our footing is another way of talking about a change in our frame for events" (Goffman, 1982, p. 128).

As mentioned earlier, Zimmer (1989) noted marked differences in signing style between a lecture environment and two other less formal environments. Kluwin (1985) studied the ability of Deaf students to acquire information from a signed lecture and found that the salience of the information presented had an impact on the amount of recall. However, this impact was seen to depend not only on the sign language fluency of the presenter, but also that of the receivers. Christie et al. (1999) compared the visual representations of discourse structures of ASL, spoken English, and written English in order to facilitate the development of Deaf students' academic bilingualism. Students were asked to create a formal narrative in ASL incorporating appropriate discourse features of ASL formal register. The features highlighted were the same as those previously discussed by Roy (1989b).

Roy conducted a study looking at particular discourse features of an ASL lecture. In a general context, Roy stated that lectures are discourses with particular goals in mind, tend to be monologues that satisfy informational goals, and are content-oriented. She claimed that lectures require the use of linguistic devices to give the listener a clear idea of how an utterance fits into the lecture process as a whole. The linguistic elements are not part of the content, per se, but are used as a guide by listeners as to how they should interpret the information they are receiving. Words and phrases used as cohesive, structural devices can contribute to the listener's ability to distinguish between major and minor points, old and new information, and shifts in the flow of topics. Roy described the lecture as adhering to a particular construct, whereby the organizational structure incorporates a natural chain of events linking subtopics. She stated that there is general agreement in society that most lectures open with an introduction and some explanation of the purpose of the lecture, followed by the main body of the lecture and an obligatory summary. The naturally occurring segments of a lecture are also referred to as "episodes," which can be distinguished by the use of certain discourse markers.

In the ASL lecture, Roy found that the sign for "now" was most often used as a discourse marker, as it was used to mark a shift into a new subtopic, rather than just indicating the present time in an ongoing discourse. The sign for "now that," however, was used to signify a shift into a group of episodes within the discourse. Bienvenu (1993) described similar features of formal ASL discourse to those outlined by Roy (1989b) in terms of "opening, middle, and closing features"; "developmental episodes"; and the need for repair strategies (cited in Christie et al., 1999).

Although it is acceptable that signed language lectures would adhere to a particular construct in much the same way as spoken lectures, it could be argued that the discourse markers suggested by Roy (1989b) are not characteristics of a formal register, but rather idiosyncratic use of formal language. It is inevitable that lectures presented in signed languages will incorporate discourse markers to indicate the formality of the situation, but the characteristics may vary from person to person. Lecturers may therefore conform to shared notions of the organizational structure of a lecture, indicative of a formal register, such as pausing or repetition, but may use individual preferences for signs to indicate a shift in topic or subtopic. For example, with reference to the signs "now" and "now that" mentioned by Roy, it is possible that people may choose to sign "okay," "right," "well," or "so" in much the same way as people might use these words as discourse markers in spoken English.

Nonetheless, sign language interpreters need to incorporate their knowledge and understanding of the lecture as a discourse genre into any interpretations they provide, taking into account the linguistic features of the language register; specifically, the potential for the lecture source text to be "lexically dense."

Lexical Density

Lexical density represents the complexity that is typical of written language (Crystal, 1995; Gerot & Wignell, 1995; Halliday, 1985), and it can be used as a measure of difficulty of a piece of text (O'Loughlin, 1995; Richards, Platt, & Flatt, 1992). The notion of lexical density is discussed here in the context of university lectures and how information is presented. It has been established that lectures are often read aloud, whereby the presenter will read verbatim from a written text. Alternatively, due to environmental influences, academic lecturers may present spoken language using a written language structure. Halliday (1985) made the distinction between spoken and written English by asserting that "most written English does not sound too good in speech" (p. 77). He contended that although they are both kinds of the same language, written and spoken English have different characteristics, yet speech is no less structured than writing: "Spontaneous speech is unlike written text. It contains many mistakes, sentences are usually brief and indeed the whole fabric of verbal expression is riddled with hesitations and silences" (p. 76).

Lakoff (1979) suggested that some of the major factors influencing differences between spoken and written discourse are the "informality," "spontaneity," and "inconsequentiality" of speech in comparison with writing (cited in Beaman, 1984). Typically spoken text has complex sentences with simple words, whereas written text has complex words in simple sentences, which Halliday (1979) suggested is because writing is static compared with speech, which is dynamic. As a consequence, spoken language tends to be less lexically dense than written language. Ure (1971) stated that the lexical density of an English text is a function first of the medium (i.e., spoken or written), and second, a function of the social environment (i.e., pragmatic language use). This statement highlights how academic lecturers may be influenced working in an environment where pragmatic language use is often based on technical research, which therefore allows their spoken language production to be influenced by the written language medium.

Language can be divided into lexical items (content words) and functional items (grammatical words); therefore, the number of lexical and functional items in a text determines its lexical density. A lexically dense passage, for example, would feature a higher number of lexical items than functional items. Halliday (1985) stated that, typically, written language is dense and spoken language is not, in that "written language displays a much higher ratio of lexical items to total running words" (p. 61). Therefore, "the more 'written' the language being used, the higher will be the proportion of lexical words to the total number of running words in the text" (p. 64).

Grammatical words in a language function in closed systems of the language; that is, they can be identified as determiners, the majority of prepositions, conjunctions, and some classes of adverbs and finite verbs (e.g., *the, has, to, on*). Content words, however, operate in open systems of the language, where different classes of the language cannot be closed off (e.g., *door, gate, window*, etc.). As content words, lexical items can be constituents of variable length and, therefore, can consist of more than one word; for example, the phrase *stand up* functions as one lexical item. Modal verbs, such as *always* and *perhaps*, are on the borderline between lexical and functional items; thus for the purpose of any analysis, a decision needs to be made about which category the modal verbs will be incorporated into, and there must be consistency in the counting. One generally identifiable difference between lexical and functional items is in the spelling. Lexical items usually have a minimum of three letters, whereas functional items can have only two.

In reporting lexical density of text, calculations can be presented in the following way: If a piece of text has a ratio of twelve lexical items to eight functional items, the proportion of lexical items can be seen to be 12 out of 20; therefore the lexical density of that particular piece of text would be 60%.

Ure (1971) used the above application to analyze alternate spoken and written texts and developed a list of typical density percentages. The various spoken texts (including informal dyadic conversation, storytelling, radio interview, and sports commentary) were found to have a range of lexical density from 23.9% to 43.2%. The written texts (including school essays, children's stories, manuals, and newspaper reports), however, had a range from 35.8% to 56.8%. Therefore, Ure found that spoken text has an average lexical density of 33%, and written text has an average lexical density of 46%. In relation to the spoken texts, he found that all the texts with a density of 36% or more were monologues, whereas all those under 36% involved some form of interaction. A typical spoken lecture had a lexical density of 39.6%.

INTERPRETING FOR LEXICALLY DENSE TEXT

According to Messina (1998), previously prepared texts that are read out verbatim create more problems for interpreters than spontaneous speech. He cited the "peculiarities of written texts and how they are usually delivered by speakers" as having the biggest effect an interpreter's performance (p. 148). In this regard, Messina is referring not only to the grammatical simplicity and lexical density of written text, but also to the prosodic features of speech delivery when reading text aloud. Some examples include monotonous intonation, faster rate of delivery, and lower frequency of pauses.

Balzani (1990) studied interpreters' performances when working from a written text that was read out and found that more mistakes were made (cited in Messina, 1998). The key issue for interpreters when dealing with lexically dense text is "higher risk of impaired understanding and interpretation as the interpreter's processing capacities reach saturation" (Messina, 1998, p. 156). The notion of text being read out, however, is not the only difficulty for interpreters. Spoken texts that are not necessarily read out, but are prepared, may also be lexically dense, and thus provide a challenge to interpreters.

Interpreters, therefore, may face difficulties in interpreting any spoken text that is more lexically dense than usual (i.e., has a lexical density of more than 33%). A university lecture is a good example of the kind of source text that may prove challenging for an interpreter working with any language. It is important to remember the point made by Halliday (1978) that academics often deliver lectures using a structure of language more typical of written than spoken language.

Sign Language Interpretation of Lexically Dense Text

In addition to challenges faced by interpreters in dealing with the delivery style of a lecture (such as speed, less pausing, etc.), the lexical density of university lectures has implications for how Deaf people will access information through sign language interpreters. As sign language has no conventional written orthography, a Deaf audience may have no frame of reference for what a lexically dense interpretation into a sign language should look like. This situation presents a challenge for sign language interpreters in that they have to decipher the meaning of a text and decide which lexical items are the most important to convey. Sign language interpreters have to take into account the following issues: The language contact situation of interpreting between spoken and signed languages; what the norms of sign language production would be for a lecture in general; what cultural relevance certain lexical items may hold, and thus what their linguistic and cultural equivalents may be; as well as deciding what linguistic coping strategies should be adopted in order to ensure that a Deaf audience receives the same message as a nondeaf audience. The *contextual force* or *relative impact* (Isham, 1986) of the message on the receiver ultimately should be, as much as possible, the same for both Deaf and nondeaf audiences.

Nida (1998) summarized the sociolinguistic and sociocultural contexts that require consideration throughout an interpretation into four categories: (1) the appropriate language register to be used in the context;

(2) the expectations of the target audience as to the type of translation they expect to receive; (3) distinctive sociolinguistic features of the source text; and (4) the medium employed for the translated text (i.e., written or spoken).

For sign language interpreters working with Deaf students in a university lecture, there are additional sociolinguistic and sociocultural factors to consider in addition to the lexical density of the text. Educational interpreting is unique to sign language interpreters (Bremner & Housden, 1996), and it requires special skills (Saur, 1992), as Deaf students have differing needs compared to those from other non-English-speaking backgrounds (Ozolins & Bridge, 1999). Typically in relation to education, spoken language interpreters may be used to facilitate discussion between parents and a teacher. For Deaf people, however, interpreters are used in the classroom in order to provide students with access to the actual teaching process itself.

When considering the issues faced by sign language interpreters in their everyday work in relation to managing communication, other issues can be highlighted in relation to interpreting for university lectures. The skills employed by interpreters have to be adapted to allow for conditions specific to the university discourse environment, so that educational interpreters can effectively contribute to the academic achievement of deaf students (Paul & Quigley, 1990). The interpreter needs to consider her role in an educational environment and the fact that Deaf people may be disadvantaged when compared to other university students. Although all university students may attend lectures without any background knowledge of the subject, and thus lack familiarity with subject-specific terminology, the interpreter is faced with the task of deciding how to provide an interpretation that is linguistically and culturally sensitive, incorporates meaningful equivalents, and still provides Deaf students with the opportunity to access specialized terminology that may be important for them to know in order to fully understand the subject of the lecture and pass examinations.

This context presents sign language interpreters with the dilemma of whether to freely interpret the content of a lecture or to establish a language contact situation that occasionally relies on the fingerspelling of English words and possible use of literal interpretation. In light of the interpreter's knowledge of the consumer's language and her knowledge of the topic and its terminology, the interpreter needs to decide which concepts should be interpreted into a sign language equivalent and which terms should be rendered literally. Thus, the interpreter will also need to judge the importance of lexical items presented in the lecture source text as well as when it might be appropriate to omit information for clarity. The interpreter's decision making will be influenced by how she perceives her role in this discourse environment.

As discussed earlier, the current thinking is that interpreters should present themselves as bilingual and bicultural mediators who make linguistic decisions based on their cultural knowledge of the groups for whom they are interpreting and their knowledge of interactional norms. In making decisions as to whether Deaf students need to access subject-specific terminology, interpreters should not perceive their role as educators, but rather as linguistic decision makers. Through this process of decision making, it is inevitable that interpreters will make omissions, some of which may be accidental and others that may be part of the linguistic decision-making process. Thus the interpreter will aid her decision making by employing key linguistic strategies.

I would suggest that sign language interpreters working in university lectures should switch translation style between free and literal methods as a linguistic coping strategy to enhance their decision-making process and their interpretation output. Use of this coping strategy would therefore give Deaf students access to specialized vocabulary when appropriate (through incorporation of fingerspelling in a literal interpretation), while providing a meaningful, conceptually accurate and culturally relevant message (through free interpretation). In order to enhance this process, another linguistic coping strategy would be for interpreters to employ the use of omissions strategically and delete irrelevant or redundant information, to effectively convey the message and intent of a university lecture. The notion of linguistic coping strategies and how interpreters use them is discussed further in chapter two.

Coping Strategies of Interpreters

The aim of this chapter is to elaborate on the notion of coping strategies in order to provide a clear definition of what is meant by the term *linguistic coping strategies*. By discussing the generic concept of coping strategies of interpreters, the detail of how translation style and omissions can be used by sign language interpreters as linguistic coping strategies can then be explored in more detail.

COPING STRATEGIES

The term *coping strategies* is an umbrella concept; that is, one that can encompass a plethora of discretionary facets according to individual interpretation. Little has been written on this explicit term, and alternative labels have included those such as, *coping tactics* (Gile, 1995), "strategies for the management of the communication event" (Roy, 1996, p. 63), *coping mechanisms* (Moser-Mercer, Kunzli, & Korac, 1998) and *creative problem-solving* (Mackenzie, 1998). Gran (1998), in fact, wrote about tactics as the interface between strategies and creativity. Alternative coping strategies can be used at different stages of the interpreting process. In describing the different stages, it is possible to provide a context within which to place linguistic coping strategies, and the consideration of translation style and omissions as potential linguistic coping strategies.

Stages of Coping

Coping strategies may be incorporated into any stage of the interpreting process, whether at the preparatory stage, during the assignment (in-situ), or retrospectively (Napier, 1996; Witter-Merithew, 1982), and can be defined as "those methods or techniques adopted by interpreters to ensure that: (1) they are able to carry out the task as fluidly as possible;

(2) intrusion or misunderstanding occurs as little as possible; (3) external factors are controlled; and (4) comfort and confidence is retained throughout the interpreting assignment" (Napier, 2001, p. 72).

Preparatory strategies may include obtaining papers and other preparation materials before an assignment; researching particular topics of assignments and familiarizing oneself with key terminology (through books, journals, or the Internet); keeping up with current affairs; consultation with co-workers in advance of an assignment with regard to tandem interpreting procedure;[1] or liaising with clients to establish working practices (e.g., lengths of working periods, seating arrangements, lighting, etc.). These are only a few examples of the lengths that interpreters may go to before they start working, to ensure that they have as much background knowledge about the assignment as possible and can predict and deal with any possible difficulties (Shaw, 1997).

Mackenzie (1998) emphasizes the need for thorough preparation, which "requires an analysis of the situation in which the need for translation has arisen. On the basis of this analysis the translator can decide what specific questions need to be asked" in order to locate and define any potential problems (p. 202). Turner (2001) suggests that all interpreting assignments have a dimension of "preparability" whereby "the more preparable an assignment is . . . the less complex it might be considered" (p. 68). He proposes a schema of twelve dimensions for interpreters to consider in order to decide whether they will have the strategies to cope with an interpreting assignment and, therefore, whether to accept an assignment. These dimensions include aspects such as the interpreter's familiarity with the language and context, the potential language diversity of consumers, the technicality of the language that will be used, and the sensitivity and perceived difficulty of the assignment. By identifying

---

1. Tandem interpreting is a term generally used to describe two interpreters working together on the same assignment, whereby one will be active and work for a stretch of approximately twenty to thirty minutes, while the other is passive but provides on-going support. This arrangement has become the norm for the majority of assignments lasting longer than two hours, and has transpired as a result of research illustrating that the optimum period for interpreting is twenty minutes, after which the quality of the interpreting service will decline. If only one interpreter is used, regular breaks should be provided.

various sources of demand in their assignments, interpreters will be in a better position to control their input (Dean & Pollard, 2001) and will be better prepared to cope with any challenges that may arise within that assignment.

Retrospective techniques can combine any approach that an interpreter might use to reflect on an interpreting assignment, whether that means talking to clients or co-workers and obtaining feedback on her performance, watching or listening to a recording of an assignment and applying some form of critical analysis, or just generally pondering over the effectiveness of an assignment and remembering key issues for future reference. Many authors (such as Humphrey, 2000; Labath, 1998; West, 1994) have commended the use of reflective journals as a strategy for retrospectively considering the strategies used in interpreting assignments and how one coped in a particular setting. When in-situ, however, other problems may arise that the interpreter may have to deal with spontaneously, regardless of the amount of preparation carried out, which will require the interpreter to implement other coping strategies.

Spontaneous Problem Solving

Problems can arise spontaneously due to a number of factors, including linguistic interference, such as the comprehension, productive, and receptive language skills of the interpreter and clients; sociolinguistic influences from the discourse environment, such as accent, dialect, or register of language; metalinguistic awareness of the interpreter; as well as internal or external extralinguistic interferences due to poor prediction skills, fatigue, assumed knowledge of interpreter and clients, environmental distractions, and/or effectiveness of the co-working relationship. Several researchers have brought attention to these factors, and some have proposed resolutions while others simply raised the issues for deliberation (Anderson, 1978; Blewett, 1985; Brasel, 1975; Cooper, Davies, & Tung, 1982; Darò, 1994; Gerver, 1974).

In considering the spontaneous problem-solving skills of interpreters, Gile (1995) surmised that it is inevitable that problems will arise during interpreting assignments, regardless of interpreters' amount of experience. He identified that spontaneous problems may occur due to "processing capacity limitations, errors in processing capacity management, and gaps in the interpreters' knowledge base" (p. 191). Atwood (1985) described one particular extralinguistic factor—environmental distractions—that may require an interpreter to use spontaneous coping strategies. He referred specifically to verbal interjections that an interpreter may receive from a co-worker while they are working, which contributes to a "loss of equilibrium" for the interpreter (p. 94). He suggested different methods for resolving disagreements between co-workers by discussing appropriate phrases to use for clarification, as well as appropriate times and places for confrontations of this nature. The issue of auditory interjection while working has potentially huge linguistic ramifications for any interpreter because it can interfere with the language interpretation process. Unfortunately, Atwood touched on this issue very briefly, as he chose to concentrate on extralinguistic strategies for working in tandem, such as those mentioned above.

Fischer (1993) detailed more positive methods for interpreters working in tandem by focusing on proactive rather than reactive measures. She proposed guidelines to ensure that interpreters can work effectively together to provide a satisfactory service, taking into account other extralinguistic influences such as fatigue, techniques for feeding information, and working conditions.

Mackenzie (1998) distinguished between two types of problems that may occur (open- and close-ended), but only gave an explanation for the concept of open-ended problems. She postulated that many interpreters encounter open-ended problems where there is no predetermined solution that can be consciously solved through the use of controlled conditions. Rather, Mackenzie suggested that open-ended problems require the use of creative problem solving strategies. Although it can be agreed that coping strategies require interpreters to be creative in dealing with spontaneous problems, it can also be argued that problems can be solved consciously if interpreters have the ability to monitor their language choices. That is, if interpreters possess a level of metalinguistic awareness about the interpretation process.

Scheibe (1986) elaborated on the notion of creative problem solving by suggesting several steps including assessment of the problem, recognition of areas needing change and analysis of group dynamics. Her conclusions, however, were rather unsophisticated as she recommended the development of curiosity and allowing time to daydream as strategies for creative problem solving, without any recognition for the multi-layered linguistic processes involved in interpreting and the actual problems that may occur.

Riccardi (1998), however, asserted that the creative behavior of interpreters could be regarded as a problem-solving strategy, as the interpreting process is intrinsically creative by its nature. She gave credence to problem solving being part of a conscious process by describing two specific strategies that are applied according to the type of difficulties being faced. First she referred to skill-based strategies, which are automatic responses that are stored and can be carried out routinely as part of the interpreting process (such as typical conference proceedings activities, including greetings, thanking, running through an agenda, motions, etc.). She then discussed knowledge-based strategies, which require a different approach as they are implemented in new situations relying on conscious analytical processes and "stored knowledge" (p. 174). According to Riccardi, knowledge-based strategies require much more effort than skill-based strategies, as information processing throughout the interpretation is controlled and conscious.

It is this level of consciousness and analytical attention, or *metalinguistic awareness*, that is imperative in the decision-making process of selecting coping strategies when in-situ. One focus of this study is the level of metalinguistic skill that sign language interpreters have during the interpretation process. The metalinguistic, analytical abilities of any interpreter will influence the particular strategies chosen at any one time.

Metalinguistic Awareness

The concept of metalinguistic awareness is usually discussed within the context of language acquisition and development of literacy skills. Several writers have discussed the metacognitive skills that children acquire, the metalinguistic awareness they have about their own language development, and how this impacts their literacy skills (Clark, 1978; Karmiloff-Smith, 1986; Perner, 1988; Tunmer & Bowey, 1984; Tunmer & Herriman, 1984). Malakoff and Hakuta (1991) specifically discussed the translation skills and metalinguistic awareness of bilingual children.

Garton and Pratt (1998) defined metalinguistic awareness as "the ability to focus attention on language and reflect upon its nature, structure and functions" (p. 149), and stated that "those who work with language must be able to focus attention on it" (p. 150).

Therefore, the concept can be applied to interpreters and the skills they have to self-regulate and monitor their abilities in the languages they interpret between (Peterson, 2000; Smith, 2000). Perner (1988) postulated that in order for an ability to be metalinguistic, individuals must be able to focus their attention on their language use, and reflect on it, as well as appreciate the fact that it is language that they are reflecting upon (cited in Garton & Pratt, 1998). Bialystok and Ryan (1985a, 1985b) and Bialystok (1991a, 1993) asserted that metalinguistic awareness involves key skills. These skills include ability to analyze linguistic knowledge into categories, capability to control attentional procedures that select and process specific linguistic information, as well as facility to intentionally consider what aspects of language are contextually relevant.

It can be argued, therefore, that in order to function, interpreters should have highly developed metalinguistic awareness, as they are constantly having to analyze the linguistic structure of language, as well as having to consider sociocultural contexts of language use and individual message impact. According to Garton and Pratt (1998), the development of metalinguistic awareness provides skills of choice and control of language, and in addition serves to facilitate communication. As a consequence, they believe that metalinguistic awareness depends upon social interaction, as people need to gain access to feedback on their language use.

When applying this concept to the work of interpreters, it can be seen that they would rely on some form of interaction in order to develop their metalinguistic awareness. Interpreters will typically receive feedback from Deaf clients in the form of a head nod or other affirmative sign that they understand. If the feedback is negative, rather than positive, interpreters will need to be aware of what linguistic choices they made, and how to repeat or change them to make the interpretation understandable. This concept has been alternatively referred to as "meta-competence" (Nord, 2000), or the use of "meta-strategies" (Hoffman, 1997).

One of the interests of this particular study was the level of metalinguistic awareness or *metacognition* (Peterson, 2000) that sign language interpreters had about linguistic choices they made while interpreting in a university lecture, in particular in relation to the types of omissions they made and why. Darò, Lambert, and Fabbro (1996) noted that the conscious monitoring of attention during simultaneous interpretation may affect the number and types of mistakes made by interpreters. Thus, the aim of the research study was to demonstrate what types of omissions were made by interpreters, and whether they were applying "metacognitive strategies" (Smith, 2000) in making certain omissions, or whether the process was an unconscious one.

At this point, I would like to assert that coping strategies are not necessarily used to resolve problems, as has been the implication so far. Coping strategies can be regarded as different techniques that may be used to ensure that the interpretation is as effective as possible. Although some strategies may be reactive, they can often be pro-active and enhance an interpretation, rather than just dealing with something that has gone wrong. So far, none of the literature that has been discussed has made any reference to the nature of coping strategies as part of a linguistic process. It is these coping strategies, used as part of a linguistic process intrinsic to any piece of interpretation, that are the central focus of this book; that is, *linguistic coping strategies*. It is strategies of this kind that can contribute to the effectiveness of an interpretation as opposed to being used solely for crisis management.

LINGUISTIC COPING STRATEGIES

Most studies that refer in some way to the use of coping strategies as part of the linguistic interpretation process have been sociolinguistic studies focusing on interactive communication events. All of the studies, however, have a different approach to the concept of coping strategies, which are open for interpretation. Two authors analyzed interactive discourse (Roy, 1989a, 1992, 1996, 2000a; Metzger, 1995, 1999), one concentrated on particular linguistic strategies (Davis, 1989, 1990a, 1990b), whereas another focused on the use of free interpretation in relation to culturally bound information (Napier, 1998b, 1998c). These studies can be grouped according to the use of linguistic and cultural knowledge as a linguistic coping strategy, or the use of translation style as a linguistic coping strategy.

Use of Linguistic and Cultural Knowledge as a Coping Strategy

Roy's thesis (1989a), which was further developed in papers written in 1992 and 1996 and published as a book in 2000, looked at how an ASL interpreter can have an impact on the turn-taking sequences of a face-to-face dialogue. This impact occurs when the interpreter "*manages* each turn through knowledge of the linguistic and social meaning beyond what appears in the surface form" (1996, p. 40). The study looked at the coping strategies an interpreter used in order to control the turn-taking involved in a face-to-face interaction, from a sociolinguistic point of view.

The original study (1989a) involved Roy videotaping and transcribing a tutorial session between a university professor and a student, analyzing the video footage, and interviewing all three participants involved (the professor who could hear, the Deaf student, and the interpreter) about their perceptions in relation to particular turn-taking sequences and any confusion or misunderstanding that occurred. In the discussion of the results, Roy focused on studying the interpretation as a successful communication event, and she investigated what the interpreter did successfully rather than what he did wrong. Because the interpreter was bicultural as well as bilingual, he was able to use his knowledge of conversational interaction norms among hearing and Deaf people to ensure that the flow of communication was not constrained in any way. This factor meant incorporating a range of strategies such as taking his own turn, prompting the student to take a turn, acknowledging the power differential involved by occasionally yielding turns to the professor, and using lengthy time lags before interpreting certain utterances.

Analysis of the transcript revealed that the interpreter did not rely solely on the primary participants to control the turn-taking, although regular turns in the interpretation did take place that "resemble regular turns in ordinary face-to-face conversation" (Roy, 1996, p. 47). In the retrospective interview, where the videotape was played back with Roy asking the interpreter why he had made certain decisions, she was able to elicit that the interpreter was making conscious choices about what coping strategies to use (for example, when there was an overlap in conversation). Although the central focus of the study was not the interpreter's conscious awareness of the linguistic decisions he made about his interpretation, it can be seen that the interpreter did use his knowledge of linguistic and cultural dynamics and his metalinguistic awareness about that knowledge to formulate coping strategies in relation to turn-taking exchanges. Roy summarized this finding as follows:

> Turns taken by the interpreter were shown to be a mixture of the interpreter's decisions as well as the primary speakers' tacit agreement to

accept those decisions . . . [Interpreters are] involved in interpreting conventions for language use and in creating turn exchanges through their knowledge of the linguistic system, the social situation, and the discourse structure system. (p. 63)

Thus Roy asserted that interpreters need to be not only competent bilinguals but also knowledgeable about ways of speaking in social situations, as well as possessing "strategies for the management of the communication event" (p. 63).

Qian (1994), writing on spoken language interpreting, used a similar approach to that of Roy (1989a) and described how an interpreter affects the communication process Two situations were discussed where the interpreter was deemed to have stepped out of role and, therefore, inappropriately affected the communication. Qian (1994) stated that interpreters must "suppress instincts or impulses to interact with the participants of a communication event" in order to remain professional (p. 218). Roy (1989a, 1992, 1996, 2000a), however, would encourage interpreters to recognize those instincts and utilize them appropriately in order to enhance the effectiveness of the communicative interaction.

Metzger (1995, 1999) also looked at the influence that ASL interpreters have on interactive discourse between Deaf and hearing participants, but she focused on slightly different parameters and collected her data from within another kind of interpreted interaction. Whereas Roy (1989a, 1992, 1996, 2000a) concentrated on how the presence of an interpreter impacts turn-taking, Metzger (1995, 1999) focused on what she called the *paradox of neutrality*. By using this term she was referring to the ideal that professional interpreters are expected to remain impartial throughout any interpreting assignment, and faithfully interpret every utterance; whereby "impartial rendering of the participant utterances helps ensure that interpreters do not selectively omit portions of other participant utterances" (1995, p. 9). The aim of Metzger's (1999) study was to "deconstruct the myth" of this neutrality by demonstrating that interpreters cannot remain completely impartial, thereby illustrating that the notion of neutrality is unrealistic.

Metzger (1995, 1999) argued that due to the very nature of their work, and the fact that interpreters are bilingual and bicultural, they are bound to use the knowledge they possess to make assumptions about their source language and target language audiences, and to make inferences about what an utterance will mean linguistically and culturally to each audience. This view implies that it is impossible for them to remain completely neutral within any interpreted interaction. She based this argument on the construct of "frame theory," and the notion that everybody has their own developed frames of reference for different concepts that have been shaped by their life experiences. As a consequence, interpreters will make specific choices within their interpretation as to what something means to them, and also what they assume it will mean to the interaction participants. In doing so, they are able to provide equivalent messages to each cultural group, thus making any utterance meaningful in a sociocultural context. In order to validate her argument, Metzger (1995) conducted an interactional sociolinguistic analysis of two interpreted medical interviews, one was a role-play performed by an interpreting student, and the other an actual medical appointment involving a professional interpreter. The former interview was recorded as part of an interpreter training program, with a copy given to Metzger at a later date with the permission of the participants. The interview took place in a large classroom with three participants, two hearing women and one Deaf man, and the encounter lasted for just over seven minutes. The latter interview involved Metzger being present at a real medical consultation and videotaping the interaction. The interview was held in a doctor's office with six participants—the doctor (male), nurse (female), interpreter (female), mother (female), child (male) and researcher (female), and lasted for approximately 26 minutes. The interviews were compared in order to establish the extent of the interpreters' influence on the interactive discourse, and whether they brought their own frames of reference to the communicative events.

Although Metzger (1995, 1999) acknowledged certain sociolinguistic influences on the study, such as having a researcher and/or video camera present, the language contact influence on the Deaf participants, and the differing lengths of each interview, other factors that may have affected the validity of her study were not raised. For example, the fact that each encounter involved different numbers of people, gender differences that may have influenced the dynamics, and the fact that the interviews recorded following different procedures under alternate conditions may have seriously skewed the comparability of the two cases. Another issue that needs to be taken into consideration is that comparison was made between only two interpreters, and these interpreters were at completely different skill levels. One was an interpreting student who was learning ASL as a second language; the other was a native ASL user with extensive experience as an interpreter. Thus the validity of juxtaposing two case studies that present different data can be questioned. Nonetheless, Metzger's findings highlight important qualities of an interpreter's work that can be identified as linguistic coping strategies and so still merit consideration.

Metzger found that a variety of linguistic features served as evidence of frames of reference, which included prosody, discourse sequences (such as question-answer pairs), topic initiation, and repairs. In each case study, the linguistic features used indicated that some of the participants' and interpreters' frames for events were mutual, whereas other frames were not shared. The interpreters were found to influence the interactive discourse in each case study in different ways through, for example, interruptions, clarifications, and responding to directed questions from either the hearing or Deaf participants. Metzger concluded that interpreters do bring their own frames of reference and assumed knowledge to any interpreted encounter, which can influence the dynamics of the interaction, and that some interpreters are more aware of this influence than others. She stated that because an interpreter's choice to include certain nonrenditions might be conscious, she will inevitably make choices that influence the outcome of any interaction.

When another perspective is applied to the research carried out by Metzger, it is possible to assert that interpreters use their assumed knowledge and make inferences as part of their repertoire of linguistic coping strategies. If they are making conscious decisions about finding equivalence between two languages and cultures, this implies that they have a certain degree of metalinguistic awareness about the interpretation process, and are therefore able to justify any decisions that are made.

The ramification of the decision-making process employed by interpreters in applying their linguistic and cultural knowledge to make strategic decisions to cope with a communication event, is that interpreters will invariably use their translation style as a linguistic coping strategy.

Use of Translation Style as a Coping Strategy

For my first piece of research I conducted a study of free interpretation and its use by BSL interpreters (Napier, 1998b). I adopted a similar approach to that of Metzger (1995), by applying the concept of frame theory to the process of interpretation, and questioned the ability of BSL interpreters to remain completely neutral. Methods of "free" and "literal" interpretation were discussed, and I made the assertion that interpreters should use the former if they regard themselves as linguistic and cultural mediators.

I agreed with other writers (McDade, 1995; Phillip, 1994; Pollitt, 1997; Scott Gibson, 1994), that the professionalization of sign language interpreting services has led to interpreters and Deaf people having different perceptions of what it means to be a professional interpreter, and that interpreters may no longer be meeting the needs of the Deaf community (Napier 1998b, 1998c). In relation to this point, I suggested that this phenomenon has led to feelings of mistrust between Deaf people and interpreters, in that interpreters are not trusted to do their job without having their translations checked, and interpreters feel vulnerable about their skills base. I then speculated that this mistrust manifests itself in literal interpretations being used by the majority of BSL interpreters, as this gives Deaf members of any audience the license to check their interpretation choices by lip-reading them, and then comparing the message with that of the original speaker.

I tested my theory by videotaping and analyzing the output of five BSL interpreters working from English into BSL. Each interpreter was asked to simultaneously translate a six-minute video clip that presented "culturally bound" information (Napier, 1998b, p. 60).[2] It was more than likely that the source text was lexically dense due to the fact that it was prepared text read aloud. All of the interpreters were given the opportunity to watch the clip through once before their task began, but were not told anything about the purpose of the research. Analysis of the results

---

2. The source material was deemed to be "culturally bound" in that it was taken from a British current affairs program that makes assumptions about the levels of language and life experiences of its viewers, which may not be compatible with the language levels and frames of reference of members of the Deaf community. Therefore as the information presented in the videoclip was 'bound' to the source language and culture, in order to find cultural equivalence when interpreting a piece such as this, free interpretation would be the most effective method. Similarly referred to by Cokely (2001) as "culturally rich" information.

showed that only two of the five interpreters provided what I defined as "culturally effective" interpretations (p. 66), by rendering the message using a free method of interpretation. The other three provided much more literal translations, and were found to make a larger number of inappropriate miscues.

The purpose of the study was to look at working practices of BSL interpreters in relation to their role as linguistic and cultural mediators, and to evaluate whether they meet the needs of the Deaf community. I argued that in order to effectively complement the requirements of Deaf people, interpreters should use their sociolinguistic and sociocultural knowledge of both the Deaf community and wider society to ensure any interpreted message is culturally, as well as linguistically, relevant to Deaf people's frames of reference. Although the study is an interesting one in terms of the use of free interpretation as a translation style, and the exploration of the relationship between BSL interpreters and Deaf people, in hindsight I can identify that the analysis was carried out subjectively. Although I proposed that *culturally effective* interpretations were born out of using a free interpretation approach, I did not provide any rationale for how the cultural effectiveness of the interpreted renditions was specifically defined. This weakness was taken into account for the study reported in this book, with the classification of translation "styles" of interpreters described in detail. The participants in my first study were not interviewed to determine the level of consciousness about their linguistic choices and how much was based on their sociolinguistic and sociocultural knowledge; therefore, only assumptions can be made about the interpreters' metalinguistic awareness of the interpreting process.

Nonetheless, in applying the notion of linguistic coping strategies, it can be contended that the use of free interpretation can be considered as a technique for coping linguistically with the dynamics of interpreting between two languages and cultures. As demonstrated by Napier, this is a strategy that some interpreters will employ, and others will not. In utilizing frame theory, assumed knowledge and by making inferences, interpreters should be able to make judgments about the linguistic and cultural meaning that needs to be equalized between two language communities. Therefore by using this knowledge, and employing a variety of approaches in dealing with the sociolinguistic and sociocultural information, sign language interpreters can be seen to be using linguistic coping strategies to enhance the effectiveness of their translations.

Davis (1989, 1990a) also explored influences on translation style but gave consideration to different linguistic features of a translation. He discussed language contact phenomena in ASL and the impact on interpreters' translation style when interpreting in a language contact environment by analyzing the linguistic interference and transference that took place when two lectures were interpreted from English into ASL. He used a videotape produced by Sign Media Inc., entitled *Interpreter Models: English to ASL* as the source of data for his analysis, in which two ASL interpreters could be seen to simultaneously interpret two 30-minute lectures without any rehearsal or interruptions. The interpreters were working in a language contact environment, with a mixed audience of five Deaf and nine hearing people. The audience was divided so that each interpreter was interpreting for a separate audience. Each interpreter could see the speaker and his or her audience, but could not see the other interpreter. Both interpreters were native users of ASL and were experienced, well-regarded interpreters in their profession.

Davis defined *linguistic interference* as the rules of one language being transferred to the other, as opposed to *linguistic transference*, which he defined as the transfer of material from the source language while the rules of the target language are maintained. Davis explained that for sign language interpreters working simultaneously between spoken English and ASL, some interference should be expected due to the highly divergent nature of the two languages. He surmised that "it is conceivable that a lack of ASL proficiency on the part of the interpreter can significantly contribute to linguistic interference" (1989, p. 91). He then made the assumption that native ASL users who work as interpreters will experience minimal English interference when they are interpreting into ASL, due to more thorough assimilation of both languages. However, this assumption seems naïve on Davis's part, as it is likely that some level of interference would be inevitable for all interpreters processing two languages at the same time, regardless of their language fluency, especially when fatigued.

In his analysis of the data, Davis (1989, 1990a) focused on the occurrence of code-switching, code-mixing (switching within a sentence or clause) and lexical borrowing within the interpretations of the lectures, and found that linguistic interference happened far less than linguistic transference. He identified that there is a rule-governed approach to code-mixing (transference) as both of the interpreters used it in very similar ways when making their language choices. For example, the interpreters used the mouthing of English words simultaneously with the production of ASL signs for nouns, question words, numbers and fingerspelled words. In relation to fingerspelling, Davis noted that the interpreters used a strategy of "nonce" fingerspelling for borrowing particular lexical items. In this case when the speaker introduced a word for the first time, the interpreters would fingerspell the lexical item, representing each letter (or ASL morpheme). The more the word was repeated, the interpreters either deleted or assimilated morphemes so that the fingerspelled word resembled a lexicalized sign rather than "a fingerspelled representation of an English orthographic event" (1989, p. 98). Davis described the participants, topic and setting as altering the extent of interlingual transference, due to the fact that some Deaf members of the audience may have been more bilingual than others, so the interpreters had the option to encode some spoken English words into the visual mode of ASL.

Davis's study (1989, 1990a) can be seen to effectively demonstrate how linguistic transference and interference occur throughout the process of sign language interpretation in a language contact environment. Nevertheless, it should be acknowledged that Davis's data was limited in that only two interpreters were studied, and both were native signers. Careful deliberation is needed, therefore, before extrapolating Davis's findings to the sign language interpreting population as a whole. In order to provide a more balanced perspective, an ideal study should incorporate use of both native and non-native signers. Yet it is still worthwhile considering the issues raised by Davis, as he made some interesting notes that can be discussed in relation to coping strategies.

Davis (1990b) developed his initial ideas in another paper where he described code-mixing, or *transference*, as a linguistic strategy that is used to avoid any vagueness or ambiguity within an interpretation, with interpreters encoding English forms in their ASL output, thus switching to a more literal translation style. He noted that when interpreters encoded English forms visually, they used systematic markers to elucidate discontinuities between ASL and English. For example, interpreters used the ASL sign for "quotation markers" before and after fingerspelling a lexical item in order to emphasize a lexical item that was not ASL. On the other hand, Davis described "interference" as the incorporation of encoded English into ASL output, which actually interferes with the propositional content of the message, and is "sporadic and unsignaled" (p. 308), without the patterning noted with the systematic use of markers when fingerspelling and mouthing.

It can be argued, therefore, that the transference skills that Davis (1989, 1990a, 1990b) highlighted can be regarded as linguistic coping strategies, in that interpreters made conscious decisions about the language choices they made in order to clarify information within the interpretation, and thus adapted their translation style accordingly. The selections made within the interpretation had to be conscious to some extent, as both interpreters used code-mixing in similar ways, and according to established rules of transference. Davis did not, however, follow up this theory in any of his discussions, so there is no way of knowing the extent of the interpreters' metalinguistic awareness about their own interpretation and the linguistic strategies they employed.

Various strategies that may be used to achieve cultural transfer were discussed by Ivir (1998). These include techniques such as borrowing, literal translation, substitution, addition, and omission.[3] Ivir stated that a translator's decision to select certain strategies is regulated by linguistic and communicative considerations, and translators' strategies are thus determined by a decision-making process, with each decision "made on its own merits, taking account of the context of the situation in which the translational act of communication takes place" (p. 138). For the purposes of this book, the focus is on linguistic coping strategies that require the incorporation of linguistic and cultural knowledge into an interpretation, and, therefore, give rise to a range of techniques that can be used to ensure that linguistic and cultural equivalence is achieved. The metalinguistic awareness that interpreters have about the strategies they employ, and the reasons they employ them, are also considered in relation to the use of translation style and the strategic use of omissions as part of a linguistic decision-making process.

---

3. For further discussion on additions and substitutions, see Cokely, (1985, 1992a); and for further elaboration on borrowing and literal translation, see Ivir (1998).

Use of Interpreting Omissions

One dictionary definition defines an omission as "something that has not been included or not been done, either deliberately or accidentally" (Fox, 1988, p. 547). Another describes omissions as "the action or an act of neglecting or failing to perform something, especially a duty" (Brown, 1993, p. 1994). In terms of omissions being used by interpreters, it would seem that the former definition is more appropriate as it makes a more positive statement about things not being included, rather than using negative connotations of failure.

The first definition also identifies that the act of omission can be accidental or deliberate, or to put it another way, unconscious or conscious. An example of an unconscious omission in interpreting may be that the interpreter simply does not hear a particular utterance and thus does not include it in the translation. Conscious omissions, however, would be those that are made, either deliberately or not, by an interpreter for a variety of reasons. An interpreter may be conscious of the fact that they have made an omission, but it was not necessarily a deliberate decision. For example, the interpreter may not understand the meaning of a word, or the interpreter does not immediately translate a word or concept as she is waiting for further elaboration, but as a consequence of waiting the information gets lost as more information is received. Alternatively, an interpreter may make a deliberate decision to consciously omit something as a result of evaluating the source message for cultural meaning, and determining its equivalence in the target language and culture. A conscious strategic decision can be made not to embrace certain concepts within the interpretation; that is, to omit those that have no relevance to the receivers of the interpretation, or those that are not central to the message and would prove more detrimental to understanding if left in. It is these strategic omissions that can be considered as strategies used by interpreters to cope with lexical density, and linguistic and cultural relevance.

There has been little research looking at this specific area of interpreting, nonetheless a few studies have been found and are reviewed here. Although it has been established that omissions can be used as a positive strategy to ensure effective interpretations, it is worthwhile comparing literature that looks at omissions from different perspectives. The studies that are reviewed here can be categorized as follows: those that place interpreting omissions within the context of errors or mistakes, and those that regard omissions as linguistic coping strategies that are intrinsic to an interpreter's work. Initially, the literature looking at omissions as mistakes is discussed, followed by a discussion of those studies that regard the use of omissions as a linguistic coping strategy.

OMISSIONS AS ERRORS

In order to discuss omissions as errors, it is helpful to explore the concept of error and language interpretation in general. Kopczynski (1980) concentrated a large part of his writing on errors made by interpreters. In establishing a context, he defined an error as "any utterance of the speaker-learner which deviates from the adopted norm" (p. 63). He identified two different kinds of errors: those that violate the rules of the norm that are not known to the learner (systematic errors) and those that violate the rules known to the learner (mistakes). Systematic errors were defined as those errors committed regularly by people at the same level of proficiency and with the same learning experience, also referred to as errors of competence. Mistakes, however, were categorized as occurring due to other influencing factors such as inattentiveness, stress and fatigue; otherwise known as errors of performance.

In introducing the notion of error analysis, Kopczynski stated that the only utterances that can be considered as erroneous are those that violate the known rules, (i.e., errors of performance). Kopczynski used a taxonomy of errors, originally proposed by Barik (1975), which distinguishes between three major types of errors where an interpreter may depart from the original source language message. These are omissions, additions, and substitutions, each of which is broken down into certain types. Additions include qualification, elaboration, relationship and closure additions; whereas substitutions incorporate mild and gross semantic errors based on lexical items or chunks of speech (such as phrases or sentences). The omission taxonomy detailed four types of errors: skipping (of a single lexical item); comprehension (omission of a larger unit of meaning as a result of an inability to comprehend the source language message); delay (omission of larger unit of meaning due to lagging too far behind the speaker); and compounding (conjoining elements from different clauses or sentences).

Kopczynski (1980) noted that Barik (1975) studied the number and type of omissions made by professional and amateur interpreters.

Barik found that both groups omitted approximately the same amount of material when working into their dominant language, as they did when working into their second language. He also identified that prepared translations experienced more omissions than those rendered spontaneously, with greater time lags resulting in a larger number of omissions.

Kopczynski (1980) conducted his own study, using Barik's (1975) error analysis taxonomy, in an attempt to determine the borderline between correct and erroneous translation. He selected a piece of text giving political toasts from a diplomatic reception and asked eight students of interpreting to perform the task of translation between English and Polish. The study used a lexically dense piece of text relying on formal register of language, which Kopczynski (1980) described as the "type of text that may be classed as a written monologue intended for oral delivery" (p. 76).

The findings of Kopczynski's study detailed different types of errors that occurred within the translations, including syntactic and phrasal errors of competence, lexical errors, errors of performance (e.g., hesitation, repetition, etc.), additions and omissions. In concentrating on omissions, it is worth noting that Kopczynski made the distinction between "obligatory" and "optional" omissions that arose as a result of differences between the structure of the two languages being interpreted (p. 85). These types of omissions were deemed more or less appropriate according to whether key words within a piece of text were translatable. The results demonstrated that more omissions were made than additions, regardless of the piece being translated simultaneously or consecutively. When omissions of whole or parts of sentences were looked at more closely, however, a much higher proportion of omissions took place within the consecutive interpretations. In his summary, Kopczynski defined omissions under both umbrellas of errors of performance and errors of receptive competence. He claimed that omissions could be regarded as performance errors because they can be affected by memory lapses, failure to choose the optimal moment of interpreting, time pressure and fatigue. He also asserted, however, that they can be regarded as receptive competence errors if they occur due to failure to understand the source language message (on the part of the interpreter).

In detailing Kopczynski's perspective on omissions, and how and why they occur, it is clear that he regarded omissions as errors or mistakes that occur during an interpretation. Apart from a fleeting mention of "optional" omissions, no indication is given within his writing that omissions may be used as a conscious part of the interpreting process, or as a linguistic coping strategy. There is no consideration that omissions may be used effectively to ensure that cultural equivalence is obtained as part of a successful interpretation. In order to gain insight into the interpretation process, it is possible to break down any interpretation and analyze for meaning and accuracy. Kopczynski should be commended for his detailed analysis and comparison of different interpretations, nonetheless it should be recognized that a more positive analysis can be done, still breaking down any interpretation into smaller components, but looking at the success of the interpretation rather than the mistakes. Other writers (Altman, 1989; Moser-Mercer, Kunzli, & Korac, 1998; Russell, 2000) have adopted a similar approach to Kopczynski (1980), in that they have looked at errors made by interpreters, and omissions have been categorized as mistakes rather than strategies. This study highlights the different types of omissions made by interpreters, those that could be defined as strategic, and others that could be identified as potential errors.

Cokely (1985, 1992a, 1992b) conducted qualitative linguistic analyses on interpreters working between English and ASL, and he developed an analysis technique similar to Barik's (1975), refining it for the purposes of analyzing sign language interpretation. This technique is known as a *miscue taxonomy*, which by its very name has negative connotations, as the term implies that the taxonomy is looking for mistakes or errors made by interpreters. Miscues were defined by Cokely as being "deviations from the original text" (1992a, p. 73) and five general miscue types were identified. These included additions, omissions, substitutions, intrusions and anomalies. Omission miscues were then broken down further into morphological, lexical and cohesive omissions.

In a specific study of the effects of lag time on interpreter errors, Cokely (1992b) applied his miscue taxonomy to the analysis of four videotaped individual interpretations from English to ASL in a conference setting. Cokely identified that two of the interpreters maintained an average lag time of two seconds, whereas the other two maintained a consistent lag time of approximately four seconds. He then compared the number of miscue occurrences in relation to the amount of lag time used by the interpreters.

In terms of omission occurrence, Cokely found that lexical omissions were the most prevalent for both groups, followed by cohesive omissions and a much smaller number of morphological omissions. Interestingly, the study shows that those interpreters using a two-second lag time made more omissions than those with a longer lag, with over twice as many total miscues. This point is worthy of note as it contradicts the findings of Barik's earlier study (1975) that demonstrated that a longer lag time leads to more omissions being made. Cokely (1992b) stated that a naïve assumption of simultaneous interpreting would be that fewer omissions are made with a shorter lag time. He asserted, however, that "a compressed lag time places the interpreter in a quasi-shadowing task, in which differences in speech articulation and sign production rates may result in increased omissions, as the interpreter strives to 'keep up' with the speaker" (p. 54). Alternatively, Cokely argued that an increased lag time augments the overall comprehension of the source language message, which, therefore, sanctions the interpreter to "determine the informational and functional value of morphological and cohesive as well as lexical units" (p. 54).

Although Cokely (1985, 1992a, 1992b) recognized that interpreters may use additional lag time to make decisions about the interpretation, which implies a level of metalinguistic awareness, his various studies all referred to omissions as errors, with discussion of possible causes for the miscues; thus inherently recommending ways to prevent omissions occurring within a piece of interpretation.

The benefit of studying interpretations for success and effectiveness has been established earlier in this chapter. This section has discussed studies that count the number of mistakes, as opposed to looking at omissions as successful strategies. As long ago as 1973, Enkvist questioned whether analysis of interpretation should count the number of errors or measure the success in communication. In supporting a goal-oriented approach to analysis, Enkvist suggested the concept of contextual appropriateness as a "yardstick" to assess the seriousness of an error, by looking at the appropriateness of an utterance in the context of situation. Enkvist claimed that as a consequence of interactions being goal related, errors should only be considered as such in relation to functionally relative objectives, rather than just as errors themselves. Baker (1992) has also recognized the occasional need for interpreters to "translate by omission," thus recognizing that the use of omissions can indeed be strategic.

STRATEGIC OMISSIONS

In giving an account of interpreter-mediated communication, Wadensjö (1998) explored the responsibilities of the interpreter and the expectations of both the participants and the interpreter involved in the interaction. She analyzed the interpretation of an interaction between a police officer and a Russian immigrant applying for a residency permit, which took place at a hearing at the immigration department of a police station in Sweden. Wadensjö discussed the concept of community interpreting, the role of an interpreter, interactional norms, the premise of communication and the interpreter's influence, turn-taking, and linguistic and cultural equivalence. This study has been highlighted in relation to strategic omissions, because Wadensjö suggested her own taxonomy for use in determining the successful outcome of an interpreted event. She developed a taxonomy that incorporated similar components to those of Barik (1975) and Cokely (1985, 1992a, 1992b), yet she used an alternative terminology that had more positive connotations.

First of all, Wadensjö (1998) established the interpreter's utterance as a *rendition*, which relates in some way to the immediately preceding original utterance. The relation between the rendition and the utterance of the originator was classified into distinct sub-categories. She stated that source texts can be considered as "context(s) in a chain of utterances" (p. 106), which condition and influence additional discoursal and contextual development. Wadensjö claimed that although "original" utterances are heard (or seen in sign language) in a particular context, it is necessary for interpreters to de-contextualise each original utterance to a certain extent, so that it is a separate unit and can be re-contextualised as a new utterance in the "flow of talk" (p. 107).

Thus, in order to compare interpreters' utterances with the originals, Wadensjö defined a taxonomy of eight sub-categories of *renditions*. These included close renditions, expanded renditions, reduced renditions, substituted renditions, summarized renditions, multi-part renditions, non-renditions and zero renditions. These sub-categories enable the analyst to explore the successful nature of an interpretation by looking at the appropriateness of particular renditions in the context of the interpreted interaction.

In relation to strategic omissions, the category of most interest is that of *reduced renditions*, similarly referred to by other authors as *condensing strategies* (Sunnari, 1995) or *selective reductions* (Hatim & Mason, 1990).

Wadensjö (1998) defined reduced renditions as "less explicitly expressed information than the preceding 'original' utterance" (p. 107). It has been noted that omissions can be regarded as strategies whereby a conscious decision is made to leave something out, or to reduce the amount of information included from the source language message into the target language interpretation. Ergo, Wadensjö's approach to an interpreter deciding to provide a *reduced rendition* applies positive connotations to the concept of making deliberate omissions.

Wadensjö argued that the interpreter in her study used reduced renditions in order to meet the communicative goals of the interaction. This coping strategy involved the interpreter using her linguistic and cultural knowledge about the participants and their communities, as well as her knowledge of communicative norms in different situations. Wadensjö gave an example of a reduced rendition that involved the source language message (in Russian) saying: ". . . and anyhow if—even if I live in the USSR, to my mind I am anyhow not Russian I am Greek, anyhow, so officially I am Greek." (p. 114); to which the interpretation into Swedish was as follows: ". . . even if I have been living all of my life in the USSR I am anyhow counted as a Greek, and not as a Russian" (p. 114). Wadensjö explained that this interpretation was contextually, linguistically and culturally appropriate as the communicative goals of the original statement were achieved in the interpreter's rendition of the message. She stated that the reduced rendition placed emphasis on the most recently articulated of the two communicative goals indicated in the original utterance. She justified the interpreter's decision to focus on the second goal, because the information met the needs of a police officer, "to record quickly and unambiguously the facts of the case (rather than, for instance, his possible wish to understand the ways in which the applicant in front of him is reasoning)" (p. 115).

Thus Wadensjö justified the omission made on the part of the interpreter by explaining why the translation was appropriate, and how it enabled the interaction to be maintained without cognitive dissonance occurring for any of the participants. Again, Wadensjö did not explore the metalinguistic awareness that the interpreter had about the strategic omissions or reduced renditions that she was making. Nonetheless, it can be assumed that if the interpreter was aware of the necessity to omit certain utterances in order to deliver an equivalent message to the receiver, the strategic omissions made must have been conscious to some extent.

The previous section discussed various types of omissions that could be made by interpreters, as suggested by different researchers, which include omissions at the morphological, lexical, syntactical, cohesive, and contextual levels. It has been established that interpreters may make conscious or unconscious omissions while they are processing information from the source into the target language, which can be respectively considered as strategies or errors. As a consequence of the research study reported in this book, a new omission taxonomy has been developed, identifying potential interpreting omissions based on levels of consciousness and strategicness (Napier, 2001).

1. *Conscious strategic omissions*—omissions made consciously by an interpreter, whereby a decision is made to omit information in order to enhance the effectiveness of the interpretation. The interpreter incorporates his or her linguistic and cultural knowledge to decide what information from the source language makes sense in the target language, what information is culturally relevant, and what is redundant.

2. *Conscious intentional omissions*—omissions made that contribute to a loss of meaningful information. The interpreter is conscious of the omission and makes it intentionally due to a lack of understanding of a particular lexical item or concept or due to an inability to think of an appropriate equivalent in the target language.

3. *Conscious unintentional omissions*—omissions made that contribute to a loss of meaningful information. The interpreter is conscious of the omission and makes it unintentionally, whereby he or she hears the lexical item (or items) and decides to "file it" before interpreting it, to wait for more contextual information or depth of meaning. Due to further source language input and lag time, however, the particular lexical item (or items) is not retrieved and so is omitted.

4. *Conscious receptive omissions*—omissions made that the interpreter is aware of, but he or she cannot properly decipher what was heard due to reported poor sound quality.

5. *Unconscious omissions*—omissions made that contribute to a loss of meaningful information. The interpreter is unconscious

of the omission and does not recall hearing the particular lexical item (or items).

These omission categories were developed as a consequence of the task reviews conducted with the interpreters and as a result of the comments they made about their levels of consciousness about the omissions they made, all of which are discussed further in chapter 5, which focuses on the methodology of the study.

This chapter has introduced the notion of coping strategies, in order to provide a context for the study of translation style and omissions as linguistic coping strategies. It has been suggested that different strategies are used by interpreters during different stages of the interpreting process, either before, during or after an interpreting assignment, in order to cope with various linguistic and extralinguistic factors that may affect their interpreting performance. As well as being used as a reactive measure for spontaneous problem solving, it has been mooted that coping strategies can also be used as a pro-active measure to enhance an interpretation. Several studies have been presented that explore linguistic coping strategies used by interpreters, incorporating use of linguistic and cultural knowledge and use of translation style.

It has been argued that interpreters may choose to use these processes as linguistic coping strategies, in order to enhance the effectiveness of their interpretations, and to ensure that the "meaning potential" of any utterance is achieved. In order for interpreters to engage in this decision-making process, and actively select linguistic strategies, it has been suggested that they must have a level of metalinguistic awareness. By drawing on their metalinguistic awareness, interpreters will monitor their language use and their language choices, and thus make adaptations to the interpretation accordingly, and select the appropriate strategies to use to cope with the linguistic demands of the discourse environment.

Further studies that evaluated the occurrence of interpreter omissions have been discussed, and it was pointed out that the majority of studies focus on omissions as errors. It has been argued that as well as being erroneous, omissions can be used as a linguistic coping strategy, whereby interpreters deliberately choose to omit information in order to ensure that the target language rendition is linguistically and culturally relevant. To be able to make the decision to use this omission type, interpreters must be engaging in a conscious meta-linguistic process of strategic selection. Thus, this omission type has been named a "conscious strategic omission."

As a consequence of being metalinguistically aware, interpreters may be conscious of making erroneous omissions, although they may not have been intentional. The taxonomy introduced in this chapter places conscious strategic omissions within a spectrum of omission types.

Now that the notion of how an interpreter copes linguistically has been discussed, and it has been established that this study focuses on the translation style and types of omissions produced by interpreters when interpreting for a university lecture, it is worth examining the discourse environment in more detail. In giving consideration to discourse-specific research, it is possible to identify the linguistic features of discourse environments comparable to university lectures. Conferences are renowned for using high (formal) registers of language, and often provide similar environments to that of university lectures, whereby the source text will often be written initially, then read out to an audience. Chapter four reviews various investigations of conference interpreting before discussing the area of educational interpreting and exploring issues faced by sign language interpreters when interpreting in university settings.

Chapter 3

Discourse-Specific Research: An Overview

This chapter gives an overview of research that has been conducted in the types of discourse environments relevant to this study. Although this study focuses on interpreters working in university lectures, literature is also reviewed that looks at interpreters working in conference settings. It is worth reviewing literature on conference interpreting because interpreters often have to work under similar conditions to those encountered in universities, in that they are having to deal with more formal registers of language, precise social discourse expectations, and will also invariably be working unidirectionally. The similarities between these discourse environments have been recognized in the field of sign language interpreting for over 25 years, with Sutcliffe (1975) stating that the same translation style should be adopted in conference and university settings. Thus, consideration is given first of all to conference interpreting, followed by discussion of educational interpreting in general, and then more specifically, university interpreting.

CONFERENCE INTERPRETING

Conference interpretation officially began during the First World War as a result of negotiations taking place between people who could not converse fluently in the diplomatic language of French. Initially it is thought that interpretation was provided consecutively, using a sentence-by-sentence process (Gentile et al., 1996; Herbert, 1978). The process of simultaneous interpretation was formally introduced to conferences for the purposes of the Nuremberg trials in 1946 (Gentile et al., 1996; Moser-Mercer et al., 1998), where equipment such as booths and headphones was used to avoid the need for protracted consecutive translation. Over the years many papers have been written on the issues faced by simultaneous conference interpreters (Gerver, 1969; Kopczynski, 1994;

Kurz, 1993; Moser, 1978; Paneth, 1957). A seminal work in relation to conference interpreting, however, is that of Danica Seleskovitch (1978). Written from the perspective of an extremely accomplished conference interpreter, Seleskovitch gives anecdotal examples from her own experiences to emphasize the need for conference interpreters to search for the meaning within any message, and to find equivalents between languages and cultures. Seleskovitch raises intelligibility of language as one of the major barriers that conference interpreters must face. She stated that "intelligibility, which is the goal of the spoken language, is not merely expressed by a greater or lesser degree of explicitness—it takes other forms as well . . . The speaker's desire to accommodate, to adjust to the situation, leads him into error" (p. 20).

As well as errors made by producers of the source language message, interpreters have to deal with conference terminology or "jargon," which may also make the source language unintelligible. Seleskovitch equated this difficulty to the feelings of isolation experienced when people are in a situation where they know nobody else, when the language used often assumes familiarity with the subject and context. She gave examples of family members or work colleagues who can understand one another although they may use "elliptical expressions and imprecise terms" (p. 21). Familiarity such as this will often give rise, for example, to the use of acronyms, or at Deaf conferences the use of name signs[1], which an interpreter may not be familiar with, and will obviously have a bearing on the interpretation she is able to provide. To compensate for this unknown element of language use, Seleskovitch maintained that interpreters need

---

1. The use of name signs in sign languages has been discussed by Meadow (1977) and Mindess (1990), among others, and it can be described as identity symbols in the Deaf community. As Deaf people rely on a visual-gestural language, it is common for them to identify each other through "visual" names that they give to each other, as well as their orthographic names. These name signs may be descriptive, in that signs will be used to describe a particular feature of that person (e.g., a large nose or curly hair). Alternatively the signs may be arbitrary, in that there is no visual reference to the person, and there will usually be some kind of story behind why they were given a particular name sign. Therefore if an interpreter is unfamiliar with name signs of Deaf people in their locality, it can be difficult to follow a conversation as they may have no idea who is being talked about.

to sustain a wide range of general knowledge, and must be prepared to devote time to preparation and research before a conference in order to raise awareness over topics that may be discussed. She asserted that, first and foremost, interpreters must concentrate on analyzing the meaning of any message, and should use their knowledge of the subject to support, rather than take over, the interpreting process.

Seleskovitch described how interpreters are generalists, who need not have expert knowledge at the same level of specialists, but must understand everything. As interpreters do not originate information, but rather they organize information rationally, they should not judge "the accuracy, the originality or the cogency of the message" (p. 62). Instead they should assess what the message seeks to prove, and for this they must have a "comparable level of intellectual ability" (p. 63) to that of the speaker. According to Seleskovitch, interpreters can be faithful in their renditions of the source language utterances primarily through logical analysis, and secondarily through familiarity with the subject. She stated that it is this power of reasoning, rather than the command of the facts, which must correspond with that of the speaker.

Thus it can be seen that Seleskovitch has highlighted the need for conference interpreters to use their linguistic and cultural knowledge, as well as any specialist knowledge they may have, to ensure a more effective interpretation. She identified language use as one of the most challenging aspects of conference work. The same analogy can be applied to interpreting in university settings, whereby the interpreter may flounder if she does not have some awareness of the specialist topic being discussed (Harrington, 2001a). Additionally, she should be prepared to draw on her own knowledge of the languages and cultures involved to provide a meaningful interpretation. The intelligibility of language will always be a factor as university lectures tend to be delivered in a more formal register, and certain assumptions will be made about the knowledge of the target audience. Seleskovitch mentioned "comparable level of intellectual ability," which when applied to university settings, can be argued to mean that interpreters should have completed university education themselves before being able to work in that environment. As a result, they should then be familiar with language use in universities, and be able to anticipate how language use in that setting may influence their interpretation process.

Sanderson, Siple, and Lyons (1999) referred to the need for interpreters to be suitably qualified for working in postsecondary education with

Deaf students. This should include, as well as having studied in a university environment in a spoken language, a demonstrable equivalent communicative competency in a sign language. Cummins' (1980) categories of "cognitive/academic language proficiency" (CALP) and "basic interpersonal communicative skills" (BICS) can be applied to the linguistic proficiency of sign language interpreters. It is necessary for interpreters to have achieved sociolinguistic communicative competence at a level of CALP in, for example, both English and Auslan in order to effectively interpret for university lectures.

To return once more to the issue of language use at conferences, Llewellyn Jones (1981a) explored the phenomenon of BSL as a naturally occurring language and whether it is a suitable language to use in conference settings. At the time of writing his paper, there was great debate amongst the British Deaf community over whether BSL made use of a formal register, and therefore whether it was an appropriate conference language. Llewellyn Jones referred to work by Deuchar (1979) that stated that the diglossia of sign language use in Britain dictates that Signed English is regarded as the most prestigious form of sign language, with BSL being the lowest. Llewellyn Jones (1981a) argued, however, that Signed English is not necessarily used amongst the Deaf community, and queried the authenticity of Deuchar's (1979) data, as she observed Deaf people using BSL in a local Deaf club (informal) and a hearing person using Signed English in a religious environment (formal). In his own study, Llewellyn Jones (1981a) demonstrated that there is in fact "a 'repertoire' of styles within BSL" (p. 51), after recording interaction amongst Deaf people in formal, semi-formal and informal settings and noting a significant difference in their sign language production. The differences included such factors as increased use of fingerspelling and lip patterns within the formal setting. This language contact variety of BSL is now commonly referred to as Sign Supported English (SSE), which incorporates English syntax and is regarded as the code-mixing of two languages to produce an inter-language (Corker, 1997).

As a consequence of his findings, Llewellyn Jones (1981a) postulated that for interpreters working in conference settings, the decisions made regarding target language output are a lot more complex than simply differentiating between BSL (informal) and Signed English (formal). To illustrate his point, he checked the comprehension levels of prelingually Deaf sign language users when observing BSL interpreters at work.

The findings revealed that a high rate of incomprehension occurred when the interpreters chose inappropriate target language production forms. Llewellyn Jones noted that those interpreters who did not have an extensive enough repertoire in BSL (i.e., competency in both BICS and CALP) resorted to a manually coded form of Signed English, rather than code-mixing to produce a formal SSE variety of BSL, which resulted in misunderstanding on the part of the consumer. In conclusion he stated that in order for Deaf people to gain equal access to information at conferences and meetings, interpreters must produce an interpreted rendition of the message in the form of language "most meaningful to the majority of the deaf community" (p. 59). Llewellyn Jones' conclusion can be equally applied to the interpretation of university lectures for Deaf university students.

Moser-Mercer et al. (1998) investigated the "coping mechanisms" that conference interpreters use when dealing with stressful situations, and the impact on the quality of the interpreting service. They introduced their study by establishing the working practices of conference interpreters, which have been established "to alleviate fatigue and help ensure high quality of output" (p. 48). Working conditions for conference interpreters incorporate key recommendations that interpreters work alone for a maximum of 40 minutes when interpreting a single speech, or if working in tandem at an all-day meeting, should take turns approximately every 30 minutes.

The investigation looked at the quality of interpreters' output, the physiological and the psychological stress levels that interpreters experience after prolonged turns of over 30 minutes; as well as looking at how interpreters' coping mechanisms manifest themselves in an experimental situation. The subjects of Moser-Mercer et al.'s study were experienced conference interpreters who had worked as interpreters for a minimum of 12 years between the languages of English and German. They were asked to interpret four speeches given by German politicians to determine quality of output, as well as being asked to fill in a questionnaire to determine psychological reactions to the environment, and donate saliva samples to ascertain physiological levels of the stress-induced secretion of the hormones cortisol and immunoglobulin.

Moser-Mercer et al. developed a taxonomy to evaluate the quality of the interpretations based on rating scales used by other researchers (e.g., Barik, 1971). The taxonomy focused on meaning errors, and its categories include *contre-sens* (saying exactly the opposite of what the speaker said); *faux-sens* (saying something different from what the speaker said); *nonsense* (not making any sense at all); and *imprecision* (not capturing all of the original meaning). As well as these categories, the study also included analysis of omissions, additions, hesitations, corrections, grammatical mistakes and lexical errors.

The qualitative findings of the study indicated that the more prolonged the interpreting task, the higher the number of errors, with omissions being the most frequent. The number of omissions rose from 59.5 during the first three minutes, to 80 when the interpreter had been working for over 60 minutes. Moser-Mercer et al. (1998) concluded that interpreters' metalinguistic ability to judge the quality of their interpreting output was extremely unreliable after longer periods of interpreting. They found that the interpreters were generally unaware of the decline in the quality of their work, especially as three out of the five subjects continued to interpret for a further 30 minutes. The interpreters decided to stop only when they were so fatigued that they could not continue to interpret.

In summary, Moser-Mercer et al. emphasized the effectiveness of the study in demonstrating the qualitative coping strategies of conference interpreters when working for prolonged periods of time. They claimed that due to the number of meaning errors increasing in accordance with interpreter fatigue, and the fact that the interpreters were not aware of the decrease in their qualitative output, "interpreters, at least on prolonged turns, cannot be trusted to assess their performance realistically" (p. 61).

They attributed this lack of awareness to cognitive overload, and hypothesized that interpreters only become aware of the decreased quality of their output when their fatigue reaches such a level that they can no longer mentally process the source language message. As a result, Moser-Mercer et al. recommended shorter turns to be taken by conference interpreters to ensure a consistently high quality of output. This study can be equally applied to interpreters working in university settings, as they often have to work through two or three hour lectures with minimal breaks. A coordinator for interpreting services at an Australian university confirmed that it is very rare for universities in Australia to consider providing more than one interpreter per lecture (V. Woodroffe, personal communication, December 8, 1999), therefore this practice will obviously have an impact on the quality of service provided.

Although the study conducted by Moser-Mercer et al. (1998) revealed that interpreters have a lack of metalinguistic awareness when it comes to their interpreting performance, it needs to be remembered that these findings can only be applied to interpreters working under stressful conditions. This is not to say that interpreters, when working under optimum conditions, will never have a certain level of metalinguistic awareness. In the context of this particular study, it can be argued that it is appropriate for Moser-Mercer et al. to discuss the incidence of errors, as they have demonstrated that fatigued interpreters are not able to make judgments about their output. Thus any omissions, additions or hesitations that are used are unlikely to be part of any conscious linguistic strategy, and can therefore be regarded as mistakes.

In looking at qualitative outcomes of conference interpreting from another perspective, Moser (1996) conducted a survey that explored the expectations of users of spoken language conference interpretation. Moser sought to prove his hypothesis that different user groups would have different qualitative expectations of a conference interpreter, particularly for highly technical conferences. In administering a questionnaire to approximately two hundred participants attending conferences and seminars of alternate typologies, Moser found that the responses covered a range of requirements.

Forty-five percent of respondents expected any interpretation to be faithful to the original source text, with 34 percent stating that regular delivery, absence of hesitation, correct grammar, use of complete sentences, and clarity of expression all gave the impression of a good interpreter. In addition, over one third of the respondents mentioned that interpreters should demonstrate the features of a lively, non-monotonous voice with clear enunciation in order to effectively convey the feeling of the original message. The findings also demonstrated that approximately one third of respondents found it irritating when the interpreters' lag time was too long, and felt that it was important for interpreters to retain synchronicity (that is, keep up with the speaker).

Moser correlated the amount of experience that people had of attending conferences, with the different expectations they held. Although those with less experience rated good voice, synchronicity, and good rhetorical skills as being just as important as those who were more experienced users of interpreters, there were significant differences in expectations about the faithfulness of an interpretation. Of the more experienced group,

53 percent stated the importance of a faithful interpretation, compared to only 35 percent of less experienced respondents. Moser concluded,

> It would appear that users who do not often have occasion to use interpretation rank synchronicity, voice, rhetorical skills and faithfulness to meaning more or less equally, whereas highly experienced users rank content match a long way ahead of the other factors. (p. 157)

Some respondents stated a preference for completeness of renditions, whereas others flagged the importance that the interpreter should concentrate on the expression of the essentials of any message. Older, less experienced respondents had a stronger expectation that the essentials should be conveyed. When asked their opinion on how long interpreters should work before letting another interpreter take a turn, over half the respondents stated 30 minutes as the optimum time. Not surprisingly, a large proportion of respondents rated terminological accuracy as being important, with women attending technical conferences being the greater advocates of this feature. Moser found that less literal interpretations were preferred, with more importance attached to interpretation of the meaning of a message, regardless of whether respondents were at general or technical conferences.

Although Moser highlighted potential flaws in the validity of the data due to different circumstances, two general conclusions can be made about the results of the survey. First, experienced users of conference interpreters had higher expectations of the service they should receive and what it should entail; and second, participants at different types of conferences do not necessarily require alternative methods of interpretation. Moser's original hypothesis assumed that the more technical the conference, the more respondents would prefer a literal interpretation incorporating technical terms. The survey results demonstrated, however, that the conference delegates involved in his study preferred faithful interpretations, which conveyed the meaning of the message.

In applying these findings to Deaf consumers of conference interpretation, it can be assumed that survey results would be very similar in that they would prefer to receive a high quality interpretation that focuses on meaning. Universities provide an analogous setting in that, as mentioned earlier, information is often presented in a similar way to how it is presented at conferences. It is possible, therefore, to assume that users of interpreters in a university lecture would have similar expectations to those users of conference interpreters.

The studies of conference interpreting that have been reviewed establish the comparability of service that interpreters are expected to provide when working in universities. It is now possible, therefore, to review any literature that specifically looks at interpreters working in educational settings.

It has been noted that there is a dearth of research in the sign language interpreting field, yet within the research that exists, the majority of papers focus on educational interpreting. One can surmise that this is due to the fact that educational interpreting is unique to sign language interpreters.

EDUCATIONAL INTERPRETING

According to Stewart et al. (1998), "more interpreters practice in schools than in any other setting" (p. 189). There is high demand for the provision of sign language interpretation in educational settings, ranging from primary through to tertiary educational institutions (Ozolins & Bridge, 1999), and some interpreters carry out the majority of their work in educational institutions (Chafin Seal, 1998; Hayes, 1992; McIntire, 1990). For those Deaf children who require sign language interpretation, they will invariably receive their education in an integrated setting, usually in some kind of special unit for "hearing impaired" children within a mainstream school (Bowman & Hyde, 1993; Chafin Seal, 1998). A task force on interpreting provision for Deaf students in the US described educational interpreting as "an enabling factor" in integrating Deaf students with their hearing peers (Stuckless, Avery, & Hurwitz, 1989, p. 1). The issues facing interpreters working in primary and secondary schools are different from those they are confronted with in postsecondary institutions. Stewart et al. (1993) described the different demands placed on sign language interpreters when working with children. These demands include: adaptation of their linguistic output; the types of information they will be expected to interpret (e.g., story reading); their role as support workers; their ability (or inability) to remain completely impartial; and potential lack of knowledge of subjects taught at secondary school level (e.g., biology and geometry). These issues may equally apply to interpreters working with Deaf adults in universities, especially the matter of inadequate background knowledge of the subject being interpreted. Paul and Quigley (1990), for example, have questioned what subjects educational interpreters should study before working with Deaf students.

Greenhaw (1985) focused on educational interpreters working with older Deaf students. In response to a lack of research at that time, Greenhaw administered a survey to postsecondary educational institutions providing interpreting services to hearing-impaired students in the US. The survey covered a gamut of questions in an attempt to collect data on every aspect of educational interpreters' work, including employment conditions, interpreter reliability, interpreter student ratios, specializations, evaluation of services, supervisory issues, and costs. In her summary of the findings, Greenhaw stated that "the survey indicates a lack of programmatic standardization . . . in all aspects of interpreting services in the postsecondary setting. This situation causes dilemmas for interpreters . . ." (p. 53). Although Greenhaw did not elaborate on the resulting dilemmas for interpreters, it can be assumed that she is referring to their roles and responsibilities, as mentioned by Stewart et al. (1998) in relation to younger children.

Many writers (Compton & Shroyer, 1997; Dahl & Wilcox, 1990; Harrington, 2001b; Scheibe & Hoza, 1986; Stewart et al., 1998) have suggested that the role of an educational interpreter incorporates the need for a range of skills and knowledge, which can be in contradiction with the conventional role of an interpreter working in other settings, and that interpreters are not always prepared enough for interpreting in education.

Hayes (1992) conducted a survey of 32 educational interpreters in Western Pennsylvania to ascertain how these interpreters felt about their work, and any problems or concerns they may have had. She found that the majority of educational interpreters were under-qualified for the job, and generally did not understand their roles and responsibilities. Jones, Clark, and Soltz (1997) also conducted a survey of educational interpreters to collect their demographic characteristics and their perspectives on their responsibilities. The findings were similar to those of Hayes (1992); they found that the majority of respondents to the survey had insufficient training to meet the needs of their role. Wells (1996), however, looked at the role of the educational interpreter from a different perspective, by discussing consumer awareness of the responsibilities of an educational interpreter, and identified a need to educate consumers about the role of the educational interpreter.

Siple (1993, 2000) acknowledged issues faced by interpreters working in college classrooms, in relation to working with college teachers or lecturers who may not have an adequate understanding of the interpreter's role. She identified issues such as the different communication needs of deaf students, the visual "distraction" for other students of having an interpreter in the classroom, use of visual aids in the classroom, difficulties in interpreting for rapidly paced presentations, and strategies for interpreting classroom discussions to avoid more than one person speaking at a time. Siple suggested that teachers should regard having an interpreter in their classroom as an opportunity to enhance the communication dynamics, and should perceive the role of the interpreter as a contributor rather than an unnecessary distraction.

In addition to the complicated role of an educational interpreter, another complex aspect requiring consideration is the skills base of educational interpreters. The notion of a "skills base" has been explored from several different perspectives, with individual writers focusing on alternative competencies that an educational interpreter is required to develop. Taylor (1993, 2002), in writing about skills that are required of sign language interpreters in any given situation, delineates the concepts of "knowledge-lean skills" and "knowledge-rich skills." The former are required in portions of an interpretation and refer more specifically to technical language and interpreting skills, whereas the latter are requisite throughout the whole of an interpretation and rely on contextual knowledge of the communities and cultures involved within any interaction.

More specifically in relation to educational interpreting, however, Maroney and Singer (1996) discussed the development of a tool for assessing the skills of educational interpreters. Four areas of skill were identified: message equivalency, linguistic competency, fluency and process management. In developing an assessment tool, Maroney and Singer asserted that it is possible to improve and maintain quality interpreter services for deaf children, increase the number of qualified educational interpreters, encourage appropriate placement of these interpreters, and feed into a professional development structure for educational interpreters. Unfortunately, they were frustrated with the initial application of the tool, due to interpreters' anxieties at being videotaped, lack of a Deaf target audience for the interpreters to sign to, and the criteria used to identify message equivalence.

Schick, Williams, and Bolster (1999) explored the skills of educational interpreters in terms of what should be considered the minimum skill level requirement for interpreters before they can work in the North American public school system. A pool of interpreters was assessed using a specific tool developed by Schick and Williams (1994) to evaluate the performance of educational interpreters. They found that less than half the interpreters assessed in their study "performed at a level considered minimally acceptable" (p. 151). They argued, therefore, that educational interpreters should be properly trained and accredited before working with Deaf children, as they can have a major impact on the effectiveness of a Deaf child's educational experience.

Cokely (1983a) applied an alternative analysis technique to looking at a different set of skills. Cokely analyzed the skills that interpreters possess in effectively conveying metanotative qualities when interpreting from English into ASL. He defined metanotative qualities as "the perceived qualities of messages and speakers rather than the literal or implied meanings of messages"; that is, metanotative qualities are seen as "those non-content characteristics that influence or determine a person's overall impressions of the speaker" (p. 16). In order to demonstrate the extent to which interpreters accurately conveyed the metanotative qualities of speakers, Cokely presented the analysis of two interpreters who were asked to interpret a series of five lectures delivered in English. A group of Deaf and hearing raters were asked to make judgments about the speakers by filling in a questionnaire, with the aim of determining whether the same speaker was perceived differently when interpreted by different interpreters.

Cokely found that there were different perceptions of the speaker according to which interpreter was being watched. For example, "deaf raters perceived Speakers 1 and 2 more positively than the hearing raters when [interpreter] 1 was working" (p. 20). Cokely concluded that this result could have occurred for two reasons: (1) interpreters are not aware of the effect of some of their behaviors and, therefore, consciously or unconsciously display mannerisms that conflict with the metanotative qualities of the speaker, and (2) interpreters may not be aware of how metanotative qualities can be conveyed by certain linguistic features of sign language and, therefore, may use grammatically correct linguistic features that do not accurately express the qualities of the speaker. These findings obviously have an impact on Deaf students, as their perceptions (as well as understanding) of college lecturers may be skewed by relying on the potentially inaccurate metanotative qualities conveyed by their interpreters.

The skills of an interpreter also need to be considered in relation to skills in translation. Livingston, Singer, and Abrahamson (1994) compared the effectiveness of ASL interpretation (free interpretation) versus transliteration (literal interpretation), in giving college students access to lectures. They defined transliteration as working "between spoken English and one of several contact varieties that incorporate linguistic features from both English and ASL" (p. 2), whereby interpreters will tend to follow English word order using signs for individual words and concepts. Conversely, interpretation was classed as the process for digesting meaning from the source language and reproducing it in the target language, therefore ignoring the individual words used. Livingston et al. stated the need for Deaf students to receive appropriate interpretation, otherwise they will not have access to the same kind of instruction as their hearing peers. They determined that one reason why interpreters might use transliteration was that Deaf students would get access to the same pool of vocabulary as hearing students, as well as potentially helping them to improve their knowledge of English.

The study involved 43 students, divided into those who expressed a preference for one translation style or another, watching a lecture presentation either interpreted or transliterated by experienced interpreters, and answering questions on the information received. The results showed that the students understood more when the information was interpreted into ASL freely, rather than literally. This was the case even for those students who had expressed a preference for the latter method of signing, but who watched the lecture in the former.

In analyzing successful interpretations of the lecture, Livingston et al. noticed that omissions did not necessarily lead to less understanding of the message. In fact, they reinforced the concept of omissions being used consciously as part of a strategic linguistic process. They explained that certain information might be omitted from an interpretation for two reasons. First, the interpreter may make a conscious decision to delete information because she feels that an equivalent message would be difficult to find. Second, the interpreter makes an omission based on her estimation of what would be meaningful to the particular audience she is serving. Therefore in asserting that interpretation, rather than transliteration, is a more effective method of conveying information to Deaf students to ensure higher levels of understanding, Livingston et al. condoned the use of omissions as part of a strategic linguistic process that can enhance an interpretation. They stated that "omissions were not necessarily indications of a poor interpretation. For this interpretation, it appeared to be just the opposite" (p. 28).

In taking a more positive view of transliteration (or literal interpretation) and its usage, Winston (1989) analyzed one interpreter who regularly worked with the same Deaf student in a university course. Winston wanted to focus on the features that occur in a transliteration when an interpreter is familiar with both the subject and the client, in order to discuss "conscious strategies used by transliterators during analysis and production of the target form, rather than random productions or errors" (p. 152). She hypothesized that transliterations incorporate a language contact mixture of English such as word order and mouthed English words, and ASL features such as lexical items, head and body shifting, and use of location. She highlighted particular strategic choices that are used to achieve certain types of transliteration. These strategies included conceptual sign choice, use of additions and omissions, restructuring, and mouthing.

Winston borrowed from the work of Casagrande (1954) in order to define four different types of transliteration. The first type is "pragmatic transliteration," whereby the source message should be translated "as efficiently and accurately as possible, with a focus on the meaning rather than on the form of the message" (Winston, 1989, p. 151). The second type, "linguistic transliteration," is described as a translation where grammatical concerns, rather than meaning, influence the target language output. The goal of the third type, "aesthetic-poetic transliteration," is to achieve an aesthetically similar form in the target language to that which was produced in the source language. Finally, "ethnographic transliteration" seeks to include explanations of cultural background and text from one language to the other. Winston stated quite clearly that these transliteration types are not mutually exclusive but should be combined within any translation in order to achieve a balance of all the stated goals.

To prove her hypothesis, Winston (1989) transcribed 25 minutes of a lecture presented in English and transliterated into ASL, then chose two particular segments for further analysis. She then consulted with the transliterator about her reasons for incorporating particular linguistic features in order to retrospectively identify whether her strategies were conscious, "as opposed to being randomly or erroneously produced" (p. 148). She also recognized the importance of checking the consumer's comprehension of the transliteration to validate its adequacy, and she accepted the "apparent satisfaction" of the consumer involved in the study as a valid measure (p. 153).

In her analysis of omissions, Winston found that certain portions of the source language that were redundant in the target language were omitted. She claimed this strategy was used to achieve the transliterative goal of efficiency, to provide a pragmatic translation even though direct lexical equivalents for transliteration purposes were available. The redundancies noted included repeated past tense markers; plural markers; linking verbs, such as *be*; prepositions, such as *of*; and previously established subject pronouns. Thus, the omission strategies outlined by Winston can be regarded as "conscious strategic omissions." Although the study was carried out specifically on transliteration, rather than interpretation, the conclusions are equally relevant.

Siple (1995, 1996) further investigated Winston's (1989) findings, but focused solely on transliterators' use of additions. She stressed the appropriateness of transliteration as a method of interpretation to be used in educational settings. She also wanted to demonstrate that interpreters used additions strategically in order to clarify the message and provide cohesion and emphasis where necessary, as well as rendering the message in a visually appropriate manner. Siple sought to identify different types and frequencies of additions by analyzing and comparing the transliterations of a lecture of 15 experienced and 15 novice interpreters. The interpreters were asked to imagine that they were transliterating to three Deaf individuals who were known to them, and "all possessed PhDs, were professionals in the academic environment, and had strong English language skills (reading, writing, and sign), and preferred a more English-like transliteration" (1996, p. 33).

As a consequence of her analysis, Siple (1995, 1996) defined five categories of additions: (1) cohesion, where an addition provides discoursal links; (2) clarification, where an addition makes the message clearer with less ambiguity; (3) modality adaptation, where an addition visually communicates an auditory aspect of the message; (4) repetition, where an addition provides emphasis by repeating a key word or phrase; and (5) reduplication, where an addition requires the re-formation of a sign to indicate pluralization. The most common additions were those in the first three categories.

In her discussion of the results, Siple gave specific examples of words or concepts in English, and how they had been transliterated into ASL. She stated that the transliterated texts often contained information that was not present in the source text, which therefore proved that interpreters utilized additions strategically to "provide supplemental information in recognition that a verbatim message would be incomplete" (1996, p. 39). This statement is based on supposition, however, as Siple did not interview the interpreters on completion of the interpreting task. There is no recognition in her discussion of the different factors that may affect an interpreter's linguistic decision-making process. Nevertheless Siple's study is commendable due to the focus on interpreter strategy, rather than interpreter error.

Viera and Stauffer (2000) discussed the expectations of Deaf consumers in relation to the use of transliteration. In their paper, they asserted that transliteration is a complex process that requires more than a verbatim rendering of the message from spoken into manually coded English. Viera and Stauffer recognized the imperative that interpreters utilize additions and omissions strategically in order to elucidate meaning, whether they are interpreting or transliterating. They conducted a small survey of a range of consumers with different levels of deafness in the US, and found that a high percentage preferred to receive transliteration, rather than interpretation. The survey was sent out, however, to colleagues of one of the authors, the majority of whom were employed in a professional capacity. Thus the results may be misrepresentative because if the majority of the survey respondents were professionals, they were more likely to be bilingual as they would need university qualifications to do their job. If they were bilingual they would therefore be more likely to be comfortable with, or require, transliteration so they could access English terminology. Nonetheless, Viera and Stauffer's study does raise a valid point in relation to why transliteration may be preferred, which is especially relevant to this study.

Viera and Stauffer asked survey recipients what they hoped to achieve when using a transliterator, rather than an interpreter, in a meeting, and found one of the most typical answers was that consumers wanted to be able to access the English language that their peers were using.

In doing so, they could participate in the discourse using the same language and thus ensure mutual understanding of terminology. The survey respondents stressed the importance for interpreters to have an excellent command of the English language at graduate-level proficiency with a wide vocabulary. Viera and Stauffer's findings may also be applicable to Deaf university students, in that they may prefer to receive information through a more literal interpretation, (i.e., transliteration), in order that they can access the subject-specific terminology and academic English used in the university discourse environment. This requirement would necessitate interpreters working in university settings to have the appropriate level of language proficiency (CALP) and to be suitably qualified to work in such an environment.

It can be seen from the various studies reviewed thus far, that there has been great interest in the field of educational interpreting in general. All have touched on research conducted in primary, secondary, or post-secondary college settings. However, fewer studies have focused on sign language interpreters working in university settings.

UNIVERSITY INTERPRETING

One of the major considerations for interpreters working in universities, according to Stewart et al. (1998), is subject matter. In an ideal world it would be possible to place interpreters with Deaf students according to their background knowledge. Unfortunately, in reality, with the shortage of available interpreters, this is not the case. Due to the wide range of subjects studied by Deaf students (Bremner & Housden, 1996), interpreters are often assigned to interpret for subjects they know nothing about and are given very few opportunities for preparation.

Lawrence (1987) conducted a study of 10 educational interpreters with fewer than 300 hours of interpreting experience, and 10 with over 1500 hours experience, in order to document differences in prepared and unprepared interpretations. Five interpreters from each group were provided with specialized training on terms and concepts related to the subject of cell division, and the next day all 20 of the interpreters translated this topic in a university lecture on cell biology. Lawrence analyzed the interpreted renditions of the lecture for the number of achieved "semantic equivalent units," and compared the mean number of each group. His findings showed that out of a total of 50 available semantic equivalent units, the less experienced interpreters achieved an average of 10.2 units without preparation, and 24.8 units with preparation. The more experienced interpreters, however, achieved 22.2 units without preparation, and 42.0 units with preparation.

The results demonstrated that preparation and, therefore, some knowledge of subject matter lead to more accurate interpretations. In summary, however, Lawrence noted that although knowledge of subject matter is important, skill level has a major influence on achievement of accuracy. He suggested one reason why the advanced interpreters achieved a higher level of accuracy than the beginners—the advanced group "had already acquired many 'tricks of the trade' and needed only to be shown how to apply those skills to the subject" (p. 89).

In some respects, one could argue that the role of interpreters in university settings is a lot clearer than in other educational settings. As they will be working with Deaf adults who have made the choice to further their education, it can be assumed that consumers will have clear expectations of interpreters, their role, and their linguistic output. Nonetheless, interpreters have to deal with other issues such as how to interpret the meaning of something if they cannot understand it themselves; being confronted with highly specialized terminology; constantly working within formal registers of language and having to expand their own vocabulary; adapting to students' individual signing styles; and working for long periods of time without a break, to name but a few. This phenomenon leads one to ask questions about the levels of education and interpreter training that interpreters should be required to attain before being allowed to work in university settings. Eighinger (2000) clearly stated that although interpreters are often required to interpret for Deaf students studying towards a tertiary-level degree, they should never accept work that involves interpreting at an educational level higher than they have achieved themselves.

Harrington (2000) stated that it is not possible to guarantee that interpreters have attended university themselves, or that they have knowledge and/or experience of the subjects that they may be expected to interpret in university lectures. He referred to the fact that the examination and assessment board for BSL interpreters (CACDP[2]) suggests that only five

---

2. Council for the Advancement of Communication with Deaf People.

percent of educational interpreters in the UK possess a graduate level qualification. This cited figure raises questions about under-qualified interpreters' abilities to adequately understand and translate a university lecture in order to make it accessible for a Deaf student.

Chafin Seal (1998) argued that "as educational interpreters, learning should be held at a premium" (p. 193). This point is reinforced by Roy (2000b), who commented that interpreters should ideally have a general liberal arts university-level education, which should include the four literacy strands of reading, writing, listening, and speaking. She stated that an education, especially in the liberal arts, is about reading, composing, analyzing, and interpreting text. By understanding the process of creating text, interpreters are thus able to interpret text more effectively. It would be pragmatic, therefore, to suggest that interpreters should have a university-level education generally, but especially before being encouraged to work in university lectures. Patrie (1993) outlined the relationship between the education of sign language interpreters and interpreting in educational settings. She cited the need to follow the lead of the spoken language interpreting profession, where interpreter training programs usually "accept only students who have a university education in place, world knowledge appropriate to the consumers they will be interpreting for and full language proficiency in at least two languages" (p. 9).

It is surprising, therefore, that more research has not been done in a university setting, as it is probably the one area that provides more of a challenge for sign language interpreters than almost any other environment. Ozolins and Bridge (1999) emphasized this point by stating that due to the diversity of subjects undertaken by university students, interpreters need to be aware of the potential challenges they face.

> The interpreter here is in a complex linguistic environment which requires subject and discipline specific knowledge and a native like fluency in the sign language which allows adaptation and creativity in order to cope with specific terminologies and concepts. (p. 54)

In addition to subject and linguistic knowledge, understanding of the discourse environment and its language use is imperative. Roy (1987) studied the outcomes of an interpretation of a videotape of a university lecture translated from ASL into spoken English, as well as the impact of the message on two different audiences. The first audience was a group of interpreting students that listened to the interpretation "live," who congratulated the interpreter on the efficacy of her interpretation in achieving accuracy and dealing with a difficult text. When Roy played a tape recording of the interpretation to another audience that was not familiar with sign language and was not aware they were listening to an interpretation, the response was quite different. Although the second audience group clearly understood the content of the message, when they were asked for whom they thought the message was intended, the overwhelming response was "children."

Through further analysis, Roy found that the lexical choices and intonation used by the interpreter were characteristic of children's storytelling, rather than an academic lecture. Roy stated that the interpreting students had probably made judgments about the interpretation according to the linguistic choices they would have made, as they were "listening out" for appropriate English equivalents for the ASL signs they had seen presented in the original discourse, rather than listening for how the interpretation sounded. The second group of listeners, however, only made judgments according to how the message sounded, with reference to familiar discourse types. Roy's study therefore demonstrates the importance for interpreters to consider the discourse environment, and the relationship between the discourse environment and language register, in order to make appropriate linguistic choices within an interpretation. This issue applies to the interpretation of signed language into spoken language, and vice versa. With regard to the interpretation of a university lecture, it is important for interpreters to consider the "global" message and the intent of the lecturer, as well as the information presented.

Jacobs (1976) studied the efficiency of sign language interpretation to convey lecture information to Deaf students. Hearing students with no knowledge of sign language and Deaf students who would normally rely on an interpreter watched the same university lecture delivered in English. Jacobs found an imbalance of knowledge acquisition between the hearing and Deaf students, with those relying on sign language interpretation receiving 16 percent less information than those receiving the information auditorily through English. It is not clear, however, how Jacobs defined the information received and what was, or was not, accurate. It can be argued that if he was looking for exact representation in the target language of words used in the source language (i.e., a literal interpretation), it is understandable why he concluded that less information was received by the Deaf students. Yet if he focused on equivalence of meaning (i.e., a free interpretation) and this was not obtained, then the study raises a pertinent issue with regard to Deaf students accessing information in a university lecture.

Murphy (1978) conducted a study of the "transmission" skills (sign language production) of interpreters working in a university setting and found that the skills of interpreters at different levels of experience were essentially the same. In a follow up study, however, Murphy tested the receptive skills of interpreters in reading sign language (i.e., voicing over for Deaf students) to determine how well information would be conveyed if a Deaf student were in an interactive university lecture. Murphy's study was based on Jacobs's (1976) original research and reached different conclusions. Interpreters were asked to watch a lecture given in ASL, then answer ten questions on the content of the lecture. The results were then compared to the scores of the original groups in Jacobs's study. The interpreters were also subcategorized as having minimal level (less than 300 hours), moderate level (600 to 900 hours) or maximum level (over 900 hours) experience.

Murphy (1978) found that those interpreters with minimum-level experience attained receptive comprehension scores equal to the Deaf students in Jacobs's (1976) study. The comprehension scores of the moderate- and maximum-level interpreters were higher than those scores of the Deaf students. Interestingly, Murphy found that the scores of the hearing group from Jacobs's study were higher than the scores of the minimum-level interpreters in his study, yet the moderate- and maximum-level interpreters' results were approximately the same as those of the original hearing group's. Therefore, although the amount of experience did not seem to affect interpreters' abilities to produce information in sign language effectively, it did appear to influence their receptive abilities. However, Murphy used his results to demonstrate that Jacobs's conclusions may be incorrect. He argued that sign language can effectively convey the content of university lectures, and that the discrepancies in scores between Deaf and hearing participants found in Jacobs's study should not be attributed to deficiencies in sign language.

Murphy (1978) explained that the deficiencies are more likely to come from poor educational backgrounds or the basic language of Deaf people, rather than the incapacities of sign language to transmit a meaningful message. Murphy's study is significant to any research conducted on the use of sign language interpreters in universities, as it implies that interpreters are capable of getting the content of lectures across to Deaf students. As a consequence, Murphy's study validates the further examination of research that looks at the performance of interpreters in this setting.

As a result of being a Deaf student studying at university and using interpreters regularly, Johnson (1991) became interested in the performance of ASL interpreters in universities. She focused on interpreters' ability to facilitate communication in classroom interaction, as well as their ability to convey the content of a lecture. In order to analyze the extent of miscommunication in university classrooms, Johnson transcribed and analyzed 32 hours of videotaped classroom sessions, and monitored the data for discrepancies between what was said by the hearing person and what was received by the Deaf person through the interpreter. She found that miscommunication or confusion does occur between Deaf and hearing people in a university classroom when relying on the use of sign language interpreters.

The criteria used to check whether the interpreters had interpreted the lecture correctly included checking for omissions of sentences or passages, misspelled words (in fingerspelling), incorrect conveyance of concepts, and inaccurate use of signs. Johnson noted that the most consistent problems occurred particularly when interpreters were unfamiliar with the subject and when it was necessary for them to render a verbal description of a diagram into ASL.

As a consequence, Johnson argued that Deaf students are often left out of classroom interaction, or they misinterpret the content of lectures. The points raised by Johnson are extremely noteworthy, although she focused on errors and mistakes rather than positive strategies used by interpreters. This is understandable as students at a university rely heavily on interpreters to get access to information at a crucial time of their lives; therefore, it can be argued that it is important to know what kinds of mistakes are made. Johnson acknowledged, however, that not all differences in Deaf/hearing interaction are problematic for interpreters, which introduces the way for the present study.

Harrington (2000) presented initial findings of a similar study to that of Johnson (1991), whereby he analyzed the relationships and dynamics that exist between university lecturers, Deaf and hearing students, and BSL interpreters. The express goals of his study were to identify access issues for Deaf students in university settings and whether interpreters were adequately meeting the needs of Deaf students. He asserted that the aim of the study was to evaluate the dynamics of a university classroom and to assess the strategies employed by lecturers, interpreters, and students in fulfilling each of their roles in the learning process, rather than a critical analysis of interpreter errors.

Harrington videotaped 15 different lectures from a range of subject areas, which comprised a total of 32 hours of interpreting data. Within the settings recorded, 11 individual Deaf students and 9 different interpreters were involved. The gathering of evidence involved the use of two video cameras placed strategically in the classrooms in order to film not only the interpreters but also the Deaf and hearing students and the lecturers. Wherever possible, participants were also interviewed to ascertain their views on how they felt about the particular lecture, whether they felt that everybody had equal access to the information that was provided, and whether there was anything they would have changed about the situation.

Harrington recognized the bimodality of a university classroom, and the distinct dynamics that may arise within any given classroom as a consequence of a variety of influences. The influences he listed include the number of participants as a whole; the ratio of hearing to Deaf students; the ratio of Deaf students to interpreters; whether the lecturer was Deaf or hearing; the duration of the lecture; and extralinguistic factors, such as the physical environment, use of audiovisual equipment, and poor acoustics.

Ultimately, however, the focus was on what he called "the interpreted event," and the ways in which the spoken message was rendered into the target language by interpreters. Harrington observed various issues that affected the interpreters' abilities to successfully communicate the message and, therefore, had an indirect impact on the general interaction within the classroom. Examples involved interruptions from hearing students when the lecturer was addressing Deaf students, and the dilemma interpreters experienced when more than one source message was being received at the same time and they had to decide which should be given priority for translation. Another example was in relation to a Deaf student asking for clarification of a sign used by an interpreter. By the time the interpreter had explained and repeated his lexical choice, and the student asked a question about the concept, the lecture had moved on considerably, thus the question raised was regarded as an unnecessary distraction. Harrington stated that the interpreter's unfamiliarity with the subject of the lecture may have contributed to the breakdown, and noted that a common issue raised within the study was a lack of preparation materials for educational interpreters.

As the study itself was incomplete at the time of discussion in his paper, Harrington did not make any concrete conclusions. But in summary, he made a significant point that difficulties experienced by interpreters in a complex linguistic environment, such as a university lecture, are usually only noted when things go wrong, which therefore raises concerns about what mistakes or misunderstandings may be unobserved because they have less serious consequences.

Locker (1990) studied lexical equivalence in transliterations performed in university settings. She built on the work of Fleischer (1975), who described research with 40 Deaf students that determined the amount of lecture information they received from watching interpreters with or without subject-specific knowledge, and who interpreted into ASL or Signed English. Fleischer concluded that the students' level of bilingualism influenced their receptive abilities, but that ultimately, students better understood information interpreted into ASL.

Locker (1990) looked specifically at the effectiveness of transliteration (literal interpretation) for accurately conveying the content of a university lecture, and identified three types of errors that frequently occurred. These errors were defined as misperception of the source message, lack of recognition of the source form, and failure to identify a target language equivalent. These categories are almost synonymous to some of those developed as a result of the study reported in this book. The category of "conscious intentional omissions" incorporates lack of recognition of the source form, as well as failure to identify a target language equivalent. Misperception of the source message is comparable either to "conscious receptive omissions" or "conscious unintentional omissions," depending on whether the misperception is based on the interpreter being unable to hear the source message properly, or whether she mishears it. Locker focused her analysis on the identification of errors that interpreters made; therefore, no definition was suggested for any category analogous to that of "conscious strategic omissions."

Locker drew on Cokely's (1985) seven-stage model of the interpreting process and miscue analysis technique, to analyze the empirical data presented by the participants of her study. She videotaped six interpreters working in half-hour segments with three different Deaf students, two studying graduate courses and one studying an undergraduate course. The videotapes were then analyzed for "non-equivalent meanings resulting from lexical choices in the target form of the message" (p. 174). Locker found that only three of the interpreters produced lexical errors, and she focused on these three subjects for the rest of the study. She points out with interest that those three who did not produce any lexical errors had a university qualification (i.e., a bachelor's degree), whereas those that did produce errors had not studied at university level.

The next stage of the study involved retesting the three interpreters who had made lexical errors, then conducting a follow-up interview where the participants were shown their original and second translations and were asked to comment on their reasons for making the original choices. This process thus allowed Locker to determine the types of errors made and the category in which the errors fit. She found in the original test that 17 percent of miscues were misperception errors and 83 percent were sign-choice errors. The results of the retest showed that 49 percent of errors were corrected in the second translation. Of those errors that were not corrected the second time, Locker elicited information from the participants as to what the problem had been. She found that 44 percent of the uncorrected errors occurred due to not understanding the source language message, and 66 percent occurred due to failure to identify a target language equivalent. Locker noted that the lexical items that interpreters had problems with were not necessarily subject-specific terminology, but rather typical use of academic English. This point was emphasized in relation to the fact that the three interpreters did not have a general university education and were, therefore, unfamiliar with the academic discourse environment. Locker emphasized the issue that the rate of lexical errors noted could be linked to the interpreters' level of formal education and whether they were educated in the topic, or even generally university educated. She stressed the need for interpreters to familiarize themselves with the subject matter of lectures they will interpret, or at least to acquire "conceptual familiarity" with terminology and typical language use. Another implication noted by Locker is that interpreters should have "at least a bachelor's level of education, in addition to bilingual fluency as a prerequisite . . . so as to be equipped for all the contexts in which they might work" (p. 180).

This chapter focused on research both relevant and specific to the discourse environment of interest in this book, namely university interpreting. By incorporating discussion of research in conference settings, which is a similar discourse environment to that of university lectures, this chapter has considered linguistic issues for sign language interpreters in dealing with complex, formal language. The discussion of general educational interpreting research has identified specific considerations for interpreters in the educational discourse environment.

Several studies of conference interpreting were considered that highlighted issues for interpreters working in conference and university settings alike, due to the similar nature of interpreting in those contexts (for example, the formality, lexicon, and register of language). In particular, the need for interpreters to have "comparable intelligence" to that of source language presenters at conferences was raised, which highlights an equivalent ideal requirement for interpreters working in university lectures to have completed a university education themselves.

In relation to conference interpreting, another issue raised was the expectations of consumers and how these expectations can vary according to the length and type of experience in using interpreters. Nonetheless, it would seem that conference attendants count on receiving a quality interpretation that accurately reflects the meaning and intent of the original message. This presents another comparable situation for Deaf consumers relying on the use of sign language interpreters in a university lecture, whereby one would expect them to demand a similar outcome.

The theme of educational interpreting has been discussed in depth, with an overview given of different facets of the educational interpreter's work and the issues involved, including their role, language skills, and interpretation techniques. The few studies on university interpreting have described research on the comparative differences between prepared and unprepared interpretations, on the impact of interpreters on classroom interaction, as well as the effectiveness of sign language interpretation and transliteration techniques in conveying the content of university lectures presented in spoken English.

Now that an overview has been provided of the theoretical grounding for the study of interpreters' linguistic coping strategies, and the discourse environment of university lectures has been explored in depth, it is possible to discuss the results of a study of sign language interpreters' use of omissions and translation style as linguistic coping strategies while interpreting for a university lecture.

Linguistic Coping Strategies: An Analysis

The empirical study that I conducted for my PhD research (Napier, 2001) involved the analysis of data obtained from a pool of professionally accredited Auslan interpreters. The analysis concentrated on the translation style and types of omissions produced by the interpreters when interpreting for a lexically dense university lecture. I also looked at the extent to which the interpreters were metalinguistically aware of the omissions they made and why they made them. The study then focused on the impact of interpreters' educational backgrounds on their ability to effectively interpret a lexically dense university lecture and whether a university-level education or familiarity with the lecture topic influenced the type of translation style used and types of omissions produced as linguistic coping strategies.

RESEARCH QUESTIONS AND HYPOTHESES

The key research questions and hypotheses were as follows:

1. How do sign language interpreters use translation style as a linguistic coping strategy in the interpretation of a university lecture?
2. How many omissions do sign language interpreters produce (within the omission types defined as part of this study) when interpreting for a university lecture?
3. Does the translation style of sign language interpreters affect the number and type of omissions that they make?
4. Do sign language interpreters use conscious strategic omissions as a linguistic coping strategy in the interpretation of a university lecture?
5. To what extent are sign language interpreters metalinguistically aware about the types of omissions that they make while interpreting for a lexically dense university lecture?

6. To what extent do the linguistic features of the source text (that is, lexical density, subject-specific terminology, academic English) influence use of the translation style and occurrence and types of omissions produced by sign language interpreters?

7. Do sign language interpreters feel that their educational background impacts their ability to interpret for a university lecture?

8. What are the expectations of Deaf university students in relation to the translation style, omissions made, and educational backgrounds of sign language interpreters in this discourse environment?

Initially, I believed that the interpreters involved in the study would switch between using free interpretation and literal interpretation methods and that their educational background would influence the pattern of switching. From a theoretical point of view, I felt that interpreters who had studied at university would be better equipped to employ a more free translation style to effectively interpret a university lecture, as they would be more familiar with the discourse environment and the inherent use of academic English.

The hypothesis in relation to the number and types of omissions was that all the sign language interpreters would make omissions in each category. I hypothesized that subjects dominant in using a free interpretation approach would use more conscious strategic omissions than those dominantly using a literal approach, as subjects using literal interpretation would concentrate more on the form of the message than on meaningful equivalents. I also predicted that interpreters in this study who had a university qualification and were more familiar with the lecture topic would make more conscious strategic omissions because they would feel more comfortable about making strategic omissions based on their familiarity with academic English and subject-specific knowledge. In relation to conscious intentional omissions, I expected that those who were not university educated, or not acquainted with the lecture topic, would make more omissions in this category due to lack of familiarity with the academic language register and subject-specific jargon. I assumed that all interpreters would unavoidably make conscious unintentional omissions due to cognitive overload. For conscious receptive omissions, however, the expectation was that those who had knowledge of the lecture topic would make fewer of this type of omission than those without knowledge.

I hypothesized that these interpreters, who had frames of reference for the lecture content, would be able to predict what terminology they should expect to hear, and thus have fewer problems hearing and deciphering lexical items. Furthermore, I predicted that those without topic knowledge, but who were familiar with academic discourse environments, would be better equipped to infer meaning in what they heard and, consequently, would make less conscious receptive omissions. Finally, I assumed that all the Auslan interpreters would make a small number of unconscious omissions.

I envisaged that the interpreters' dominant translation style would affect the number and types of omissions produced, and that all interpreters would use conscious strategic omissions as a linguistic coping strategy. Because the use of metacognitive strategies is intrinsic to the occurrence of conscious omissions, I predicted that sign language interpreters would have a high level of metalinguistic awareness about the types of omissions they made while interpreting for the university lecture. I also suspected that the linguistic features of the source text would have an impact on the translation style and occurrence and types of omissions produced by the interpreters, and that the interpreters would be most influenced by their level of familiarity with academic English and subject-specific terminology. I also expected that the interpreters would make more omissions in the most complex (i.e., lexically dense) parts of the text. Consequently, I predicted that the interpreters would feel that their educational background affected their ability to interpret for the university lecture due to their comfort levels with the language use. Lastly, I predicted that Deaf university students would prefer interpreters to provide meaningful interpretations of university lectures while appropriately providing access to English terminology. I also expected that they would not be comfortable with the idea of interpreters making conscious strategic omissions and that it would be important for interpreters working in universities to have a good level of education, but that language and interpretation skills would be more important.

THE INTERPRETERS

I decided to select accredited interpreters only to participate in the study. Interpreters must have a minimum level of competence and sophistication in the language being analyzed before they can make an effective analysis of linguistic coping strategies and before they will be able to apply such strategies to their work. All of the chosen interpreters had responded to an earlier survey that collected information on interpreters' educational backgrounds and areas of work (Napier, 2001), and they had expressed an interest in participating in further research. The recruitment process involved contacting 18 interpreters to ascertain their availability and willingness to participate, which meant sending a letter explaining what was to be involved in the data collection. Twelve agreed to participate, but due to unforeseen circumstances, I collected data from only ten interpreters. The ideal criteria required a representation of interpreters from those who were native signers and those who were not; those who had a university qualification or were studying towards a university qualification, and those who did not; and experience interpreting in higher education. The final group of interpreters included seven native and three non-native signers, eight people with a university qualification and two without, and eight who had a lot of experience with university interpreting and two who had very little.

THE SOURCE TEXT

I selected a real lecture as the source text because it had higher lexical density than typical spoken conversation. A lecture entitled "Issues in Sign Language Acquisition by Young Children," which was presented in English as part of a master's degree program for teachers of the deaf, was recorded live on videotape. The lecture was selected with confidence that analysis would show it to be lexically dense due to the reputation of the lecturer, and my own previous experience of interpreting for this particular lecturer.[1]

At the time of the presentation, the lecture was being simultaneously interpreted by an accredited interpreter into Auslan for a Deaf student, which authenticates the "interpretability" of the lecture. In recording the data, however, the video camera was trained on the lecturer as he

---

1. I am indebted to Dr. Greg Leigh for agreeing to have his lecture videotaped and used for the purposes of the research study.

presented the material, and it did not record any of the work of the interpreter present at the time of recording. The whole lecture lasted for one hour and twenty minutes, but, for the purposes of this study, I focused on the first 30 minutes. This section was chosen knowing that many of the participants who would interpret the piece would not be overly familiar with the subject and, therefore, the first part of the lecture would contain some introduction to the area.

The chosen section was transcribed using conventional orthography. The transcription of the 20-minute section of the lecture that the interpreters would actually translate was analyzed for lexical density using the method proposed by Ure (1971). The analysis involved counting the number of words in the text, then dividing the total by the number of lexical items (content words) to work out the percentage of lexical rather than functional (grammatical) items used throughout the text. Lexical or content words are those with "full" meaning, as opposed to grammatical or function words that are "empty" of meaning (Crystal, 1995). The text was found to have slightly more content than grammatical words, giving a lexical density of 51 percent. Considering that typical spoken text has a lexical density of 33 percent, and an average lecture contains a lexical density of 39.6 percent (Ure, 1971), the chosen lecture was more than suitable to use as the source material for the purposes of the study.

THE TASK

The focus of this study was on what interpreters do well, rather than on what they do wrong. In order to evaluate the skills of Auslan interpreters, I decided to combine three different procedures—a "tough-case analysis," meaning a tricky interpreting situation (Moser-Mercer, 1997); a task of "process tracing," whereby the subject runs through the task a second time (Moser-Mercer, 1997); and a "retrospective interview" (Hoffman, 1997). After conducting several pilot studies to ensure that the methodology was sound, the data collection took place over a period of two weeks.

Each participant in the study had to interpret the same twenty-minute segment of the chosen videotaped lecture, as this is the optimum period for interpreting before the qualitative output begins to suffer (CACDP, 1997). All the participants learned of the purpose of the data collection when arrangements were being made for them to be involved in the study. The notion of researching omissions as a positive linguistic coping strategy, rather than a negative outcome, was emphasized.

Whereas linguists researching spoken languages will often use tape recorders to preserve data for future reference, in this instance it was necessary to videotape each subject, due to the visual nature of signed languages. In this way, a simultaneous recording could be made of both the spoken English source message and the signed target message, and the tape could be referred to by the researcher and the participants "to elicit . . . explanations or spontaneous comments" (Stokoe & Kuschel, 1979, p. 19).

Each participant was recorded individually in a room with a television and video camera. The only other people in the room were the researcher and a Deaf person acting as the receiver of the interpretation.[2] The interpreter was positioned so he or she could be filmed during the task but still comfortably see the television screen. The Deaf person sat next to the video camera facing the participant, and I sat in the corner of the room slightly outside the interpreter's field of vision.

Before commencing the task, I gave the same instructions to each participant, following a script to ensure consistency. They were told the topic and source of the lecture but not any further preparation in relation to content. They were permitted to watch the first ten minutes of the lecture in order to familiarize themselves with the topic and the pace of

---

2. Interpreters often rely on feedback from their clients (in the form of facial expression, etc.) to gauge whether their interpretation is being understood, and whether they need to make any adaptations (Brennan & Brown, 1997). During this study, the interpreters were able to maintain eye contact with a "real" Deaf person, thus making the interpretation process as authentic as possible. The Deaf person "received" the interpreted lecture and acted as a target for the interpreting output. Several writers have commented on the negative impact of not having a Deaf target audience when analyzing the work of interpreters (Maroney & Singer, 1996; Napier, 1998b); therefore, it was considered a necessary component of the data collection. It was important to have the same Deaf receiver for all participants, as lack of consistency may have skewed the interpreters' notions of their target audience. For that reason, one Deaf person was hired as a research assistant for the duration of the data collection. He was present at every video recording, and his role was to just sit and watch the interpretation without giving any overt comments.

delivery before interpreting the next twenty minutes of videotape. The subjects knew they would only be allowed one attempt at the exercise, whereby the videotape would be played all the way through without any pauses. Whereas in real-life interpreting situations, it is common practice for interpreters to interrupt a speaker for clarification or repetition, for the purposes of this study, it was felt that it was not necessary to ensure accuracy, as the focus was on those omissions made as part of a conscious linguistic process and the translation style used. The participants were advised that if they did miss a piece of information, they should stop, continue to listen, and begin to interpret again as soon as they had picked up the thread of what was being said.

In order to prevent distractions or unnecessary confusion for the interpreters, each subject was given a list of names mentioned throughout the lecture before beginning the task. This procedure ensured they knew how to fingerspell the names and would not be distracted from the point of the task by worrying about misspelling.

Throughout the task, I referred to a transcript of the lecture and underlined any omissions that were made throughout the interpretation. Being an accredited interpreter myself, I was able to listen to the source language message and identify anything that was omitted from the target language output through the interpretation process. Omissions were noted according to the following definition that I developed based on a review of the literature: An omission occurs when information transmitted in the source language with one or more lexical items does not appear in the target language and, therefore, potentially alters the meaning.

On completion of the interpreting exercise, the subject sat down with the researcher and performed a task review. The Deaf receiver was no longer in the room. The procedure of the task review involved the researcher and participant watching a playback of the taped interpreting task, pausing the video when omissions were noted in the Auslan rendition of the English lecture. If omissions were noted, the participant was asked to explain why he or she thought the omission might have occurred, and whether he or she was aware of it at the time; that is, whether it was conscious or unconscious. The purpose of the review was to establish whether omissions were being made on a conscious or unconscious level. If subjects identified conscious omissions being made as a linguistic strategy, they were asked to elaborate on why they had made the conscious decision to omit particular types of information.

It was emphasized once again at this point that the identified omissions did not necessarily indicate errors, but rather potential strategic decisions. The feedback from the review gave an indication of the level of metalinguistic awareness that the interpreters had about their language use, the cultural relevance of certain information, and processing skills. Notes of their feedback were added to the transcript used by the researcher at the same time that the whole review was videotaped.

A retrospective interview took place when the task review was completed. The notion of retrospective interview for the purposes of "knowledge elicitation" has been described favorably by Hoffman (1997). An interpreter interviewed in this way by Hoffman commented that "the process pulled out much of what [I] had thought, the difficulties [I] had encountered, and the ways [I] had managed [my] interpretation process" (p. 205). The ultimate goal of the retrospective interview in this study was to elicit information from the subjects about their perceptions of the interpreting task.

I conducted the interview using pre-set focus questions and videotaped it in order to provide evidence for inter-rater reliability checks at a later stage. The focus questions asked how the interpreters felt about the overall piece of interpretation; whether there was anything they were particularly happy or not happy with; what they found most easy or difficult about the piece; whether they had any particular skills or knowledge which contributed to their ability to interpret for the lecture; and whether they thought there were any other skills or knowledge that they did not possess that may have helped them to interpret the lecture more effectively. Finally, the interpreters were asked to comment on perceptions they had about their own educational background and its affect or influence on their interpretation skills. The goal of the retrospective interview was to ascertain whether the interpreters felt there was any relationship between their level of educational achievement and their ability to interpret for a university lecture, as well as their ability to objectively reflect on their work and identify strengths and weaknesses.

In relation to the task, there is one issue that should be acknowledged and accounted for. In most circumstances, interpreters work regularly with the same client when they attend university lectures. Quite often an interpreter will be booked for a whole semester, and so has the opportunity to get to know the client. This situation means that interpreters also have the advantage of being able to familiarize themselves with the content of lectures and the pace and delivery style of lecturers, and they can develop specific ways of working with a client to suit his or her needs.

Some might argue, therefore, that the scenario for this study was unrealistic. However, an entire semester of a university course may not be interpreted by the same interpreter throughout. For example, interpreters fall ill, so it is conceivable for interpreters to provide cover for one-off occasions and go into this type of assignment without any preparation and without knowing the client. Chafin Seal (1998) often referred to last-minute substitute interpreting in her discussion of educational interpreting case studies. Other situations include interpreters who withdraw from an assignment when they feel they cannot adequately understand the content to interpret effectively, or Deaf students who request that an interpreter be replaced because they cannot follow the interpretation well enough to suit their needs. One Deaf person revealed to me that during one semester at university, she had eight different interpreters for one course, for exactly these reasons (D. Thornton, personal communication, November 27, 2000). I would argue, therefore, that the best way to test interpreters' linguistic coping strategies is by testing them in a new, possibly unprepared for, situation, as it would seem that this is where their skills would be most challenged.

THE ANALYSIS

Once all the data had been collected, it was necessary to develop an analysis tool that could be appropriately applied to the data to elicit the required information. At the conclusion of the analysis, the process and results were checked for reliability. This was necessary to ascertain that the data collected was sufficient in relation to the research questions and that the subjects involved were appropriately tested.

The process of data analysis involved two stages. First, entering the number and types of omissions made by each subject into a database. Second, identifying the translation "style" of each interpreter. The information was then cross-referenced in order to compare the output of each interpreter. The database was set up to identify the patterns that emerged in the use of certain types of omissions. The omission types were

- conscious strategic omissions;
- conscious intentional omissions;

- conscious unintentional omissions;
- receptive omissions; and
- unconscious omissions.

The omission types were entered into a spreadsheet with the corresponding numbers for the lines of text where the omissions had occurred. There were a total of 176 lines counted in the source text. Using this system, it was possible to note whether an identifiable pattern of omission types emerged within particular pieces of text; for example, frequent conscious strategic omissions on line 22, and sporadic unconscious omissions on line 140. If an omission occurred across more than one line of text, it was counted on the first line that it appeared.

As well as distinguishing patterns of omissions in certain parts of the text, the purpose of the analysis was to determine the ratio of conscious and unconscious omissions made by each subject, and whether the types of omissions made were influenced by translation style. A final comparison was made with regard to the qualifications of each subject to determine whether there was a relationship between the subjects' educational background and the types of omissions made.

In order to ascertain whether the number of omissions made per subject was influenced by translation style, it was necessary to develop a system for identifying the approach used by each interpreter. The aim was to distinguish between free and literal styles of interpretation. These styles were identified according to definitions put together from a literature search. For definitions and examples of translated English sentences to illustrate how each method of translation might be applied see examples 1 and 2.[3]

EXAMPLE 1: FREE INTERPRETATION

Free interpretation: "The linguistic structure of the source language is ignored, and an equivalent is found based on the meaning it conveys" (Crystal, 1987, p. 344). In the context of discussing bilingual programs for Deaf children, the following transcription is a free interpretation of an English sentence.

We should try and encourage families to support the first language acquisition of their Deaf children.

---

3. Transcription conventions can be found in Appendix A.

ALL FAMILY HAVE DEAF CHILDREN.. WE SHOULD WHAT
(point-arc)   *(q)*
ENCOURAGE PARENTS LEARN SIGN LANGUAGE.. MEANS
(point left-middle-right)

PARENTS AND CHILD HAVE SAME LANGUAGE.. MEANS CHILD CAN
(point-left point-right)   *(point-left)*

ACQUIRE SIGN FIRST LANGUAGE
(their-left)   *(hd)*

Example 2: Literal Interpretation

Literal interpretation: "The linguistic structure of the source text is followed, but is normalized according to the rules of the target language" (Crystal, 1987, p. 344). The following transcription is a literal interpretation of the same English sentence seen in example 1.

We should try and encourage families to support the first language acquisition of their Deaf children.

WE SHOULD TRY WHAT ENCOURAGE FAMILY SUPPORT
(q)   *(point-right)*
DEAF CHILDREN FIRST LANGUAGE ACQUISITION
(point-left) *(their-left)*   *(hd)*

In order to compare the translation styles of each subject, three sentences were chosen from the source text—one from the beginning, one from the middle, and another from the end. Each sentence incorporated one terminological word relevant to the subject and culturally bound to the subject in terms of register and content.

The way that each of the ten subjects translated the sentences was transcribed and compared to the definitions and translation examples given earlier in this section. The general translation style of each subject was then judged from the transcriptions and the dominant style used. It is generally difficult to compartmentalize and state categorically that every interpreter only uses one method or another. Most of the interpreters tended to fluctuate depending on their level of comfort with the subject and the speed of delivery. Sometimes subjects could be seen to code-mix within one sentence, within one paragraph, or throughout a piece of text. It was noted, however, that the interpreters tended to be dominant in one approach, so although they might have code-mixed and switched between approaches at certain parts of the text, they tended to have a certain style in terms of their general approach and how often they code-switched between translation styles. For the purposes of this research, each subject was compartmentalized as using either free or literal interpretation. If a subject used a certain style for two or more of the three sentences selected for analysis, he or she would be judged to be dominant in that style. For example, subject one translated the first sentence freely and the second and third literally; therefore, she was deemed to dominantly use a literal interpretation approach. If, however, an interpreter used the same style for all three sentences, he or she would be judged to be extremely dominant in his or her use of a particular translation style.

This classification method was one of the unique aspects of this study, as it identified that although interpreters will be dominant in one translation style, some tend to switch style more than others, thus acknowledging that interpreters may switch translation style as a linguistic coping strategy to meet the needs of their client group within a particular discourse environment. Most literature tends to refer to interpreters adopting one particular style or another, with little recognition of the fact that interpreters can switch between translation styles and, therefore, can use more than one style in one scenario.

On completion of the analysis of the subjects' translation styles, it was necessary to ensure the reliability and validity of the findings. This was done by carrying out inter-rater reliability checks. Burns (1997) stated that "when data are obtained from a data gathering instrument or technique, we need to know what faith we can put in the data as truly indicating the person's performance or behaviour" (p. 259). He asserted that the assessment instrument must be reliable and valid, and that extraneous factors, which might influence a subject's ability to perform, are controlled as much as possible. The key to determining whether a test is reliable is whether it is dependable and can in fact be consistently emulated by other researchers. In relation to the assessment of sign language interpreters, Strong and Rudser (1992) noted that many techniques are subjective and rely on the opinion of just one person. Thus they condoned the checking of any test instrument for reliability to eliminate any potential subjective decisions of the rater.

I decided, therefore, to administer a reliability check using the "test-retest" method (Burns, 1997), whereby my scores were compared with results presented by the data analysis of another person. The reliability check incorporated the three stages of task analysis, as originally administered. The first, concentrating on the interpreting task itself, the second on the task review, and the third on the retrospective interview. The checks involved evaluating the data of three subjects, each collected at different stages of the data collection phase—the beginning, middle, and end.

An accredited interpreter was chosen to conduct the reliability checks, as she matched the criteria decided upon for the inter-rater. The criteria required the rater to be bilingual in English and Auslan and to have the ability to freely access each language (i.e., be able to listen to the English and watch the Auslan). It was also considered important for the rater to be a qualified interpreter with experience of analyzing and critiquing interpretations of other interpreters.

The reliability check involved four stages: the rater watching the videotapes of the interpreting task and marking the omissions of each interpreter; the rater watching the videotapes of the task review and noting the specific omission types of each interpreter according to the omission taxonomy; the rater watching the videotapes of the retrospective interview and noting the key points made by the interpreters about their perception of the interpreting task; and comparing the rater's results with my own findings. On analysis of the results, the number of omissions noted by myself and the rater were found to be 90.8 percent reliable. With regards to reliability of the task review data, the types of identified omissions were found to be 86 percent reliable with those identified by myself. The retrospective interview check was found to have a reliability of 83 percent. Thus the methodology was judged as reliable.

In order to validate the method developed for the classification of translation styles, and to check for objective reliability, a different sign language researcher who is also an accredited interpreter was asked to emulate the translation style classification process. The rater was given the original style definitions and example sentences and asked to check the written transcriptions of the three sentences for each subject using the interpreted renditions on the videotapes. He was then asked whether he agreed with the style of translation for each sentence and what he judged as the dominant translation style of each subject. This process resulted in a reliability score of 100 percent.

Interpreters' Use of Linguistic

Coping Strategies

The aim of this chapter is to give a detailed breakdown of the results of the analysis of the linguistic coping strategies, namely translation style and omissions, used by interpreters. Information is also presented on the final stage of the study, which involved discussion with a panel of Deaf people who regularly use interpreters in university lectures to ascertain their expectations of interpreters in this discourse environment and whether their expectations matched the findings of the study.

TRANSLATION STYLE

Two particular styles were identified as key methods of translation: free interpretation and literal interpretation. The interpreters in the study were classified according to their dominant translation style, as described in the previous chapter. Six of the interpreters used a dominantly free interpretation approach, with two out of the six being extremely dominant, whereby they did not code-switch between free and literal interpretation methods. The other four subjects used a dominantly literal approach, with three of the four being extremely dominant. The classification of translation style was not a test of accuracy, merely a method to identify the interpretation approach of each subject. Examples of an extreme dominant approach and a dominant code-switching approach are shown in Examples 3 and 4.

Example 3 shows how the interpreter employed the method of free interpretation for all three sentences, demonstrating the features of free interpretation as identified in Appendix B, and thus was extremely dominant in her use of this interpretation method.

EXAMPLE 3: EXTREME DOMINANT APPROACH
(FREE INTERPRETATION)

SUBJECT 9

Sentence 1 (free)
And what they did was contrast the acquisition of these these features
     WELL THREE WRITE NOTE-DOWN WHAT THEY D-O WHAT WELL
    (point-right)   *(q)*

with the acquisition of the same types of grammatical features in
COMPARE CHILDREN ACQUIRE SIGN LANGUAGE GROW-UP ACQUIRE
              (left)   *(right)*

English, and came up with, as a result of this study, with what seemed
ENGLISH (STRUCTURE) G-R-A-M-M-A-R COMPARE+ FIND THEIR
                                   (hd)   *(their-right)*

to me some quite consistent patterns of grammatical acquisition
RESEARCH SHOW HAVE+ SAME COMPARE+ CHILDREN ACQUIRE MANY

across the two languages.
SAME HOW

SUBJECT 9

Sentence 2 (free)
Er, any of you who're, er, particularly those of you that are interested
in early childhood education will be aware of the work in this area, the
work of people like Jean Piaget, who made a very very strong case
                                YOU AWARE
                            (point-middle)
KNOW WHAT J-O-H-N P-I-A-G-E-T WORK.. PERSON WRITE A-LOT-
    (q)   *(his-middle) (point-middle)*

for . . . the, erm, for a binding relationship between early sensory-
OF-TEXT STRONG* TALK OVER WELL.. RELATIONSHIP WITH WHAT WHEN
                                       (q)

motor development and early language acquisition.
BABY CHILDREN GROW-UP THEIR HANDS EYES ARMS-MOVE EARLY MOVE
                (their-right)

RELATE-TO EARLY ACQUIRE LANGUAGE.
(point-right)

SUBJECT 9

Sentence 3 (free)
If you look at the work of someone like Steve Krashen, even in second
            DOESN'T-MATTER SECOND LANGUAGE

language research, his notion of, that we have to be at or just,
RESEARCH S-T-E-V-E K-R-A-S-H-E-N SECOND LANGUAGE RESEARCH
           (point-right)   *(his-right)*

just above the language receptive capacities of the language learner,
AREA WELL THEIR LANGUAGE MUST ALMOST AHEAD ME ACQUIRE+
(point-right) (their-right) (point-right)

that if we're too far above it, then the capacity for the learner to
THEIR SPEAK+ T-O ME ME-UNDERSTAND LITTLE-BIT AHEAD WHAT MY
(their-right)

actually make use of language input is certainly diminished.
UNDERSTAND ME CAN AHEAD IMPROVE WELL I-F FAR-AHEAD ME CAN'T
    (neg/hd)   *(point-right)*   *(neg)*
ACQUIRE DAMAGE MY ACQUIRE T-O LEARN SECOND LANGUAGE.

Example 4, however, provides a transcription of the same three sentences from another subject, who code-switched between a free and a literal interpretation approach, and therefore was not as extreme in her dominance of translation style.

EXAMPLE 4: DOMINANT CODE-SWITCHING APPROACH (FREE INTERPRETATION)

SUBJECT 6

Sentence 1 (free)
And what they did was contrast the acquisition of these these features
            WELL ACTUALLY COMPARE HOW PEOPLE
                                   (point-left)

with the acquisition of the same types of grammatical features in
LEARN F-E-A-T-U-R-E-S WITH HOW PEOPLE LEARN SAME G-R-A-M-M-A-R

English, and came up with, as a result of this study, with what seemed
F-E-A-T-U-R-E-S ENGLISH.. FROM.. FOUND SAME SAME HOW PEOPLE
(point-left-right)   (left) (right)

to me some quite consistent patterns of grammatical acquisition
LEARN OR LEARN DOESN'T-MATTER WHICH LANGUAGE.
(point left) (point right)   (point both)

across the two languages.

SUBJECT 6

Sentence 2 (literal)
Er, any of you who're, er, particularly those of you that are interested
in early childhood education will be aware of the work in this area, the
work of people like Jean Piaget, who made a very very strong case
MAYBE YOU..
(point-arc)

for . . . the, erm, for a binding relationship between early sensory-motor
EXPERIENCE WITH WORK O-F J-E-A-N P-I-A-G-E-T HIMSELF REALLY

development and early language acquisition.
BELIEVE.. VERY STRONG RELATIONSHIP B-I-N-D-I-N-G RELATIONSHIP
BETWEEN EARLY S-E-N-S-O-R-Y M-O-T-O-R DEVELOP AND EARLY
LANGUAGE ACQUISITION

SUBJECT 6

Sentence 3 (free)
If you look at the work of someone like Steve Krashen, even in second
language research, his notion of, that we have to be at or just, just
above the language receptive capacities of the language
I-F LOOK-AT WORK O-F S-T-E-

learner, that if we're too far above it, then the capacity for the learner
V-E SOMEONE RESEARCH.. ANOTHER PERSON HAVE-TO EQUAL-TO
(their-right)   (hd)

to actually make use of language input is certainly diminished.

SIMILAR T-O LANGUAGE LEARN I-F HIGH-ABOVE* SOPHISTICATED VERY
(point-left)

DIFFICULT CAN'T-UNDERSTAND WHAT PERSON SAY
(neg)   *(point-right)*

Table 1 provides a summary of the dominant translation style of each interpreter, plus information on their level of education. There did not seem to be any major relationship between the translation style and level of education of each interpreter. Four of the subjects who were dominant in their use of free interpretation held postgraduate qualifications, and two held undergraduate qualifications. Two of the subjects who were dominantly literal in their interpretation approach also held university qualifications. Only 2 of the 10 subjects had no postsecondary qualifications at all, and both of them used an extremely literal approach. Although I originally hypothesized that those with less education might rely more on literal translation if they were less comfortable with the academic discourse, this assumption was negated by the fact that one other subject with a postgraduate qualification also employed an extremely dominant literal approach.

It is possible to speculate on why these interpreters might have chosen to employ such a literal method and the issues that informed their decision-making. For instance, the subjects who were university qualified may have made a decision to use literal interpretation as they felt

TABLE I. *Dominant Translation Style and Educational Background of Each Subject*

Subject	Translation style	Level of postsecondary qualification
1	Dominant free	Postgraduate
2	Extreme dominant literal	None
3	Extreme dominant literal	None
4	Dominant free	Postgraduate
5	Extreme dominant literal	Postgraduate
6	Dominant free	Postgraduate
7	Dominant free	Undergraduate
8	Dominant free	Postgraduate
9	Extreme dominant free	Postgraduate
10	Extreme dominant free	Undergraduate

it was the more appropriate method to use in a university context, not because they lacked understanding of the academic discourse. The two interpreters who were not university educated may have made their decision based on lack of familiarity with the discourse environment. They could, however, just as easily have made their decision based on their understanding of university lectures and what they felt was the appropriate translation style to be used.

Although there does not seem to be a tangible link between translation style and educational background, consistent patterns could, however, be identified between translation style and what Davis (1989, 1990a, 1990b) referred to as linguistic transference, in this case, fingerspelling.

Translation Style and Linguistic Transference

Aside from fingerspelling names, which would be the norm (Johnston, 1998), and the use of lexicalized fingerspelling where fingerspelled English words have been assimilated into Auslan (Schembri, 1996), certain lexical items were consistently fingerspelled by the majority of the subjects. The amount of fingerspelling used by the subjects was consistent with typical Auslan use, in that borrowing of English words into Auslan in the form of fingerspelling frequently occurs. Johnston (1998) stated that the manual alphabet is used in Auslan for the "fingerspelling of English words for which no direct sign equivalent exists or when there is a particular need to use an English word" (p. 591). The same type of borrowing has also been observed in BSL (Brennan, 2001) and ASL (Lucas & Valli, 1992).

It can be argued that in a university context it would be important for a Deaf student to receive key English words, as the terminology would be central to the comprehension of the topic. This argument would be supported by Bremner and Housden (1996), who reported that Deaf postsecondary students preferred interpreters to fingerspell technical or subject-specific words that did not have an existing sign, rather than making up a sign.

Notwithstanding the appropriateness of fingerspelling in sign languages, it emerged that the interpreters used a different pattern of fingerspelling, depending on their translation style. Initially, it was thought that dominant literal interpretations incorporated more fingerspelling of a particular type. For example, it could be seen that one subject who was extremely dominant in using a free approach (i.e., did not code-switch at all) used far less fingerspelling when compared to another subject who was extremely dominant in a literal approach. Example 5 shows that the interpreter using a dominant free interpretation approach only employed the use of fingerspelling on one occasion, whereas Example 6 shows that an interpreter who used a dominant literal approach incorporated the use of fingerspelling for eight different words in the same sentence.

EXAMPLE 5: DOMINANT FREE APPROACH

SUBJECT 10
And what they did was contrast the acquisition of these these features with the acquisition of the same types of grammatical features
WHAT WHAT RESEARCH WHAT COMPARE WITH
 (point arc)   *(q)*

in English, and came up with, as a result of this study, with what
G-R-A-M-M-A-R LIST IN ENGLISH COMPARE WITH SIGN LANGUAGE HOW

seemed to me some quite consistent patterns of grammatical
LIST COMPARE.. RESEARCH FOUND LIST ALMOST SAME LANGUAGE
                       (left)

acquisition across the two languages.
ACQUISITION BOTH LANGUAGE ALMOST SAME
         (their right) (their left)   *(hd)*

EXAMPLE 6: DOMINANT LITERAL APPROACH

SUBJECT 2
And what they did was contrast the acquisition of these these features with the acquisition of the same types of grammatical features in
WHAT THEY.. RECEIVE
            (point-right)

English, and came up with, as a result of this study, with what seemed
F-E-A-T-U-R-E WITH SAME TYPE C-F G-R-A-M-M-A-T-I-C-A-L F-E-A-T-U-R-

to me some quite consistent patterns of grammatical acquisition

E-S IN ENGLISH AND COME UP WITH.. BECAUSE O-F STUDY WHAT S-E-E-
M-E-D T-O B-E WHAT CONSISTENT P-A-T-T-E-R-N O-F G-R-A-M-M-A-T-I-

(q)

across the two languages.

C-A-L ACQUISITION ACROSS AREA
(hd)

I counted the number of times each subject fingerspelled a lexical item throughout the whole 20-minute piece of interpretation and found that there was in fact no direct relationship between translation style and the amount of linguistic transference. Table 2 provides a breakdown of the number of fingerspelled lexical items produced by each subject.

On closer analysis, however, a distinct pattern could be seen in what lexical items the interpreters chose to fingerspell, according to their translation style. It is questionable why some subjects would incorporate more fingerspelling into their interpretations than others. First of all, they may have made a conscious decision, as a linguistic strategy, to fingerspell key words that they identified as being important for the student to know. Alternatively, they might not have been aware of an existing equivalent

TABLE 2. *Number of Fingerspelled Lexical Items per Subject*

Subject	Translation style	No. of finger-spelled lexical items	No. of aborted fingerspelling attempts
1	Dominant literal	100	2
2	Extreme dominant literal	271	5
3	Extreme dominant literal	93	5
4	Dominant free	114	2
5	Extreme dominant literal	141	3
6	Dominant free	172	1
7	Dominant free	83	2
8	Dominant free	115	1
9	Extreme dominant free	85	1
10	Extreme dominant free	78	2

Note. An aborted fingerspelling attempt was counted when an interpreter began to finger-spell a word then stopped, and either began fingerspelling a lexical item again, or chose to use a sign instead.

sign for those words; or they may not have understood the meaning of the words in the context of the lecture and, therefore, did not know the most appropriate equivalent sign to use. The major difference noted, however, between those dominant in using a free or literal interpretation approach was in relation to the fingerspelling of lexical (content) or function (grammatical) words.

I expected the interpreters to fingerspell a corpus of lexical words (names of people or places), regardless of their translation style, because it would be the norm to fingerspell a name at least once when it is first introduced. Their linguistic strategy could then involve either establishing the person or place as a location in space, after which the same location would be referred to every time the name was used, or they could choose to fingerspell the name each time it is mentioned. In relation to function words, a sign language linguist and a sign language teacher confirmed that various words are commonly fingerspelled by deaf people. For example, fingerspelling the words *if* and *do* is considered appropriate as they are commonly recognized as words that have been lexicalized into Auslan. Similarly, the word *to* is fingerspelled in specific contexts as a function word when it is not automatically incorporated into a directional verb, such as *give to*. In the context of the sentence beginning "a mother will adjust her language to meet the needs of," it would be acceptable to fingerspell *to*. With regard to the word *so*, this function word is commonly used in Auslan as a discourse marker to signify the beginning of a new topic or for emphasis, but it is fingerspelled because no sign exists for it.

It was expected, therefore, that the interpreters would fingerspell the lexical and function words described above, regardless of their translation style. The biggest difference noted was the way in which the interpreters who were dominant in a free approach seemed to use linguistic transference as a linguistic coping strategy, especially in relation to lexical words. As mentioned earlier, all the interpreters tended to fingerspell lexical words that could be classed as technical, subject-specific terminology, such as *cognitive, modality, co-actional dueting,* and *motherese.* It seemed, however, that the interpreters using a dominant free approach strategically switched to literal borrowing from English in order to convey information and enhance the meaning of the message, while accounting for the needs of university students to access academic English. I noted that the interpreters in this group tended to translate the concept into a meaningful visual Auslan rendition, plus fingerspell the lexical item to introduce the English terminology. Those interpreters dominant in a literal approach, however, only fingerspelled the subject-specific lexical words and did not translate the meaning. They also experienced more linguistic interference and fingerspelled English function words other than those identified above that would not ordinarily be fingerspelled in Auslan, including conjunctions such as *if, so, or, then, that, than, but*; prepositions such as *at, of, by*; and auxiliary verbs such as *be* and *did*.

As a consequence of the findings outlined above, two points can be made: (1) Interpreters that dominantly used a free interpretation approach seemed to use linguistic transference as a linguistic coping strategy, and they switched to a literal approach in order to complement paraphrasing with a fingerspelled lexical item and enhance the contextual force of a message, thus supporting the findings of Davis's (1990a) study of interpreters, and (2) free interpretation can be regarded as a method of interpretation appropriate for use in the context of a university lecture if interpreters use code-switching between free and literal methods to provide access to English when appropriate.

The issue of translation style merits further discussion in relation to the other focus of this study; that is, the types of omissions produced by interpreters while interpreting for a university lecture, and the occurrence of omissions used as a linguistic coping strategy. Interpreting omissions were analyzed on several levels taking a range of factors into consideration, including the number and type of omissions made by each interpreter; the relationship between each interpreter's translation style, educational background, and familiarity with the topic and the number and types of omissions made; the lexical density of the text and its impact on the number and type of omissions made; and the interpreters' level of metalinguistic awareness about omission occurrences and their linguistic decision-making process.

INTERPRETING OMISSIONS

Hatim and Mason (1990) suggested that translators working on written texts use a process of selective reduction to decide which portions of source text should be omitted. They stated that translators "can and do take responsibility for omitting information which is deemed to be of insufficient relevance" (p. 96). The same suggestion can be made for interpreters working between signed or spoken languages, yet it should be acknowledged that interpreters inevitably make some omissions that they do not necessarily make strategic decisions about, due to the more spontaneous nature of their work and the time constraints involved.

For the purposes of analyzing interpreting omissions, I used a new omission taxonomy (see chapter four). The taxonomy included five key omission types, which incorporated omissions made during a process of selective reduction, as well as those made inadvertently — *conscious strategic, conscious intentional, conscious unintentional, conscious receptive,* and *unconscious omissions.*

A total of 341 omissions were made by all ten subjects, across all five categories, with an average of 34.1 omissions made per subject. The highest number of omissions made by one subject was 50, and the lowest number was 18. Table 3 provides a breakdown of the total number of omissions made by all ten subjects in each omission category. From these figures, it can be seen that the most commonly occurring omissions were unconscious, closely followed by conscious strategic, conscious intentional, and conscious receptive, with the least occurring omissions being conscious unintentional. Thus, over half of the omissions made by the subjects were at opposite ends of the spectrum in terms of strategic use of omissions.

Analysis of the number and types of omissions made by individuals involved in the study shows a common thread, with minor exceptions, that unconscious and conscious strategic omissions are the most frequently occurring omission types. Table 4 provides information on the number of omissions made by each subject in the different omission categories. The figures demonstrate that interpreters do consciously employ the use of omissions as a linguistic coping strategy, and so not

TABLE 3. *Total Omissions Made by All Subjects across All Categories*

Omission categories	Omissions (%)
Unconscious	92 (27%)
Conscious strategic	87 (26%)
Conscious intentional	61 (18%)
Conscious receptive	52 (15%)
Conscious unintentional	49 (14%)
Total	341 (100%)

TABLE 4. *Total and Types of Omissions per Subject*

	Subject									
Omission type	1	2	3	4	5	6	7	8	9	10
Conscious strategic	11	7	8	13	3	8	10	9	7	11
Conscious intentional	9	15	7	7	3	2	8	2	5	3
Conscious unintentional	5	5	4	8	5	5	4	5	4	4
Conscious receptive	1	11	9	5	4	6	4	3	4	5
Unconscious	8	12	16	8	3	9	7	10	9	10
Total	34	50	44	41	18	30	33	29	29	33

all omissions should be counted as errors. The figures also demonstrate, however, that a large proportion of omissions made by interpreters are not intentional.

There is one important point to consider — the total number of omissions made by each interpreter is not the central issue; rather the focus is on the types of omissions made. An evaluation of the total number of omissions may be misleading if judged on its own. Importance is placed on the proportion of those omissions that are strategic, intentional, unintentional, due to receptive difficulties, or are unconscious. Nevertheless, it is worth reflecting on the overall omission occurrences of each interpreter, as this evaluation can provide early indication of any patterns that may emerge during further analysis of individual omission types. Table 5 provides a ranking according to the total number of omissions per subject.

The most obvious pattern that emerges from evaluating the total number of omissions per subject is the relationship between the number of omissions and the subjects' familiarity with the lecture topic. The total omission occurrence of those interpreters who were less familiar with the topic was higher than others with more familiarity, who made less than the average number of omissions (mean = 34.1). The two subjects who made the highest number of omissions also had no university qualifications (subjects 2 and 3) and, one can assume, were less familiar with the academic discourse environment. Lack of qualifications is not necessarily linked to the total number of omissions due to the fact that one subject with a postgraduate qualification also made a high number of omissions (subject 4). Nevertheless, apart from one anomaly, the majority of subjects with postgraduate qualifications made less than the average number

TABLE 5. *Total Number of Omissions and Background of Subjects*

Subject	Subjects' Background			
	Familiarity with topic	University qualification	Translation style	Total Omissions
1	No	Undergraduate	L	34
2	No	No	EL	50
3	No	No	EL	44
4	No	Postgraduate	F	41
5	Yes	Postgraduate	EL	18
6	Yes	Postgraduate	F	30
7	Yes	Undergraduate	F	33
8	Yes	Postgraduate	F	29
9	Yes	Postgraduate	EF	29
10	No	Undergraduate	EF	33

Note. EL = Extremely literal approach; L = Dominant literal approach;
EF = Extremely free approach; F = Dominant free approach.

of omissions, and all those with undergraduate qualifications also made less than the average number of omissions.

It would seem, therefore, that there is a relationship between educational background and the total number of omissions made by each subject. In relation to the translation style of the interpreters, however, the figures do not show any distinct pattern. Thus an association cannot be made between the total number of omissions made and whether an interpreter was dominant in using a literal or free interpretation approach.

When studying the occurrence of the discrete omission types more closely, it can be seen that the patterns begin to shift, with different factors influencing the rate of particular omission occurrences by each subject. In proposing the concept of *conscious strategic omissions*, I would advocate that all interpreters use this omission type as a linguistic coping strategy, regardless of their translation style, educational background, or familiarity with the topic. I originally hypothesized, however, that the rate at which conscious strategic omissions are used when interpreting for a university lecture would be affected by these factors. I further hypothesized that subjects dominant in using a free interpretation approach would be more likely to use more conscious strategic omissions than those dominantly using a literal approach. The process of free interpretation necessitates the search for linguistic and cultural equivalence, whereby interpreters judge what is relevant and meaningful to their target audience. Thus interpreters using a free approach would make conscious decisions to make strategic omissions for the sake of clarity of a message. Alternatively, I proposed that subjects using a more literal interpretation would make less conscious strategic omissions, as they would concentrate on the form of the message and the accuracy of the interpretation, rather than meaningful equivalents. Further, I predicted that interpreters who had a university qualification and were more familiar with the lecture topic would make more conscious strategic omissions when interpreting for a lexically dense university lecture than those subjects with no qualifications or lack of knowledge of the lecture topic. I assumed that interpreters with more exposure to the general academic discourse environment would feel more comfortable about making strategic linguistic and cultural decisions with regard to making omissions, especially if they had subject-specific knowledge and could thus judge the importance of terminology used. Table 6, however, demonstrates that these hypotheses were incorrect. There is no identifiable pattern between the rate of occurrence of conscious strategic omissions and either the translation style, educational background, or lecture topic familiarity of the interpreters.

As can be seen in Table 6, the number of conscious strategic omissions ranged from 3 to 13, with the average being 8.7. The majority of those

TABLE 6. *Occurrence of Conscious Strategic Omissions in Decreasing Order*

Subject	Subjects' Background			
	Familiarity with topic	University qualification	Translation style	Omissions
4	No	Postgraduate	F	13
1	No	Undergraduate	L	11
10	No	Undergraduate	EF	11
7	Yes	Undergraduate	F	10
8	Yes	Postgraduate	F	9
3	No	No	EL	8
6	Yes	Postgraduate	F	8
2	No	No	EL	7
9	Yes	Postgraduate	EF	7
5	Yes	Postgraduate	EL	3

Note. EL = Extremely literal approach; L = Dominant literal approach;
EF = Extremely free approach; F = Dominant free approach.

who made more than the average number of conscious strategic omissions dominantly used a free interpretation approach, but it can also be
seen that subjects using the same approach made less than the average
number of omissions. The two subjects with no qualifications (subjects
2 and 3) made less than the average number of this omission type, yet so
did other subjects with postgraduate qualifications (subjects 5, 6, and 9),
and surprisingly the three subjects who made the most conscious strategic omissions were less familiar with the lecture topic (subjects 1, 4, and
10). Thus it would appear that conscious strategic omissions are used
as a linguistic coping strategy by all interpreters, and in the particular
discourse environment of a university lecture, the translation style, educational background, and topic familiarity of the interpreters does not
influence the rate of occurrence of conscious strategic omissions.

The other four omission categories cannot be considered as strategic, even if the interpreters were conscious of making the omissions.
Therefore, the fewer the number of omissions made intentionally, unintentionally, receptively, or unconsciously, the better for a meaningful and
accurate interpretation of the message. By identifying any patterns in
relation to the occurrence of erroneous omissions, this information can
be incorporated into education and training programs for sign language
interpreters, to allow them to assess their strengths and weaknesses and
enhance the quality of their interpretation output.

Along with conscious strategic omissions, there also does not appear
to be any particular pattern with the occurrence of *conscious intentional
omissions*, as demonstrated in Table 7. On average, each subject made
this type of omission 6.1 times, with the highest number at 15, and the
lowest at two. I had hypothesized that those who were not university
educated or were not acquainted with the lecture topic would make more
omissions in this category due to lack of familiarity with the academic
language register and subject-specific lexicon, yet this was not the case.
Although the subject who made the most omissions was not university
educated and not acquainted with the lecture topic (subject 2), and the
two who made the least were educated to postgraduate level with familiarity of the topic (subjects 6 and 8), there is not enough consistency in
the data to suggest that these factors influenced the outcome; translation style seemed to have no bearing at all. Conscious intentional omissions were made by subjects who had university qualifications and who
were familiar with the subject area, yet they still made omissions because

	Subjects' Background			
Subject	Familiarity with topic	University qualification	Translation style	Omissions
2	No	No	EL	15
1	No	Undergraduate	L	9
7	Yes	Undergraduate	F	8
4	No	Postgraduate	F	7
3	No	No	EL	7
9	Yes	Postgraduate	EF	5
5	Yes	Postgraduate	EL	3
10	No	Undergraduate	EF	3
8	Yes	Postgraduate	F	2
6	Yes	Postgraduate	F	2

Note. EL = Extremely literal approach; L = Dominant literal approach;
EF = Extremely free approach; F = Dominant free approach.

they could not understand lexical items or concepts, or did not know the meaningful equivalents in the target language.

Conscious unintentional omissions were made consistently by all subjects, regardless of their translation style, educational background, or familiarity with the lecture topic. Almost all subjects made either four or five conscious unintentional omissions, except for subject number four who made eight omissions (see Table 8), giving rise to an average number of 4.9 conscious unintentional omissions per subject.

This problem of unintentionally making omissions is a cognitive information processing issue that could not necessarily be improved upon with better educational background or increased knowledge of the topic being interpreted; nor does it depend on translation style. All the subjects in the study agreed that they had every intention of interpreting that particular piece of information, and they had been trying to make a strategic decision in waiting for further contextual information, but the information somehow eluded them.

In relation to both conscious intentional, and conscious unintentional omissions, Peterson (2000) suggested that metacognitive strategies can be used by interpreters as "tools for 'repairing' incomplete information or for compensating for messages that are not clearly comprehended" (p. 136). Peterson argued that by having knowledge about how their

TABLE 8. *Occurrence of Conscious Unintentional Omissions in Decreasing Order*

| Subject | Subjects' Background | | | Omissions |
	Familiarity with topic	University qualification	Translation style	
4	No	Postgraduate	F	8
2	No	No	EL	5
1	No	Undergraduate	L	5
5	Yes	Postgraduate	EL	5
8	Yes	Postgraduate	F	5
6	Yes	Postgraduate	F	5
7	Yes	Undergraduate	F	4
3	No	No	EL	4
9	Yes	Postgraduate	EF	4
10	No	Undergraduate	EF	4

Note. EL = Extremely literal approach; L = Dominant literal approach;
EF = Extremely free approach; F = Dominant free approach.

cognitive processes function, interpreters can monitor their information processing, and thus be in a better position to process meaning and make inferences about meaning according to their linguistic and cultural knowledge.

An average of 5.2 *conscious receptive omissions* were made by each subject, with the highest being 11, and the lowest being 1, as seen in Table 9. Conscious receptive omissions occurred due to reported problems in hearing the source text, which some of the subjects attributed to the poor sound quality of the videotape used. However, it is worth considering the fact that the two interpreters who made well above the average number of conscious receptive omissions had no university qualifications and did not have any familiarity with the lecture topic (subjects 2 and 3).

The three subjects who made the average number of conscious receptive omissions were unfamiliar with the lecture topic, but had a university education (subjects 4 and 10). All those who made less than the average number of conscious receptive omissions had a university education and were also familiar with the lecture content (subjects 5, 7, 8, and 9), except for one subject who was unfamiliar with the lecture topic (subject 1). There did not appear to be any relationship between the number of receptive omissions and the translation style used.

TABLE 9. *Occurrence of Conscious Receptive Omissions in Decreasing Order*

Subject	Subjects' Background			
	Familiarity with topic	University qualification	Translation style	Omissions
2	No	No	EL	11
3	No	No	EL	9
6	Yes	Postgraduate	F	6
10	No	Undergraduate	EF	5
4	No	Postgraduate	F	5
5	Yes	Postgraduate	EL	4
7	Yes	Undergraduate	F	4
9	Yes	Postgraduate	EF	4
8	Yes	Postgraduate	F	3
1	No	Undergraduate	L	1

Note. EL = Extremely literal approach; L = Dominant literal approach;
EF = Extremely free approach; F = Dominant free approach.

In applying the notion of frame theory to this process, it is possible to assume that those who were more familiar with the discourse environment and lecture topic may have been better equipped to make predictions about the information being presented and to "second-guess" lexical items that could not be heard properly. Even those without familiarity of the topic but who had an inherent understanding of general academic discourse may have been able to infer meaning and "fill in the gaps" of what they could not hear properly. Those without the advantage of prior knowledge of the topic or familiarity with the language register, however, would have been relying solely on what they could hear, which is why it is understandable that an omission would be made if the lexical item could not be heard properly.

Finally, each subject made an average of 9.2 *unconscious omissions*, ranging from 3 to 16 omissions, which was a figure much higher than envisaged. Although it was hypothesized that the subjects would make a number of unconscious omissions, it was surprising to note that this type was as prevalent as the use of conscious strategic omissions. Table 10 shows that, again, the two interpreters with no university qualifications or lecture content knowledge made the most omissions in this category (subjects 2 and 3). Apart from these two subjects, however, the distribution of omission occurrences was not consistent with the level of

TABLE 10. *Occurrence of Unconscious Omissions in Decreasing Order*

| Subject | Subjects' Background | | | Omissions |
	Familiarity with topic	University qualification	Translation style	
3	No	No	EL	16
2	No	No	EL	12
10	No	Undergraduate	EF	10
8	Yes	Postgraduate	F	10
9	Yes	Postgraduate	EF	9
6	Yes	Postgraduate	F	9
4	No	Postgraduate	F	8
1	No	Undergraduate	L	8
7	Yes	Undergraduate	F	7
5	Yes	Postgraduate	EL	3

Note. EL = Extremely literal approach; L = Dominant literal approach;
EF = Extremely free approach; F = Dominant free approach.

qualification held or familiarity with the topic. The dominant translation style of the interpreters did not seem to affect the number of unconscious omissions made.

It is generally accepted among interpreters and interpreter educators that it is not necessary to interpret every lexical item received, but rather the source language message should be "chunked" into meaningful parts, and thus equivalent intent should be sought in the target language (Winston & Monikowski, 2000). The notion, however, that interpreters are making omissions when interpreting a university lecture because they do not hear the information in the source language, regardless of their level of qualifications or subject knowledge, has implications for interpreter training and raising levels of awareness as to why this happens.

Thus far, the evaluation of omission occurrences has demonstrated that the translation style of an interpreter does not significantly influence the rate of omissions in any omission category. The educational background of interpreters is not a major factor on its own that affects the rate and type of omissions made, and the interpreters' previous knowledge of the lecture topic only seems to have a slight impact on the rate and type of omissions produced. When the two factors are combined, however, it is apparent that there is more likelihood of an increase in erroneous omissions, especially with conscious receptive and unconscious omissions. A combination, therefore, of interpreters' familiarity with the general academic discourse environment and the subject-specific content and terminology of a lecture would appear to be the most consistent factor affecting the rate of occurrence of omissions.

Omission Patterns and Familiarity

Closer examination of the relationship between omission patterns and familiarity revealed specific examples that demonstrated the link between the features of language use, which are bound both to the lecture topic and the discourse environment, and the occurrence of different omission types. Not surprisingly, a pattern emerged that specific features of language use elicited the occurrence of particular omissions, implying that interpreters used their knowledge of language use to identify the significance of the message in the context of the university lecture, which had an impact on the types of omissions they made. Figure 1 illustrates the pattern of omissions when aligned with the interpreters' familiarity with the lecture topic and their educational background.

In order to identify the specific language features it was decided to concentrate on key parts of the text that featured a high number of omissions, regardless of the omission type, and look for identifiable relationships with the number of omissions and the text itself. The printed version of the source text had 176 lines of text, with only 32 percent of the lines producing no omissions at all from the ten subjects. The number of omissions made by each subject on each line of text was totaled to find which lines featured the most omissions. For example, subjects 4 and 6 both made an omission on line 4 of the text, for a total of two omissions on that line of text. On line 79 of the text, subjects 2, 4, 8, 9, and 10 each made one omission, meaning that this line had 5 omissions. All totaled, the subjects made 341 omissions, with an average of 1.95 omissions per line of text. The analysis showed that seven particular lines of text featured the highest number of omissions, with seven or more omissions per line. These seven lines (lines 59, 90, 104, 116, 117, 139, and 169) are underlined in Example 7, which contains the sentences or paragraphs in which these seven lines appeared.

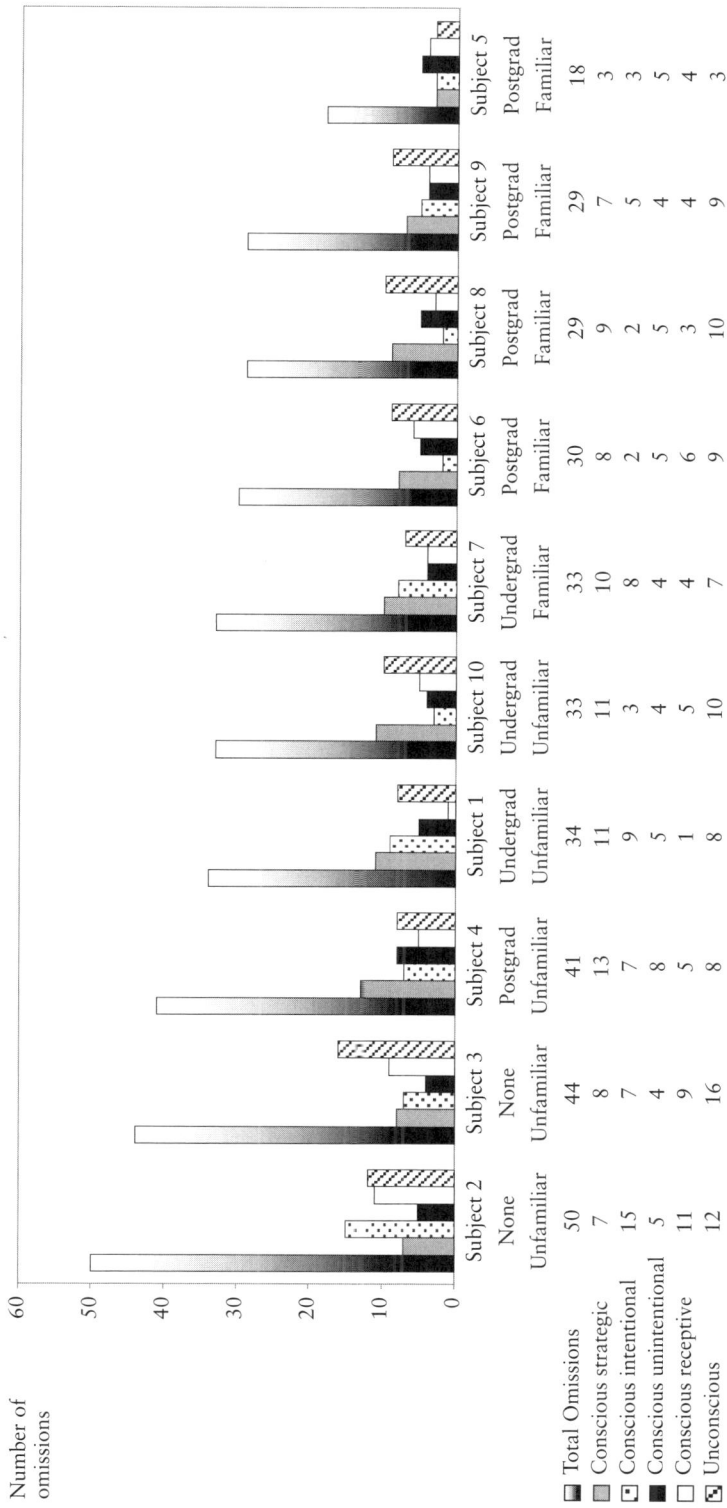

FIGURE 1. *Comparison of type of omissions and subjects' education and familiarity with the topic.*

EXAMPLE 7: LINES OF TEXT FEATURING HIGHEST
PROPORTION OF OMISSIONS

One

Line 57:   The second issue I'd like to look at is, partly by way of

Line 58:   exploding a myth, is the notion of early acquisition. What some people, or we can refer to

Line 59:   <u>as precocity or precociousness in, erm, sign language acquisition. There's very much a</u>

Line 60:   sort of an idea there in people's minds that children learning a sign language, acquire sign

Line 61:   language earlier than children acquiring a spoken language. . .

Two

Line 87:   Erm, as I said, we don't have time to go into it tonight, but some of the work on early sign

Line 88:   language acquisition has, erm, made some interesting points in that regard and led a lot of

Line 89:   researchers to challenge the notion that that's the necessary relationship in quite the, the

Line 90:   <u>lock-step way that Piaget and others were suggesting. And the last issue that, again, we</u>

Line 91:   won't have time to go into tonight is the. . . issue of nativization and denativization.

Three

Line 103:   Where there's been a long tradition of oral education and

Line 104:   <u>very little El Salvador! El Salvador! And very little, er, use of sign language, and there's</u>

Line 105:   evidence on kids acquiring, sort of, linguistic or universal characteristics of sign language

Line 106:   in the absence of good input, and then gradually as more and more exposure to a formal

Line 107:   sign language occurs, denativizing and moving towards that particular, erm, set of sign

Line 108:   language rules and features.

Four and Five

Line 114: Erm, and a number of authors over a long period of

Line 115: time have, and Snow, that we talked about last week, Catherine Snow? Who's been so

Line 116: vocal on the issue of erm, er. . . critical period hypothesis, thank you! (*refers to student*),

Line 117: has done an enormous amount of work on this. So, over to you for a minute. What do we

Line 118: know about the characteristics of caregiver input that makes it, that seems to be a critical

Line 119: component of language acquisition?

Six

Line 137: But the actual nature of

Line 138: the features does seem to differ slightly across certain cultural groups. (*student question*)

Line 139: It was definitely a 60s thing, I'm not suggesting you were in the 60s, but there was a 60s/

Line 140: 70s thing, a of, sort of, seeing pop psychology time, you know, making the child a genius

Line 141: type thing, which advocated a particular level of discourse with a child.

Seven

Line 167: Well you tell me, what are the features of mother/child,

Line 168: motherese babytalk? (*student comment*) Repetition. . . (*student comment*) Erm, to a certain

Line 169: extent, imitation figures more highly in mother/child, you know, "say such and such"

Line 170: (*Babytalk intonation*) or "say daddy, say mummy" (*babytalk intonation*).

The types of omissions made by all subjects on each of these lines of text were noted in order to identify any patterns between omission categories and linguistic features of the text. Although a pattern could be seen with omissions being made on certain lines, not all the omissions were the same, with the highest proportion of omissions being *conscious strategic* or *unconscious* omissions. Twenty-two percent of omissions on line 59 were conscious strategic and 78 percent were conscious intentional. Line 90 had 28.5 percent conscious intentional omissions, 28.5 percent conscious receptive omissions, and 43 percent unconscious omissions. Line 104 had 40 percent conscious strategic omissions, 10 percent conscious unintentional omissions, and 50 percent unconscious omissions. Line 116 had 28.5 percent conscious receptive omissions and 71.5 percent unconscious omissions, and line 117 had 14 percent conscious unintentional omissions and 86 percent unconscious omissions. The omissions on line 139 were 50 percent conscious strategic, 12.5 percent conscious receptive, and 37.5 percent unconscious; and on line 169, 64 percent were conscious strategic, 9 percent conscious unintentional, 18 percent conscious receptive, and 9 percent unconscious.

Table 11 provides information on the total number of omission types made on each of the seven lines of text. The exact omission types made by each subject can be seen in Appendix K. The highest number of omissions occurred on the following lines of text with particular features of language use:

1. Unfamiliar (possibly academic English) or subject-specific terms; for example, *precocity* and *precociousness* in line 59 and *critical period hypothesis* in line 116.
2. Idiomatic English; for example, *lock-step way* in line 90.
3. Names of people or places; for example, *Piaget* in line 90, and *El Salvador* in line 104.
4. Repetition in English; for example, "it was a 60s thing, I'm not saying you were in the 60s, but it was a 60s/70s thing" in line 139.
5. Ambiguities in English; for example, "say such and such" in line 169.

Identifiable patterns of omissions can be seen on these lines of text according to the linguistic feature presented. In relation to unfamiliar or subject-specific terms, line 59 contained the terms *precocity* and *precociousness*, and the highest proportion of omissions on this line were in the conscious intentional category. All the subjects who made this type of omission reported that they either did not understand the use of the term in this context or did not know how to find an equivalent sign in Auslan. Line 116 produced mostly conscious receptive or unconscious omissions, and the most commonly omitted lexical item was the academic term *hypothesis*. Most subjects explained that because the concept was

TABLE 11. *Total Number of Each Omission Type on Key Lines of Text*

	Line number						
Omission type	59	90	104	116	117	139	169
Conscious strategic	2	0	4	0	0	4	8
Conscious intentional	7	2	0	0	0	0	1
Conscious unintentional	1	0	1	0	1	0	0
Conscious receptive	0	2	0	2	0	1	1
Unconscious	0	3	5	5	6	3	1
Total	10	7	10	7	7	8	11

unfamiliar to them, they had focused on the preceding two words, which they considered to be important (*critical* and *period*), and did not hear the word *hypothesis*; or they were unfamiliar with the term *hypothesis* and could not hear it clearly enough to decipher it.

All but one of the omissions that appeared on line 117 were unconscious and occurred with the phrase, "So, over to you for a minute . . ." All the respondents remarked that they probably had not heard this phrase because they were still concentrating on the difficult interpretation of the previous sentence in line 116, and they experienced cognitive overload.

With regard to repetition in English, lines 104 and 139 both predominantly featured unconscious omissions or conscious strategic omissions, meaning that subjects either did not hear the repetition of the words/ concepts, or heard them and chose to delete them. All subjects who had made a strategic omission reported that the repetition was redundant, and thus had made a conscious decision to omit as it would not detract from the message.

In relation to ambiguities in English, line 169 featured the phrase "say such and such," and the majority of omissions were conscious strategic. Subjects unanimously commented that it was impossible to interpret such a phrase into Auslan as it was too abstract, so they opted to omit this information in favor of the subsequent phrase "say mummy, say daddy," which presented concrete information that could be clearly interpreted into Auslan.

Finally, although line 90 did not present any consistency in the omission types that occurred, it did demonstrate a pattern when compared with the other lines of text. Several omission types occurred due to the fact that some subjects omitted the term *lock-step way*, whereas others omitted the name *Piaget*. The conscious receptive omissions were made because they were not familiar with the name Piaget and could not hear it pronounced clearly enough, whereas the term *lock-step way* was either not heard at all or was omitted consciously and intentionally because the subjects were not familiar with this idiomatic expression and were unsure how to represent it in Auslan.

It was predicted that the type of patterning discussed thus far would also occur in other lines of text that had fewer omissions. Therefore, other lines were chosen at random from those with less than seven, but above the average number of omissions (mean = 1.95). As envisaged, the number of omissions were higher on lines using subject-specific or unfamiliar terms, such as *pronouns* (line 6), *denativizing* (line 99), and *motherese* (line 143). Omissions were also present on lines using English idioms, such as "photocopy powers that be" (line 10) and "in a nutshell" (line 12); as well as in lines using names such as Reilly, McIntire, and Bellugi (lines 15 and 16) and Caselli and Volterra (line 66). Omissions were found on lines featuring repetition, as in line 166: "there's that principle in, in *mother/child*, or *caregiver/child* interaction." The same was found with redundant repetition, where two different words that were perceived by the interpreters to mean the same thing were used one after the other; for example, "what happens to kids when they have *incomplete* or *inadequate* input in their first language" (line 95). English words such as *saliency* (line 151) and *consumable* (line 166), which were regarded by the interpreters as being ambiguous in this context, also appeared in lines with above the average number of omissions.

It can be stated, therefore, that one explanation for the pattern of omission occurrence in this text is in relation to interpreters' familiarity with the features of language use that are bound both to the lecture topic and the academic English used in the university discourse environment. Although the interpreters' familiarity with the discourse environment alone did not necessarily affect the number of omissions they produced, it certainly seemed to affect the types of omissions that occurred in different parts of the text in relation to the linguistic features presented.

Omission Patterns and Lexical Density

Lexical density is another linguistic feature of the discourse environment that was thought to have influenced the prevalence and types of omissions occurring in different parts of the text. It refers to the complexity of language (Halliday, 1985), and it is a concept that can be used to measure the difficulty of a piece of text (Richards, Platt, & Platt, 1992). I hypothesized that more omissions would be made on the most lexically dense parts of the text, and if this was the case, that more omissions would be made in the most complex parts of the text. In order to validate this assumption, it was necessary to calculate the average lexical density of a line of text and then compare the number of omissions on an average line of text with the number of omissions on those lines with higher than average lexical density. I expected that a relationship would be found between the number of omissions and the lexical density of a line of text.

Adopting the method proposed by Ure (1971), I added up the total number of words on the first line of each page of text, then divided each total by the number of lexical items on that line to arrive at a percentage. These calculations found that the overall lexical density of the university lecture text was 51 percent, and the average lexical density for a random line of text was 47.6 percent. Of the eight lines of text selected at random, three were of average lexical density, two were above, and three were below (see Table 12). In order to test the relationship between the number of omissions and the lexical density of text, the seven lines identified earlier with the highest number of omissions were analyzed for lexical density (see Table 13). The results showed that, apart from one anomaly, all the lines of text with the highest number of omissions had a lexical density higher than the average line of text. Then, to identify whether those lines of text with a lower percentage of lexical density produced a smaller number of omissions, all the lines of text featured in Tables 12 and 13 were compared for lexical density and omission rates (see Table 14).

Apart from the anomalies in lines 117 and 139 (as mentioned in the discussion of Table 11), Table 14 shows that the lexical density of the text does seem to influence the number of omissions. It can be seen that the issue is not whether the text is higher than the average lexical density, but rather the extent to which it is higher than the average. The lines of text of below (lines 1, 4, and 21) or average lexical density (lines 67 and 136) presented 0–2 omissions. The increased relationship between omissions and density begins when the lexical density of a line of text reaches 57 percent, almost 10 percent above the average, with an almost exponential increase in the number of omissions in relation to an increase in lexical

TABLE 12. *Lexical Density per Random Text Line*

Line number	Number of lexical (content) words	Number of function (grammatical) words	Lexical density
1	5	10	33%
44	6	10	37.5%
21	7	8	46%
67	9	10	47%
136	9	10	47%
113	7	7	50%
159	9	7	56%
90	10	6	62.5%
	Average lexical density of text		47.6%

TABLE 13. *Lexical Density of Text Lines with Highest Number of Omissions*

Line number	Number of lexical (content) words	Number of function (grammatical) words	Lexical density
117	4	15	21%
139	10	10	50%
116	8	6	57%
59	10	6	62.5%
90	10	6	62.5%
104	12	5	71%
169	11	3	78.5%

density. Interestingly, those lines with the highest lexical density (104 and 169) featured the highest number of conscious strategic omissions in proportion to the total number of omissions on that line.

From this superficial analysis, it seems that the lexical density of text does influence the occurrence and types of omissions produced by Auslan interpreters to some extent. If, as stated by Halliday (1978), university lectures are typically presented in lexically dense text, the results of this study illustrate that it is inevitable that sign language interpreters will make omissions, some of which will be strategic.

It is arguable, however, that lexical density alone influences the rate and type of omissions; the lexical items themselves also have an effect, as demonstrated with regard to familiarity with academic discourse and subject-specific terminology. If interpreters are familiar with the content words used in lexically dense parts of text, they are less likely to

TABLE 14. *Number of Omissions Compared with Lexical Density of Text*

Line number	Omissions	Lexical density
117	7	21%
1	0	33%
4	1	37.5%
21	2	46%
67	0	47%
136	1	47%
113	1	50%
139	5	50%
159	0	56%
116	7	57%
59	10	62.5%
90	7	62.5%
104	10	71%
169	11	78.5%

erroneously omit the meaning of those particular lexical items, but they might choose to strategically omit them as part of the linguistic decision-making process. Interpreters may, however, generally experience difficulties in interpreting lexically dense text, depending on the presentation style and whether the text is spontaneous or read out loud. In order to establish the extent to which the lexical density of a text affects the rate and occurrence of omissions, it would be necessary to analyze the omissions made by interpreters when interpreting a lexically dense piece of prepared text that is read out, or when interpreting different texts with alternative percentages of lexical density. These preliminary findings do suggest, however, that the lexical density of the source text has a bearing on the omissions made by interpreters.

Thus far it has been established that the lexical density of source text and familiarity with the source text affect the number of omissions made by interpreters. Findings show that the discourse environment influences the number and types of omissions made by sign language interpreters — interpreters make different types of omissions based on their conscious monitoring of the discourse, the application of their knowledge of the discourse environment, and the linguistic and cultural expectations of the discourse participants.

METALINGUISTIC AWARENESS DURING
THE INTERPRETING PROCESS

The concept of metalinguistic awareness refers to the ability to monitor and change language use, and it has been suggested that interpreters need to apply their metalinguistic knowledge and use "meta-strategies" (Hoffman, 1997) or "metacognitive strategies" (Peterson, 2000; Smith, 2000) while interpreting, to monitor the linguistic choices they make during the interpretation process.

The very nature of this study has demonstrated the fact that the participants had a level of metalinguistic awareness while performing the interpreting task. This awareness is evident in the categories developed for defining the types of omissions identified, which referred to whether the omissions were conscious or unconscious. The categories were developed as a consequence of reviewing the interpreting tasks with the subjects and asking them whether they remembered making certain omissions. Through discussion of the interpreting task, it was possible to ascertain the interpreters' level of consciousness about the linguistic choices they were making and, thus, the extent of their metalinguistic awareness.

All of the subjects involved in the study were highly cognizant of their linguistic choices and were particularly conscious of the omissions they made and why they made them. In fact, because of the interpreters' level of metalinguistic awareness, I was able to explore why omissions were being made. If the subjects had not been so metalinguistically aware, it would not have been possible to develop the categories of omissions in the first place. All the subjects referred to an internalized self-critical commentary that accompanied the interpreting process, whereby they were constantly reevaluating and commenting on their linguistic decision making during the process. The results of the study imply that the subjects engaged in using metacognitive strategies as a linguistic coping strategy to monitor and enhance the effectiveness of their interpreting output, as they were able to engage in the task review and refer to the commentary in their head about the linguistic choices they made. Additionally, it can be stated that the interpreters must have been applying their metalinguistic awareness to the interpreting process in order to consciously make the decisions to use strategic omissions, due to the fact that conscious strategic omissions comprise a larger percentage of the total omissions they made. Nonetheless, it is interesting to reflect on some of the interpreters' comments made with regard to their own level of metalinguistic awareness. One subject commented that during the task review she became more conscious of the process of making omissions, and, therefore, she might have been more conscious during the study than she normally would be when interpreting elsewhere. It could be argued, however, that although the review process may have heightened the interpreters' awareness, all interpreters were able to reflect on their thought processes during the interpretations and on whether they were conscious of the omissions they had made. This ability implies that they are comfortable with this process and that they probably consistently engage in it while interpreting, but perhaps on a less conscious level.

Another subject also reported that her metalinguistic awareness was heightened due to being able to watch the video of herself interpreting. She stated that the knowledge that she would be able to review her work prompted her to remember how she felt and what she was thinking during the interpreting task. She noted that it may have been more difficult to reflect on the experience without the visual prompt of the recorded interpretation.

All interpreters involved in the study expressed an interest in the types of omissions made, their level of awareness at the time of making the omissions, and their ability to reflect on their interpreting decisions. A few of the subjects expressed amazement at the extent to which they relied on the commentary going on in their head while they were interpreting; they said that participating in this study made them realize it for the first time.

Although the extent of metalinguistic awareness is difficult to measure, the comments made by some of the subjects are worthwhile considering for any future study on interpreting. Comments made by the study subjects in relation to their educational backgrounds are also worth considering.

SOCIOLINGUISTIC AND SOCIOCULTURAL INFLUENCES ON INTERPRETERS: EDUCATION

The ten subjects involved in the study had diverse educational backgrounds; some held undergraduate or postgraduate qualifications, while others had not studied since they left school. In the retrospective interview,

I asked the interpreters to comment on their educational backgrounds and how their ability to interpret for the university lecture segment was affected by that background. I hypothesized that they would comment on how their comfort and confidence during the interpreting task was predominantly affected by their level of familiarity with the language used and the lecture topic itself. This prediction was substantiated, as comments revealed unanimous agreement that their educational backgrounds did influence their ability to interpret for the lecture. Some of their comments are shown in Example 8.

EXAMPLE 8: SUBJECTS' COMMENTS REGARDING
EDUCATIONAL BACKGROUND

I was hindered by my lack of higher education. . . . I haven't studied since I was fifteen. I found this task hard because of the academic language used in universities. I didn't have enough knowledge of the subject matter, the English language or the terminology used.

I am not familiar with university language and jargon, especially subject-specific words. . . . I don't have a strong educational background . . . I didn't understand the language sufficiently enough to "freely" interpret; I think I could have gone for the meaning more.

I've had a university education and that contributes greatly. But I'm not overly familiar with academic language as I don't work much in universities, so that threw me a little. . . . My English skills would need to be improved to the register of university-level language.

Knowledge about the subject helped a lot . . . and having been to university myself helped me to deal with the language register. . . . It helps the more familiar you are with the topic. . . . I think a lot of interpreters are under-qualified to interpret. In an ideal world interpreters would be matched with situations or subjects they have studied or are familiar with. . . . [For university interpreting] I think you need either a university education yourself, or plenty of experience interpreting in university settings — you can't do justice to difficult concepts if you don't understand them.

I have a university education . . . so I am familiar with the language use and with university situations, so I wasn't intimidated by that, but the ideal is to have knowledge of the content. I was comfortable with the level of language because I have interpreted this type of lecture lots of times before. . . . Plus my educational background helped me to deal with the level of language — I'm used to the university environment and the language use.

My education supports me in what I do. . . . I couldn't have coped without a university education background.

My ability to interpret has improved dramatically since studying at H.E. level. . . . I have a greater understanding of language and how culture and language are linked. I have more familiarity with university-level discourse and a better understanding of how someone can use a creative lexicon.

It can be seen from the comments in Example 8 that the subjects involved in this study felt that their educational backgrounds made a difference in their ability to interpret for the university lecture segment. It can be stated, therefore, that a university education, plus knowledge of the subject, meant that the subjects felt more able to cope with the linguistic demands of the interpreting task. Even without subject-specific knowledge, it is apparent that subjects with a general university education were less perturbed by the linguistic pressures of the task due to their familiarity and comfort with the university discourse environment.

Although the subjects felt that their educational background influenced their ability to interpret the lecture, the results of this study have not shown that educational background on its own is a major factor. Larger numbers of subjects would need to be tested in order to determine the extent to which educational background affects the quality of interpretation of a university lecture. Nevertheless, the reporting of the subjects involved in the study is valid, and it provides insight into interpreters' self-perceptions of the relationship between education and interpreting skills.

EXPECTATIONS OF INTERPRETING SERVICE CONSUMERS

In order to validate the findings of this study for discussion of wider implications, it was important to ensure that the perspective of Deaf university students was taken into consideration. Various European and North American studies have assessed the expectations of consumers of interpreting services. Moser (1996) found that users of spoken language interpreters at conferences had different qualitative expectations of the interpreting service, depending on their experience of attending conferences and using interpreters, and the type of conference they were attending. Viera and Stauffer (2000) found that Deaf people using interpreters in professional arenas had very particular preferences in relation to the translation style used by interpreters, so that they could access English terminology. Locker (1990) found that American Deaf students had similar expectations of the interpreters they used in university settings, especially in regard to the type of errors made and translation style used. It can be assumed, therefore, that Australian Deaf people would have particular expectations in terms of the interpreting service they would expect to receive in a university context.

University lectures and conference presentations are both situations that offer potentially complex information. If participants choose to attend a conference presentation or a university lecture, it can be assumed that they will have a clear idea of how they would like to access the information. Consequently, a panel of Deaf university students was brought together to discuss the issues introduced during this study.

The panel included four Deaf people from different backgrounds — two native signers and two non-native signers — in order to provide a representative sample of the Deaf community. Two had been educated using some form of signed communication in a deaf unit within a mainstream school, and the other two were educated orally in a mainstream school; three of the panel members were studying towards undergraduate degrees at the time the research took place, and the fourth had completed both undergraduate and postgraduate study and was still studying toward another university qualification. Two of the participants were familiar with the subject of language acquisition, which was the lecture topic in the interpreting task.

The panel watched two extracts of interpreting taken from the data collected as part of this study. In the first, the interpreter used an extremely dominant free interpretation approach, and in the second, the interpreter used an extremely dominant literal interpretation approach. The panel members were asked to discuss the different interpretation methods, their preferences, and reasons for those preferences. I asked a series of questions, which I adapted from Moser (1996) and Locker (1990), in order to prompt discussion in relation to the issues of translation style, interpreting omissions, educational background of interpreters, and expectations in university settings.

When asked which of the interpretation approaches they preferred, the panelists concurred that they liked both approaches but that each was more appropriate in different contexts. They stated that the extremely dominant free interpretation approach would be fine for more general interpreting situations, but that the literal approach was more suitable in university lecture situations. The reason posited was that a literal approach incorporated more use of fingerspelling, thus allowing the students to access technical vocabulary and academic English. The panel members also trusted that they were receiving more information from the interpreter using the extremely dominant literal approach, as she seemed to be keeping up with the pace of the lecturer and pausing less, thus conveying that she was confident to interpret the information.

One person stated that it was important for key concepts to be interpreted using a more free approach, but that terminology should be fingerspelled (i.e., the interpreter should switch to a more literal interpretation at key points of the text). The general consensus seemed to be that the extracts they had been shown were both too extreme, and that they would prefer to receive information in conceptually accurate Auslan, with the use of fingerspelling and English mouth patterns when appropriate, for conveying terminology and academic terms (i.e., a dominant free interpretation approach with occasional code-switching into a literal approach).

When the panel members were asked to discuss in more depth whether interpreters should be more free or literal in their interpretation approach, many contradictions seemed to occur. One member, who had previously stated a preference for a literal approach, proceeded to say that concepts should be freely interpreted because it made it easier to absorb more complex information. Another member pointed out that a free interpretation approach was sometimes more appropriate, but it made taking notes difficult as Deaf students would have to re-interpret the information into written English. In relation to this point, the other three panel members agreed and asserted that a mixture of free and literal interpretation approaches was required. Two people went on to explain that the appropriate mix should fit the needs of the student, and interpreters could work towards this by building a close relationship with their clients. The panel was then asked to consider whether a free or literal approach was more desirable in interpretation of university tutorials. One person remarked that an interpreter needed to be extremely fluent in Auslan to cope with the demands of a tutorial, and that an interpreter who worked effectively in a lecture was not necessarily the best choice for a tutorial.

When asked how much they understood when following an interpreted university lecture, one panel member said she felt she got about 80 percent of the lecture material, whereas another said he accessed between 50 and 70 percent and had to follow up what he had missed on his own time through additional reading and study. Another person claimed to understand 80 to 90 percent of her lectures, which she was happy with. The first person who said she followed 80 percent stated that she was very satisfied with what interpreting provides, and that the 20 percent she missed was mostly due to her own inattention. Another person commented that the brain could only take in a limited amount of information anyway, and that how much you understand of a lecture can depend on yourself, not just the interpreter's skills.

Although the panelists stated that they understood a high percentage of university lectures through sign language interpretation, their comments were subjective and based only on reported, rather than definitive, understanding. Sign language can effectively convey the content of university lectures, yet a Deaf person's actual level of comprehension may contradict his or her reported understanding (Murphy, 1978). Steiner (1998) conducted a study of Deaf viewers' understanding of sign language production on television in the UK and found that the expressed preference of Deaf viewers in relation to signing style did not always correspond with their actual level of comprehension. The comprehension of sign language on television will invariably be influenced by different factors than the comprehension of a university lecture because the medium of television provides less clarity of depth, which is crucial to the effective articulation of sign language (through use of signing space, location, etc.). Nonetheless, the key issue is the fact that the respondents in Steiner's study contradicted themselves in terms of how much they understood and how accurately they received information from their preferred signing style. Livingston et al. (1994) studied North American Deaf postsecondary students' understanding of a lecture and found similar results. Further empirical study would be needed, therefore, to ascertain the actual extent of comprehension of Australian Deaf students in university lectures.

In relation to the Deaf students' reported level of understanding, all of the panel members conceded that they never accessed 100 percent of a university lecture, thus raising questions about their perspective on interpreting omissions. When asked what they thought about various kinds of omissions that may occur during interpretation of a university lecture, the responses from the panel members were varied. One panel member stated that occasional omissions do not matter, but that she was not comfortable with the idea that interpreters might choose to omit something, as she was afraid she might miss out on information. Two other panel members felt that fewer omissions would occur if the interpreter was familiar with the subject, and they said it was more important for the interpreter to have an understanding of the lecture content than to convey every single piece of information.

Opinions differed in relation to the concept of conscious strategic omissions and whether it was appropriate for interpreters to consciously omit information. One panel member felt that some omissions were linguistically and culturally appropriate, whereas the other three were not convinced. One of these three admitted it was appropriate if an interpreter chose to omit "trivia"; and everybody agreed that it would be difficult to interpret everything in a lecture anyway. The question was not really answered, however, as three of the panel members seemed uncomfortable with the idea that interpreters might make judgments about what information should be imparted and so make omissions accordingly.

With regard to the occurrence of omissions, the panelists in this study seemed reluctant to comment, probably because they assumed that omissions would always be erroneous. This parallels Locker's (1990) findings that Deaf students involved in a study regarded omissions negatively. Interestingly, the one panel member in my study who acknowledged that omissions could be used strategically was studying for a degree in linguistics and, therefore, was likely to have had a better understanding of the linguistic processes involved in interpreting. Although reluctant to comment with regard to interpreting omissions, the panel members had very clear opinions about the education of interpreters and their expectations of interpreters working in university settings.

The issue as to whether interpreters should have some knowledge of the subject matter they are interpreting provoked varied responses. One person claimed that subject knowledge definitely helps in a lecturing situation, but perhaps it is less necessary in a tutorial situation. Another person complained that she has had many different interpreters over several years as a part-time student, even as many as eight different interpreters for one subject. Yet she has never hesitated to reject interpreters who did not have adequate background knowledge to be able to cope with the subject matter of her studies. One panel member explained that, in an ideal world, students would be able to choose the interpreter most suited to their needs from a whole "army" of different interpreters. It was recognized that this is not the current reality, however, and that the mismatch between supply and demand must be acknowledged. The other members expressed the view that regardless of the reality, it is best to aspire to have an interpreter with the appropriate subject knowledge, although it is not the only criteria.

In response to the question of whether interpreters should have a university qualification before being allowed to interpret in universities, the panel unanimously agreed that it was necessary, although one panel member admitted that perhaps knowledge and skills equivalent to having a university qualification were also appropriate. Two people pointed out that a high school certificate should be the minimum requirement. Another three panel members reasserted their opinion that interpreters really ought to have a university background themselves if they aimed to work in that environment. One person gave an example of an experience in which a non-university educated interpreter could not recognize a word that was fingerspelled and was even unable to pronounce it.

This discussion was followed with a debate about whether interpreters should have a university qualification to interpret in general, again with differing perspectives. One person agreed that all interpreters should have a university education, stating that it was especially important if interpreters were going to work in medical and legal settings. Another person added that for working in linguistically demanding interpreting situations, interpreters must be university educated. The other two panel members were unsure. One person felt that, as a university educated professional, she preferred to have an interpreter with a similar background in a range of interpreting situations so that the interpreter's language skills can convey her skills and education to her colleagues and workmates. Another person argued that the reverse of this problem was that some over-qualified interpreters misrepresented the language skills of grassroots Deaf people by interpreting their limited signing into a formal and sophisticated variety of English, giving the impression that they were more educated than they actually were.

In relation to the educational background of interpreters, there was general agreement that interpreters should have a university education, especially if they are going to interpret in university contexts, and that familiarity with the subject they were interpreting was preferable, although not mandatory. This finding is comparable to that of Locker (1990), who stated that interpreters ideally should be familiar with the content of the lectures they interpret; and also to that of Bremner and Housden (1996), who reported that Deaf students felt that subject-specific knowledge would be an advantage to educational interpreters and that interpreters should be encouraged to specialize in interpreting for subjects they have studied.

Ultimately, the panel agreed that there were fundamental prerequisite skills an interpreter needed to work in a university context. The panel also recognized the importance of knowing the context of a situation by stating that, ideally, skills would be prioritized differently according to whether the interpretation happened in a lecture or tutorial situation.

In summary, the panel described the ideal skills of interpreters working in university lectures. All members of the panel generally agreed that interpreters should have a good university education, and good skills in both languages, especially in fingerspelling. They should be able to code-switch between free and literal interpretation as the situation, consumer, and content of the message required, using clear mouth patterns and fingerspelling when appropriate. They should be expressive, confident, and assertive. They needed to be able to develop a good rapport with the Deaf student and have a reasonable degree of knowledge of the subject.

In evaluating the outcome of the discussion panel, it would seem that Australian Deaf university students have differing expectations, depending on their experience and the university setting they are in, much like users of conference interpreters (Moser, 1996). The participants in this panel agreed with the Deaf students in Locker's (1996) study, that information should be interpreted conceptually into sign language for ease of understanding, yet they also agreed with respondents in Bremner and Housden's (1996) study, which found that Deaf students also wanted access to English terms. It would seem, therefore, that the university students involved in this study would endorse the notion of interpreters utilizing a dominant free interpretation approach, and switching into a literal approach as a linguistic coping strategy, to deal with the complexity of the information received, and the demands of the context of situation. The students would also advocate for interpreters to have a university qualification in general, especially if they are working in a university context.

With regard to the use of conscious strategic omissions, the Deaf university students were reluctant to accept that interpreters might use omissions strategically. One possible explanation for this is the issue of trust. It also might be that more time was needed to explain the concept properly, so that the students could make an informed decision about their perspective on the use of omissions as a linguistic coping strategy. It is understandable that Deaf students would want to ensure that they are receiving all the information presented in a university lecture, as they rely solely on interpreters for access to information in this type of environment. It is also understandable that Deaf people might not trust an interpreter's decision to omit information, especially because of the historic relationship between the Deaf community and hearing "helpers" who have made decisions on their behalf.

Chapter 6

Issues to Consider

The aim of this research was to study particular linguistic coping strategies of sign language interpreters working in lexically dense university lectures, with the goal of highlighting issues in relation to working practices of sign language interpreters in higher education settings and also in relation to the training and education of sign language interpreters in general. Some of the results of the study have not been particularly surprising, and they have corroborated findings of other studies of sign language interpreter working practices. Other results, however, have yielded new information with regard to interpreters' use of translation style, types of omissions produced, and metacognitive strategies used while interpreting. This chapter seeks to further explore and summarize the results presented in chapter five, leading to a discussion of the relevance of this study to Deaf consumers and sign language interpreter education and training.

LINGUISTIC COPING STRATEGIES: DISCUSSION

Chapter two introduced the notion of linguistic coping strategies as those linguistic processes used by interpreters as a pro-active measure to cope with the interpreting task at hand. It was suggested that linguistic coping strategies are consciously used by interpreters to cope with the sociolinguistic and sociocultural influences on any communicative event. One of the linguistic coping strategies discussed was the use of translation style and how linguistic transference could be used in combination with code-switching between free and literal interpretation approaches in order to meet the needs of Deaf students in university lectures. Interpreters should recognize that a free interpretation approach is probably the most effective translation style for interpreting information with cultural sensitivity. Yet interpreters should also recognize that the literal approach is just as valid, especially when used in combination with free interpretation (i.e., code-switching) to ensure the interpreted message achieves its meaning potential.

The concept of omissions being used by interpreters as a conscious linguistic coping strategy has been one of the main threads throughout the book. My research showed that in order to work effectively as linguistic and cultural mediators using an interactive model of interpreting, interpreters employ the use of *conscious strategic omissions* to decide what information is translatable and relevant to each language and culture. The level of metalinguistic awareness that interpreters have about their use of omissions has been another thread throughout the book, with particular focus on their level of awareness about the types of omissions made and why they were made. I also found that interpreters must engage in metalinguistic processing in order to monitor the source language they are receiving and their target language output in order to make strategic decisions based on linguistic and cultural knowledge and to make conscious strategic omissions appropriately.

The results of this study revealed that sign language interpreters do use linguistic coping strategies while interpreting for a university lecture. The extent to which they use these strategies varies depending on their level of familiarity with the subject and with university lectures as a discourse environment.

Translation Style and Translational Contact

The results of the analysis showed that the interpreters involved in the study had a dominant interpretation approach, using either a free or literal interpretation method, even if they code-switched between approaches during the interpretation. I identified a spectrum that demonstrated that the interpreters were either extremely literal or extremely free, or they code-switched between literal and free, but were still dominant in one style or the other. Of the ten subjects involved in the study, one was dominant in using a literal approach, three were extremely dominant in using a literal approach, four were dominant in using a free approach, and two subjects were extremely dominant in using a free approach.

The majority of recent literature on spoken and sign language interpreting advocates for a free, equivalence-based approach to interpreting, as this allows interpreters to make linguistic and cultural decisions based on their knowledge of the communities with whom they work. It can be argued, however, that sign language interpreting in university settings may require a more flexible approach due to the sociolinguistic and sociocultural factors within the discourse environment. This study has advocated that it might be more appropriate for both free and literal interpretation methods to be used in combination in a university context. By switching between free and literal methods as a linguistic coping strategy, interpreters can provide conceptually accurate interpretations of lecture content, as well as give access to academic jargon or subject-specific terminology. This suggestion was corroborated with discussion on the issue of language contact in relation to sign language. Arguments have been presented from several authors (Davis, 1989, 1990a, 1990b; Fontana, 1999; Lucas & Valli, 1989, 1990) that code-mixing or linguistic transference often occurs in sign language in more formal situations, leading to the use of more mouth patterns and finger-spelling than would be expected, for example, in conversation. Davis's (1989, 1990a, 1990b) research showed that interpreters used linguistic transference appropriate to the formality of the interpreting context. Therefore, in relation to this study, it could be argued that those subjects who incorporated fingerspelling (i.e., linguistic transference) for key lexical items of the text were using the most appropriate translation style for a university lecture. Given the fact that university lectures will often utilize subject-specific terminology that is central to the understanding of the subject matter, it is imperative that Deaf university students are given access to terminology in the form in which it is delivered. It is also essential, however that Deaf students receive information in semantically and syntactically correct sign language structure. Therefore an interpretation approach that introduces subject-specific lexicon through the use of fingerspelling, incorporating patterning as appropriate to the formality of the situation, would be an effective way of transmitting this information.

Pollitt (2000b) discussed the appropriateness of switching between an interactive interpretation model (free) and a conduit interpretation model (literal) according to the context of the interpreting situation. She cited university settings as one context where it would be appropriate to employ both literal and free interpretation approaches, depending on the content; for example, whether it was a lecture or tutorial. Rather than proscribe the use of one translation style in the university context,

I would agree with Pollitt and suggest that interpreters should switch between different styles as a linguistic strategy for coping with the context of the situation. This study has found that interpreters using a dominant free interpretation approach switched to a more literal style at key points of the message in order to borrow English lexical items, as well as interpreting the concept visually into Auslan. For example, idiomatic English such as the term *in a nutshell* was fingerspelled, followed by a conceptually accurate translation of the meaning of the term. The same process also occurred with the interpretation of subject-specific vocabulary, such as the term *critical period hypothesis*. This linguistic transference allowed the interpreters to provide a meaningful rendition of the message in Auslan, as well as access to the discourse-specific lexicon. It would seem, therefore, that it is appropriate for interpreters to use a free interpretation approach in the context of a university lecture, as long as they employ the linguistic coping strategy of switching to a more literal technique when they judge that it is suitable to do so. According to Bremner and Housden (1996), it is this kind of translation style that Deaf university students prefer, as they want interpretation into "an Auslan framework with English terms" (p. 13). I would interpret Bremner and Housden's statement to mean interpretation using a free translation style with code-switching into a more literal style for the introduction of English terms.

As a consequence of this study, I have concluded that it may not be appropriate to discuss translation styles as distinct entities, but rather interpretation approaches should be considered within a continuum. I would favor a free interpretation approach as the most effective method for translation, but I recognize that a literal approach can also be effective and may in fact be preferred by some Deaf consumers. Although extreme forms of free and literal interpretation may be appropriate for some contexts of situation, I would suggest that for university lectures, a combination of the two approaches is the most appropriate. In giving consideration to language contact between signed and spoken languages, and the notion of a continuum of sign language use, I propose a translation style continuum (see Figure 2). I would posit that the use of code-switching between translation styles should be used particularly in contexts presenting features of language contact in formal discourse environments, such as university lectures. A suggested term for this type of code-switching is *translational contact*.

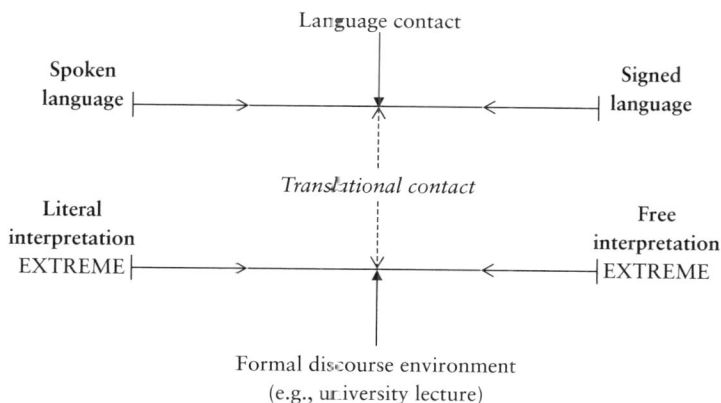

Language contact

Spoken
language ⊢————→————↥————←————⊣ Signed
language

Translational contact

Literal
interpretation
EXTREME ⊢————→————↧————←————⊣ EXTREME
Free
interpretation

Formal discourse environment
(e.g., university lecture)

FIGURE 2. *Translation style continuum.*

Steiner (1998) goes some way toward acknowledging the need for translational contact in his five-pronged model on motivational strategies. He proposed ways of presenting information to meet the needs of a target audience through *purist, empowerment, education, conglomerate,* or *holistic* attitudes toward the Deaf community and sign language. Steiner described the purist perspective as one that is driven to preserve language in its purest form, without any interference from other languages. In the example of Auslan, ASL, or BSL, the borrowing of English would be reduced to a minimum, and the use of visualization would be maximized. This suggestion seems somewhat idealistic as it is debatable whether "pure" forms of language exist. The empowerment aspect, however, is explained by Steiner as one used by people that understand "the linguistic struggles of the Deaf community and their needs within wider society" (p. 108). Steiner suggested that people using an empowerment approach produce language that benefits the community "beyond the production of the message itself" (p. 108), by explaining concepts believed not to have been accessed by the Deaf community to the same extent as the hearing majority, through the use of paraphrasing, anecdotes or simplification. Alternatively, the educational aspect is used by somebody who is aware that the Deaf community cannot acquire English in the same way that hearing people do, but recognizes that they do have exposure to English, and, therefore, allows a Deaf audience to acquire new English vocabulary through a visual medium. This is done by "shadowing the source language or selecting specific lexical items that will need to be borrowed into the target language" (p. 108); that is, the use of linguistic transference. The conglomerate belief incorporates understanding of both the empowerment and educational needs of the Deaf community, which is reflected in the language production dependent on the context of the situation, whereby code-mixing may occur between, for example, Auslan and English. Finally, the holistic belief means that a person is aware of all four of the categories outlined and attempts to produce a language that best reflects all categories.

By taking the essence of Steiner's categories and applying them to sign language interpreting, it is possible to identify approaches that would meet the needs of interpreting in different contexts. It is possible to equate the empowerment aspect with the use of an extremely free interpretation, and the educational aspect with a dominant free interpretation approach that incorporates code-switching into a literal style in order to introduce fingerspelling. The conglomerate strategy can be thought of as a succinct way of describing the linguistic coping strategy used by interpreters in deciding when to switch between the empowerment and educational approaches, or the free or literal interpretation models, depending on the content and intent of the message. Thus the aspects suggested by Steiner can be considered within a translation style continuum in order to account for the issue of translational contact.

In recognizing that sign language interpreters can use different interpretation approaches and adapt their translation style to meet the needs of Deaf consumers in different contexts, it is possible to accept that they are continuously making linguistic decisions based on the sociolinguistic and sociocultural influences on the interpreting situation. With the acceptance that interpreters can use translation style as a linguistic coping strategy, it is also possible to acknowledge that interpreters consciously utilize other linguistic coping strategies, such as the use of omissions. Steiner reinforces this point as follows:

> The "Educational Aspect" and "Empowerment Aspect" would certainly influence a signer to make informed omissions or additions to a translated presentation. Cultural, social, and educational notions about the D/deaf community are used to modify approaches to the interpretation or translation. (p. 109)

By conceding that omissions may be used as a linguistic coping strategy, it is important to discuss the use of *conscious strategic omissions* within a specific interpreting context.

Interpreting Omissions and Omission Potential

The concept of omissions being made by interpreters has been discussed in detail, with consideration given to omissions produced as errors and those produced strategically as part of the linguistic process to find meaningful equivalence for the target audience. This study has, for the first time, determined interpreters' levels of consciousness while producing omissions within a context of omission types.

It has been acknowledged that although interpreters might use omissions as a conscious linguistic strategy, it was inevitable that they would make other omissions for different reasons. Through a process of conducting an immediate task review with the interpreters involved in this study, it was possible to categorize the different types of omissions made during the interpreting task. During the study, it became obvious that the interpreters were conscious of various omissions they made, but only one omission type could be considered as a linguistic coping strategy.

All of the interpreters made omissions in each category; the highest number of total omissions were made by subjects who had no university education and were unfamiliar with the lecture topic. The most common omissions were unconscious omissions (26.9 percent) and conscious strategic omissions (25.5 percent). Conscious strategic omissions were used as a linguistic coping strategy by all the subjects, regardless of their educational background, familiarity with the topic, or translation style. The prevalence of unconscious omissions was noted with astonishment by both myself and the subjects, as it was not foreseen that such a large proportion of omissions would be unconscious. This level of unconscious omission production reinforces the notion that an interpretation never can convey 100 percent of the information imparted in a message; there will always be a level of information loss of which even the interpreter is unaware. It was surprising, however, to find that as much information is lost unconsciously as is selectively omitted as part of a conscious linguistic process.

Overall, there were no obvious patterns of omission occurrences in relation to influencing factors, although the results showed that the most erroneous omissions tended to be made by subjects with no university education and no knowledge of the lecture topic. It would seem, therefore, that the most influential factor is a combination of familiarities—familiarity with the discourse environment and familiarity with the topic itself.

The results of the empirical study demonstrate the importance of considering omissions within a context of omission types. It can be seen that interpreters do use omissions proactively, making conscious decisions as a linguistic coping strategy, as an inherent part of the interpreting process. Conscious omissions can be used effectively by interpreters to manage the communication event; therefore, in this context, the use of omissions is something that interpreters can do well. Nevertheless, it must still be recognized that interpreters also make other omissions, conscious or unconscious, intentional or unintentional. The fact that omissions can be used strategically does not negate the fact that erroneous omissions do occur, some of which interpreters are aware of, and others not. This study corroborates that within the framework of an interpretation, erroneous omissions do occur. The key issue to note, however, is that a high percentage of the omissions made by interpreters in this study were conscious strategic omissions—the second most-frequent category. When considering interpreting omissions, we should recognize that for every item of information mistakenly excluded, there are several more that are omitted consciously and strategically to enhance the equivalence of the message.

In accounting for the occurrence of omissions within a context of omission types, I suggest that omissions should be considered within a framework of *omission potential*, as seen in Figure 3. By doing so, it is

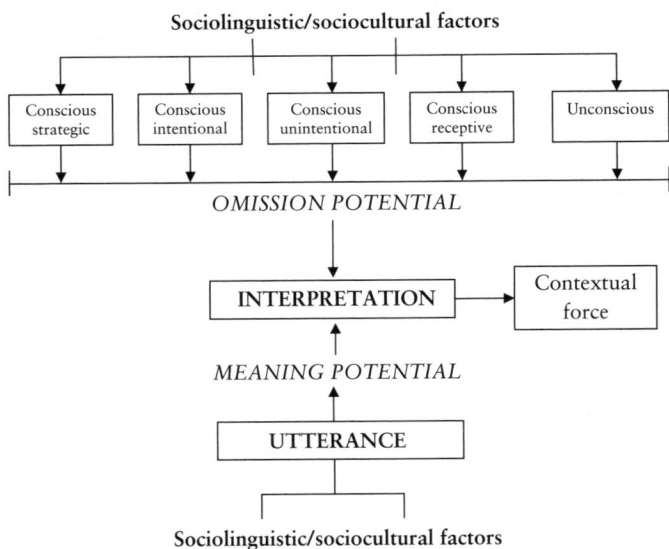

FIGURE 3. *Omission Potential Framework*

possible for interpreters to recognize the sociolinguistic and sociocultural factors that may influence their production of different omission types. The framework allows for recognition of the fact that omissions can be used strategically to achieve the meaning potential of an utterance, but that there is also the potential to make erroneous omissions that may skew the contextual force of the message.

Another major issue to take into account when evaluating the prevalence of interpreting omissions is the context of situation; in the case of this study, the context was a lexically dense university lecture. The results showed that the highest number of omissions tended to occur on higher than average lexically dense lines of text (mean lexical density of line of text = 47.6 percent), and on lines of text featuring subject-specific terminology or academic terms. In other words, more omissions occurred on the most grammatically complex and unfamiliar parts of the text. Interpreters made seven or more omissions on each of seven lines of text featured line. This finding is not particularly surprising, as any interpreting scholar would expect interpreters to struggle when dealing with factors contributing to "cognitive overload" (Moser-Mercer et al., 1998). What is a revelation, however, is the fact that some interpreters in this study seemed to use conscious strategic omissions to cope linguistically with the density and complexity of information featured on particular lines of text. For example, line 169 had a lexical density of 78.5 percent and featured 11 omissions in total. Nearly 73 percent of these omissions were conscious strategic.

Although the interpreters in this study did produce more omissions on lexically dense lines of text, consideration needs to be given to the actual lexical items omitted before making any concrete conclusions with regard to lexical density. The highest number of omissions occurred on higher than average lexically dense lines of text that featured English terms that were unfamiliar to the interpreters. Therefore, it would seem that lexical density may only have a bearing on the number and types of omissions in combination with interpreters' familiarity with the text. If interpreters were assessed on their production of omissions when interpreting non-lexically dense text, it would be possible to evaluate the extent to which density influences omission occurrence.

Nonetheless, it can be seen that the linguistic features of the source text do have an impact on the use of omissions. Thus, in order to make better use of omissions as a conscious linguistic strategy while inter-preting for a university lecture, an interpreter needs to be familiar with academic discourse, and preferably with specific subjects, before inter-preting in a university context. It can be reasonably assumed, therefore, that interpreters who are more familiar with the context of situation and the characteristics of the discourse environment will make more use of conscious strategic omissions and will produce less erroneous omis-sions, whether they are working in educational, legal, medical, political, or other arenas.

The interpreters involved in this study had a high level of metalin-guistic awareness of when and why they produced omissions. Although the interpreters did not discuss their level of metalinguistic awareness in relation to the translation style they chose to use at any given time, the level of awareness exhibited while discussing their interpreting omissions would imply a similarly high level of awareness with respect to choice of translation style. This assumption would need to be verified, however, with further study.

SOCIO-EDUCATIONAL INFLUENCES: DISCUSSION

This study sought to answer the question of how interpreters would cope linguistically in a university setting if they had not studied at univer-sity themselves. I compared the interpretations of the study participants and then interviewed them to ascertain the impact of their educational backgrounds on their ability to cope linguistically with the lecture seg-ments. Throughout this book I have mentioned that other researchers have recommended that a postsecondary qualification should be a pre-requisite for all sign language interpreters, especially if they work in higher education (Chafin Seal, 1998; Eighinger, 2000; Patrie, 1993; Roy, 2000b; Sanderson et al., 1999). These researchers suggest that studying at university would enable interpreters to attain a level of cognitive and academic linguistic proficiency that would provide the range of linguistic sophistication needed to work effectively as an interpreter.

It can be considered, therefore, a necessity for interpreters to have a university-level education in order to be able to cope linguistically with the various situations they encounter in their interpreting work (Locker, 1990). If it is deemed necessary for interpreters to have a university qualification to be linguistically better equipped to do their job, it can be stated that the requirement of interpreters to have a university qualification before working in university settings is of paramount importance, and "should be preferred, if not required" (Stuckless et al., 1989, p. 12). This point is reinforced in the World Federation of the Deaf policy statement on the education of Deaf people (Aquiline, 2000).

> Ensure that Deaf students in mainstream educational settings (particularly secondary schools and universities) have access to the services of sign language interpreters who are: (a) fully trained and qualified as sign language interpreters; and (b) *have themselves attained a level of education appropriate to the situation in which they are interpreting* [emphasis added].

The results of a survey of Auslan interpreters (Napier, 2001) found that only 48 percent of the 125 interpreters surveyed had completed, or were studying toward, a university qualification. Of those respondents who confirmed that they accepted interpreting work in higher education, only 59 percent had a university qualification. Harrington and Traynor (1999) surveyed 142 BSL interpreters, and found that 43 percent of the respondents had postsecondary qualifications.

Almost 20 years ago, Cokely (1981) surveyed 160 working ASL interpreters participating in a convention of the Registry of Interpreters for the Deaf. He found 60.6 percent had completed four or more years at college or university. Later figures showed that things had improved, but not dramatically. Humphrey and Alcorn (1996) stated that the majority of qualified sign language interpreters in the US are university graduates, with 32 percent holding a bachelor's degree, 25 percent holding a master's degree, and 2 percent holding a doctorate. Stewart et al. (1998) cited similar numbers, referring to a survey of the 1991–1992 membership of the Registry of Interpreters for the Deaf. They stated that 8.4 percent of ASL interpreters had studied for less than two years at college, 16.0 percent had completed an associate's degree, 26.1 percent a bachelor's degree, 24.1 percent a master's degree, and 2.7 percent had attained a doctorate.

Hayes (1992) conducted a survey of 52 educational interpreters working in primary and secondary schools in Western Pennsylvania. All respondents had at least a high school diploma and over 65 percent had completed some type of college or university degree, 10 of which

(31.2 percent) were associate's degrees. Jones et al. (1997) surveyed educational interpreters working in primary or secondary schools throughout the US. They reported that 17 percent of the respondents had a high school diploma or vocational certificate, 36 percent had studied at college but had not completed a degree, 21 percent had a community college associate's degree, 21 percent had a bachelor's degree, and 5 percent had a master's degree. These statistics are extremely close to those found in the Australian context of this study; however, Jones et al. did not report how many interpreters they surveyed, so it is difficult to judge the figures accurately.

McIntire (1990) conducted an informal survey on the work and education of sign language interpreters from various countries. She surveyed 45 interpreters from 11 countries, including Canada, Denmark, Finland, Germany, Greece, Italy, New Zealand, Norway, Sweden, Switzerland, and the UK. She asked the respondents about their highest level of formal education completed and found that 31 percent had studied for one to two years beyond the national minimum of their country, 60 percent had studied at university, 9 percent had attended a vocational or technical school, and 13 percent had completed a nondegree program. Although this survey gives an interesting picture of the educational qualifications held by sign language interpreters worldwide, McIntire herself stated that the figures are not based on empirical data collection, but rather on responses received from interpreter colleagues. Therefore, the results do not necessarily accurately reflect the sign language interpreting profession. Drawing on overall figures from Cokely (1981), Hayes (1992), and McIntire (1990), it would seem that, on average, 60–65 percent of sign language interpreters hold, or are studying toward, a postsecondary qualification equivalent to that of an undergraduate university degree or above.

In my empirical study of ten Auslan interpreters, I found that familiarity with the topic, combined with educational background (i.e., familiarity with the discourse environment) did in fact influence the linguistic coping strategies used (i.e., the translation style and the rate and number of omission occurrences). It should be remembered, however, that these results only give an indication of the possible influence of educational background, as only two of the subjects did not have a university qualification. Further study would be needed with a balanced number of subjects representing people with and without university qualifications before any definitive conclusions can be made with regard to educational background.

Nevertheless, those subjects who were familiar with the topic of language acquisition presented in the university lecture commented that it helped them a great deal in processing the information. As a consequence, they felt that their knowledge of the area made their interpretation more effective. This study reinforces that familiarity plays an important part in the success of an interpreted event, as interpreters are better able to not only understand the message but also evaluate the significance of the message in relation to the context of situation and the target audience. Seleskovitch (1978) stated that interpreters must have generalist knowledge, in that they must understand everything, but not necessarily to the same extent as specialists. By having generalist knowledge, they will be familiar with language use and content but will not necessarily be experts in the area. Thus, in relation to interpreting in university contexts, it is imperative that interpreters have studied at university themselves to gain generalist knowledge in academic discourse. By completing coursework and written assignments or oral presentations, interpreters will be able to broaden their understanding of academic language use in tertiary education in general. They will also have frames of reference for discourse expectations within such a learning environment and will be able to apply their knowledge accordingly. Additionally, they should ideally interpret for lectures in subjects that they have studied themselves, giving them more than a generalist understanding of the context in which they are interpreting.

In relation to interpreters' perceptions about own their educational background, however, it can be seen that the majority of subjects involved in the empirical phase of this study felt that their level of education impacted their ability to interpret the university lecture. The general comments reveal that those who were university educated felt more comfortable with the register of language, as they were familiar with university discourse. Those interpreters who were not university educated said that they struggled with the formality of the language, especially with some of the lexical items used. The data analysis supports the views of these interpreters in particular, as it was the two subjects with no university education that made the most omissions.

The importance of education was expressly stated by two subjects who recognized that their interpreting skills began to improve when they began to study at university. They felt that their understanding, knowledge, and use of the English language was expanding. They had more mastery in English and, therefore, could focus more on meaning and searching for semantic equivalence in Auslan when interpreting from English. This acknowledgment reinforces the need for interpreters to be generally educated to university standard as it will allow them to expand their vocabulary, their familiarity with various registers of language use, and their interpretation of language.

The notion of sign language interpreters needing a tertiary education to effectively work as interpreters is certainly not a new one. The results of this study have demonstrated how interpretation of a university lecture and the use of linguistic coping strategies can be particularly influenced by interpreters' familiarity with English and subject-specific language use. The results have also shown that the occurrence of omissions can be affected by the interpreters' educational experience with regard to the exposure they have had to different subject areas and the inherent terminology. The interpreters' familiarity with language use in academic settings also seemed to influence their use of translation style. These findings endorse the necessity for interpreters to be university educated before being permitted to interpret in university settings in order to be better prepared for the range of linguistic demands presented in different interpreting scenarios.

Familiarity and Preparation

Preparatory techniques can be used as coping strategies by interpreters to deal with environmental and other extra-linguistic factors that may influence their ability to effectively interpret a communication event. The results and discussion of my study have emphasized the need for interpreters to familiarize themselves not only with the logistics of working in a particular discourse environment, but also to familiarize themselves with linguistic aspects of the discourse environment, particularly if working in university settings.

Although it has been suggested that the best way for interpreters to familiarize themselves with academic discourse and subject-specific terminology is to study at tertiary level, it should be acknowledged that additional preparation is always advisable. It is widely recognized in the literature that preparation contributes to the effectiveness of any interpretation (Frishberg, 1990; Humphrey & Alcorn, 1996; Mackenzie, 1998; Napier, 1996; Neumann Solow, 2000; Stewart et al. 1998). Interpreters should strive to prepare for specific assignments in order to familiarize themselves with idiosyncratic language use within the context of situation, regardless of their educational background or acquaintance with topics they are expected to interpret. My study concentrated on the linguistic coping strategies of interpreters working unprepared in order to reflect situations in which interpreters often find themselves. It should never be assumed, however, that a general university education guarantees interpreters the level of familiarity necessary for dealing with the linguistic aspects of the university discourse environment, or any other discourse environment. Similarly, interpreters should not presume that because they are familiar with particular topics they can predict what subject-specific terminology will be used. The ideal situation should always require interpreters to carry out preparation before any type of interpreting assignment to ensure they are prepared for all contingencies, linguistic or otherwise.

CONCLUSIONS

Thus far, the issues of translation style, interpreting omissions, educational background, and familiarity have been discussed within the context of linguistic coping strategies used by sign language interpreters when interpreting for a university lecture. In relation to the research questions originally proposed, the findings of this study have concluded the following:

1. The interpreters involved in the study were dominant or extremely dominant in using either a free or literal interpretation approach. During interpretation of the university lecture, those who were dominant in using free interpretation used their translation style as a linguistic coping strategy. They switched to a more literal interpretation at key points of the text in order to borrow English lexical items and provide access to subject-specific terms, or academic or idiomatic English.
2. The interpreters made five different types of omissions while interpreting a lexically dense university lecture segment—conscious

strategic, conscious intentional, conscious unintentional, conscious receptive, and unconscious. They made a total of 341 omissions across all five categories of omission types. Of these identifiable omissions, 25.5 percent were conscious strategic omissions, 17.7 percent were conscious intentional omissions, 14.3 percent were conscious unintentional omissions, 15.2 percent were conscious receptive omissions, and 26.9 percent were unconscious omissions.

3. The translation style of interpreters does not stand alone as a factor that affects the rate and type of omissions made.

4. The study results indicate that interpreters do use conscious strategic omissions as a linguistic coping strategy in order to deal with the linguistic features of a university lecture.

5. The interpreters demonstrated a high level of metalinguistic awareness about the types of omissions they made while interpreting the lexically dense university lecture segment.

6. The linguistic features of the university lecture source text did influence the use of translation style and the rate and occurrence of omissions. Translation style was affected by familiarity with academic English and subject-specific terminology. The lexical density of the source text, combined with the interpreters' familiarity with the discourse environment and the subject-specific terminology, influenced the rate and types of omissions produced by the interpreters.

7. The sign language interpreters in this study felt that their educational background had an impact on their ability to interpret the university lecture, whereby those with a university education felt better able to cope with the linguistic demands of the lecture due to their familiarity with university-level discourse. Those interpreters that had previously studied the lecture topic felt that their familiarity with the subject also contributed to their ability to effectively interpret the university lecture.

8. The expectations of Deaf university students with regard to sign language interpreters varies, but generally they agreed that interpreters should be fluent in both Auslan and English, should provide interpretations freely, and should occasionally switch to a more literal approach. There was general consensus that interpreters should be educated to equivalent standard to interpret

in university settings, and there was suspicion about interpreters making any kinds of omissions while interpreting.

IMPLICATIONS: AUSLAN INTERPRETER EDUCATION AND TRAINING

The findings of this study have significant implications for the education and training of interpreters in relation to the linguistic coping strategies used by interpreters. In accordance with the statement that "graduates of university programs with bachelors' and more especially masters' degrees are prepared for most interpreting tasks" (Frishberg & Wilcox, 1994, p. 18), it has been the general finding of this study that the interpreters felt they coped better with interpreting for a university lecture when they had completed a university education themselves. Deaf university students also reported that interpreters work more effectively in university lectures if they are familiar with the discourse environment. The educational background of the interpreters in the study also had some impact on the linguistic coping strategies that were used, which implies that the level of education achieved by interpreters is of significance.

Many countries do not require sign language interpreters to have completed a university degree, nor do they have university programs available in sign language interpreting. Patrie (1994) stated that interpreter education and training are two different experiences that should provide entry to the profession at two different levels. The interpreter training and education system in both Australia and the US allows people to enter postsecondary, non-university interpreter training and achieve recognition as interpreters. This system corroborates a suggestion from Patrie that community college interpreter training is sufficient for entry to the profession at a "technical" level. Patrie also suggested, however, that to enter the profession at a "professional" level, interpreters need a minimum level of undergraduate study. Education at this level would provide interpreters with a deeper and broader base of knowledge, analysis, and application. In the UK and US, it is possible to study sign language interpreting at the undergraduate level, and postgraduate study of sign language interpreting is available in the UK, US, and Australia.

The field of sign language interpreting has recognized that highly skilled interpreters must be highly educated, but it has also recognized that entry to the profession at a technical level is appropriate, if graduates restrict their work to particular areas for which they have been trained (Stauffer, 1994). The infrastructure for two levels of entry already exists in Australia, with paraprofessional interpreters assessed on their ability to interpret for one-to-one communication events, and professional interpreters assessed for their skills in interpreting more complex and linguistically sophisticated situations (NAATI, 1999). A similar system has been proposed in the UK, with a National Vocational Qualifications for BSL interpreters suggested at different levels of competence and expertise (CACDP, 1997). However, by establishing more university interpreter education programs, more practitioners can enter the field at the professional level and, thus, have the skills necessary to provide interpreting services in highly demanding discourse environments, such as university lectures.

It has also been recognized that as well as being essential for working in a university context, a university education also better enables interpreters to cope linguistically with the varied situations they face in their everyday interpreting work. Thus, another consideration of this study is that all interpreters should complete a general university undergraduate degree before they attend an interpreter education or training program. In doing so, they will have a wider linguistic repertoire with which to enter their interpreter education or training. The ideal situation would be for interpreters to have studied either a related subject at undergraduate level (such as deaf studies or linguistics) or have had a broader liberal arts undergraduate education (for example, in the social sciences) before then going on to train in a technical program or be educated as interpreters at the postgraduate level.

This study also has implications for the content of interpreter education and training programs. The study has demonstrated that interpreters use translation styles to different ends, with some interpreters switching between free and literal interpretation approaches as a linguistic coping strategy to deal with the complexity of the message and the needs of their Deaf consumers. Discussion with Deaf university students found that they prefer to receive information in a university context through a process of free interpretation, with interpreters switching to a more literal approach in order to borrow English terminology and academic terms when appropriate. The students recognized that the use of more fingerspelling and mouth patterns would be acceptable in the formal situation of a university lecture, but that a more interactive cultural approach would be necessary in university tutorials. This study reinforces, therefore, the notion that interpretation does not have "context-independent rules" (Moser-Mercer, 1997, p. 3).

Consequently, my findings suggest that sign language interpreters should be educated on the theoretical standpoints of both free and literal interpretation methods, and they should be taught how to switch between these two methods as a linguistic coping strategy, depending on the context of situation and the consumers with whom they are working. This approach is endorsed by various writers (Davis, 2000; Metzger, 2000; Pollitt, 2000a; Roy, 2000d; Winston & Monikowski, 2000) who advocate for interpreter education programs to treat interpreting as a discourse process. They suggest that interpreter education should incorporate theoretical and practical discourse analysis to better enable interpreters to understand, and develop strategies for coping with the various discourse environments they will encounter in their everyday work. In doing so, interpreters can adopt an interactive model of interpreting and make informed linguistic and cultural decisions about which interpretation approach to use in order to ensure the successful outcome of a communication event.

This study has also highlighted the fact that interpreters make different types of omissions while interpreting, one of which is used as a conscious linguistic coping strategy. The rate and type of omission occurrences were influenced by the complexity of, and familiarity with, the source text. This finding highlights the need for interpreters to be educated about the types of omissions they make and why they make them. In having a better understanding of various omission types and the sociolinguistic and sociocultural influences on their occurrence, interpreters will be enabled to use certain omissions proactively as a linguistic coping strategy. They will also have a heightened awareness of the possibilities of erroneous omissions.

With regard to heightened awareness, this study has demonstrated that although the interpreters applied their metalinguistic awareness of their language use to monitor their interpretation output, this application only became conscious through the interpreting task review. Sign language interpreter education and training should, therefore, incorporate activities to enhance the metalinguistic processes involved in interpreting. Peterson (2000) and Smith (2000) assert that by allowing interpreting students to explore and develop metacognitive strategies, they will be better equipped to evaluate their interpretation output and the linguistic and cultural decisions made within the context of the discourse environment.

WIDER IMPLICATIONS: INTERPRETING IN DIFFERENT CONTEXTS

While the focus of this study has been on the linguistic coping strategies of sign language interpreters working in university lectures, the findings can be extrapolated to interpreters working in other languages and in other contexts. Interpreters can use translation style as a linguistic coping strategy in contexts other than university settings, and they can potentially make five types of omissions, regardless of the interpreting situation in which they are working. This study has demonstrated that the interpreters involved had high levels of metalinguistic awareness while interpreting, and there is no reason to doubt this would not be the case for other interpreters in different contexts.

It should be recognized that an interpreter's ability to use translation style as a linguistic coping strategy may well be affected by several sociolinguistic issues, such as the context of situation, familiarity with the discourse environment, knowledge of the topic being discussed, and familiarity with the Deaf and hearing interaction participants. These same sociolinguistic factors could also affect the rate and types of omission occurrences, regardless of whether the interpreting takes place in a medical, legal, or political arena, or the signed or spoken languages with which the interpreter was working.

In recognizing the wider implications for this research and the fact that the findings can be applied in other areas of interpreting, it is possible to identify a limitation of the study, which consequently generates suggestions for further research that would expand on the ideas presented in this volume.

FUTURE RESEARCH

The major limitation of the study is that the findings of the empirical research are presented with the assumption that the linguistic coping strategies adopted by interpreters, in the forms of translation style and conscious omissions, are appropriate according to the interpreting theory presented in the literature. The interpretations of the participants in this study were not analyzed for accuracy and were not tested for comprehensibility. To date, there have been very few studies on Deaf people's comprehension of information received through sign language interpreting, some of which were discussed (Jacobs, 1976; Livingston et al., 1994; Llewellyn Jones, 1981; Steiner, 1998). I recognize that the ideal study would have incorporated testing Deaf university students' comprehension before reporting the effectiveness of sign language interpreters in using linguistic coping strategies. Due to time constraints, however, it was only possible to interview Deaf university students about their expectations of interpreters working in university settings and about their opinions on the use of omissions and the translation style and educational background of interpreters. Although the perspective of Deaf university students is valid, the information does not provide empirical evidence about interpreters' effectiveness at using linguistic coping strategies appropriately in university lectures.

Thus, the presentation of the research findings is done with faith that the interpreting theory is correct, and with the hope that one day further studies may be carried out on comprehension to verify the efficacy of the interpretations presented in this study. Similar studies could be carried out in different ways to analyze and cross-reference the issues raised in this study, in order to gain a better understanding of the working practices of interpreters in a range of situations. Discussion of the research findings has flagged key issues that require further analysis, as well as tangential issues of relevant interest.

One of the most important issues raised that necessitates further research is that of comprehensibility. Although this study incorporated the perspective of Deaf people in terms of their expectations and preferences, in order to verify whether interpreters are using linguistic coping strategies appropriately, it would be necessary to test Deaf people's comprehension levels. In this way, it would be possible to determine whether sign language interpreters are meeting the communicative needs of Deaf university students, in addition to how well they conform to theoretical perceptions of what effective interpreting means. A study of this kind would also provide insight into whether Deaf people's preferred translation style actually provides them with adequate access to information in a university lecture.

Another suggestion is that the panel discussion that took place with Deaf university students in this study could be extended to include debate about the expectations of Deaf consumers in a variety of different settings. Deaf people from a range of backgrounds could be brought together to discuss the translation style they prefer interpreters to use in diverse contexts, along with the reasons for these different preferences. Further comprehensibility studies could be conducted to ask Deaf people to rate their understanding of different interpreters interpreting in a range of scenarios. Information derived from this data could then be transferred into interpreter training and education programs to better prepare student interpreters for the level of flexibility required to meet the needs of Deaf people in various discourse environments.

The Deaf students in this study seemed to misunderstand the interpreters' use of omissions. To help Deaf people understand why omissions occur, a study could be conducted to engage them in a similar interpreting task and task review. By asking Deaf people to interpret a source text received in one signed language into another signed or written language, or to retell the text in the same signed language, it would be possible to identify any omissions made, reflecting the task review of the interpreters involved in this study. In so doing, it is possible to assume that the Deaf people would discover that they had made linguistic decisions about what information to omit based on their knowledge and understanding of the source text, the context of situation, and the linguistic and cultural relevance and meaning potential of the text to the target audience. Experiencing this process for themselves would better enable them to understand, and comment on, interpreters' use of omissions as a linguistic coping strategy.

In relation to the context of situation examined in this study, it would be interesting to conduct a study of Auslan interpreters working in a lecture that was not lexically dense. For example, interpretation of a conference keynote presentation could be compared with the lecture interpretation in this study to highlight the similarities and differences in use of translation style and omissions as linguistic coping strategies. Alternatively, a comparative study could be done of omissions made by interpreters interpreting a lecture read out loud verbatim from a prepared text, which would make the text even more lexically dense than the one used in this study and, thus, more complex to interpret.

Another comparative study could involve interpretations of the same university lecture, but allowing the interpreters more preparation and time to clarify terminology. This altered methodology would provide interesting contrastive data, as it would be possible to ascertain exactly how the use of linguistic coping strategies changed, and to what extent.

In terms of studying interpreting in different contexts, it would be valuable to replicate this study to analyze the rate and prevalence of conscious strategic, conscious intentional, conscious unintentional, conscious receptive and unconscious omissions in other interpreting scenarios. This would create a picture of the different factors that impact the use of conscious strategic omissions and the production of erroneous omissions in a medical appointment, a job interview, a conference paper, a board meeting, or a university tutorial. The research could then be taken one step further by contrasting interpreters working in identical situations who had received more preparation. The same replication could offer the opportunity to analyze the strategic use of free and literal interpretation approaches in different contexts.

The superficial identification of lexical borrowing, or linguistic transference, in this study provides a foundation for further research in relation to the degree of fingerspelling used strategically by interpreters and the sociolinguistic factors that influence the incidence of fingerspelling. References have been made to the amount of fingerspelling typical of Auslan and BSL use and the extent to which Auslan and BSL interpreters reflect the language use of the Deaf community with whom they work (Napier & Adam, 2002). As far as I know, however, there has been no empirical research into the amount of fingerspelling used by Deaf people in Australia and the UK. A study recording and analyzing spontaneous sign language production of Deaf people in various discourse environments would provide a picture of any fingerspelling patterns in different contexts. It would then be possible, therefore, to investigate interpreters' use of fingerspelling in comparison with the original Deaf corpus group.

Although not an exhaustive list, these few suggestions for future research are offered with the goal of discovering more about interpreters and interpreting and broadening our understanding of the various linguistic processes and factors involved. Any future research should endeavor to develop a better understanding of the relationship between interpreters, consumers, and the discourse environments in which they participate. Additional research will allow interpreters, interpreter educators, and interpreter researchers to further explore the linguistic coping strategies of interpreters and the sociolinguistic and sociocultural factors that influence the outcome of an interpreted communicative event. Rather than thinking about whether interpreters succeed or fail, research enables us to consider the strategies employed and the interpreters' contributions to the outcomes of such events. As Roy (2000a) has said, "there are no absolute criteria for defining 'good' interpretations. Different discourse events with different goals and needs and different participants require changing actions on the part of the interpreter" (p. 126).

Appendix A

Transcription Conventions

Know (conventional orthography)	Spoken English words.
KNOW	A word in small capital letters is an English representation (gloss) of an Auslan sign.
I-ASK-YOU	When more than one English word is needed to gloss an Auslan sign, the English words are separated by a hyphen.
T-R-U-E	When an English word is fingerspelled, the letters in the word are separated by a hyphen.
WHAT*	An asterisk indicates that the sign is emphasized.
KNOCK+	The plus symbol indicates that the sign is repeated.
(VERY)	When a gloss is inside parentheses, it means that the signer has started to execute a particular sign but has stopped and moved on to another sign.
LIMIT (1) LIMIT (2)	Numbers indicate that two different signs are used for the same gloss, one directly after the other.
point-left/point-right	The signer has pointed to a location to reference a specific place or established entity or entities. For example, FAMILY point-left/FAMILY FAMILY FAMILY point-arc
-left/-right	Directions following a sign indicate placement of the sign by either the left or right side of the signer's body. For example, ACQUIRE-left ACQUIRE-right

(continued)

Know (conventional orthography)	Spoken English words.
their-left/right	Directions following a possessive pronoun indicate the
his/her-left/right	the person location.
Nonmanual Grammatical Markers	
..	A noticeable pause, equivalent to a comma in orthographic English.
q	The facial expressions and head movements used to indicate a question is being asked (often rhetorical).
hd	Indicates affirmation through a head nod.
neg	Indicates negation through a head shake.

Note. These conventions are adapted and developed from Baker and Cokely (1980), Harrington (2000), Roy (1992), and Sutton-Spence and Woll (1998).

Appendix B

Characteristics of Translation Styles

Sample English sentence: *We should try and encourage families to support the first language acquisition of their Deaf children.*

FREE INTERPRETATION

Free interpretation is "the process by which concepts and meanings are translated from one language into another, by incorporating cultural norms and values; assumed knowledge about these values; and the search for linguistic and cultural equivalents" (Napier, 1998b, p. 36), whereby "the linguistic structure of the source language is ignored, and an equivalent is found based on the meaning it conveys" (Crystal, 1987, p. 344).

Linguistic Markers

- Use of possessive pronouns, placement and corresponding spatial reference, exploitation of visual metaphor, use of rhetorical questioning and nonmanual features.
- Elaboration on meaning. Interpretation provides equivalency of meaning, not necessarily equivalency of each lexical item.
- Use of fingerspelling typically is limited to glosses already lexicalized in Auslan. Grammatically appropriate use of lip pattern.

Possible translation of example sentence:

We should try and encourage families to support the first language acquisition of their Deaf children.

ALL FAMILY HAVE DEAF CHILDREN.. WE SHOULD WHAT
(point-arc) (q)
ENCOURAGE PARENTS LEARN SIGN LANGUAGE.. MEANS PARENTS AND
(point left-middle-right) *(point-left point-right)*

CHILD HAVE SAME LANGUAGE.. MEANS CHILD CAN ACQUIRE
                    (point-left)   *(their-left)*

SIGN FIRST LANGUAGE
    (hd)

LITERAL INTERPRETATION

Literal interpretation means that "the linguistic structure of the source text is followed, but is normalized according to the rules of the target language" (Crystal, 1987, p. 344).

Linguistic Markers

- Use of rhetorical questioning, possessive pronouns, spatial reference and nonmanual features.
- Less exploitation of visual metaphor and little meaningful elaboration.
- Equivalency based on lexical gloss, with a higher proportion of borrowing from English in terms of fingerspelling.
- Use of lip patterns articulating English words. This is especially noticeable when fingerspelling.

Possible translation of example sentence:

We should try and encourage families to support the first language acquisition of their Deaf children.

WE SHOULD TRY WHAT ENCOURAGE FAMILY HAVE DEAF CHILDREN
                (q)   *(point-left-middle-right)*
SUPPORT CHILD FIRST LANGUAGE ACQUISITION
    (point-left)   *(their-left)*

SENTENCES TRANSCRIBED FROM ORIGINAL SOURCE DATA

Sentence 1: *And what they did was contrast the acquisition of these features with the acquisition of the same types of grammatical features in English, and came up with, as a result of this study, with what seemed to be some quite consistent patterns of grammatical acquisition across the two languages.*

Sentence 2: *Any of you who are aware of the work in this area, the work of people like Jean Piaget, who made a very very strong case for a binding relationship between early sensory-motor development and early language acquisition.*

Sentence 3: *If you look at the work of someone like Steve Krashen, even in second language research, his notion of, that we have to be at or just above the language receptive capacities of the language learner, that if we are too far above it then the capacity for the learner to actually make use of language input is certainly diminished.*

TRANSCRIPTIONS OF THREE SENTENCES FOR EACH SUBJECT

SUBJECT 1

Sentence 1
And what they did was contrast the acquisition of these
      WHAT D-I-D LOOK A-T COMPARE ACQUISITION ACQUISITION
             (point-left)   *(left)*   *(right)*
features with the acquisition of the same types of grammatical
SAME TYPE O-F G-R-A-M-M-A-R THING IN ENGLISH.. SHOW COMPARE
                                        (point-right)

features in English, and came up with, as a result of this study, with
FROM RESULT RESEARCH RESEARCH WHAT LOOK LIKE REALLY
           (left)   *(right)*

what seemed to be some quite consistent patterns of grammatical
acquisition across the two languages.
SAME* PARALLEL HOW G-R-A-M-M-A-R ACQUIRE SAME SAME
                           (left) (right)

Sentence 2
Any of you who are aware of the work in this area, the work of
      AWARE THAT AREA PEOPLE LIKE J-O-H-N G-O-U-G-E-R MAKE
      (point-left) (point-left)
people like Jean Piaget, who made a very very strong case for a
VERY GOOD PROOF PRESENT FOR FOR.. (BECAUSE) BETWEEN EARLY
  (point-left)

binding relationship between early sensory-motor development and early
CHILD S-E-N-S-O-R-Y M-O-T-O-R AND EARLY

language acquisition.
LANGUAGE ACQUISITION

Sentence 3
If you look at the work of someone like Steve Krashen, even in
    LOOK-AT S-T-E-V-E K-R-A-S-H-E IN SECOND* LANGUAGE ACQUISITION

second language research, his notion of, that we have to be at or just
RESEARCH YOU HAVE-TO A-T O-R JUST SLIGHTLY-ABOVE LANGUAGE

above the language receptive capacities of the language learner, that if
ABILITY ACQUIRE CAN'T TOO-FAR-ABOVE ABILITY LEARN OR USE
                                (point-left)

we are too far above it then the capacity for the learner to actually
make use of language input is certainly diminished.
LANGUAGE.. (receptive difficulty)
    (neg)

SUBJECT 2

Sentence 1
And what they did was contrast the acquisition of these features with
        WHAT THEY.. RECEIVE F-E-A-T-U-R-E WITH SAME TYPE O-F
                  (point-right)

the acquisition of the same types of grammatical features in English,
G-R-A-M-M-A-T-I-C-A-L F-E-A-T-U-R-E-S IN ENGLISH AND COME UP

and came up with, as a result of this study, with what seemed to be
WITH.. BECAUSE O-F STUDY WHAT S-E-E-M-E-D T-O B-E

some quite consistent patterns of grammatical acquisition across the
WHAT CONSISTENT P-A-T-T-E-R-N O-F G-R-A-M-M-A-T-I-C-A-L ACQUISITION
  (q)   *(hd)*

two languages.
ACQUISITION ACROSS AREA

Sentence 2

Any of you who are aware of the work in this area, the work of
AWARE O-F WORK AREA.. PEOPLE LIKE P-I-A-G-E-THE MAKE
(point-right)   *(point-right)*

people like Jean Piaget, who made a very very strong case
VERY STRONG C-A-S-E FOR.. TALK-ABOUT.. WORD SOMETHING

for a binding relationship between early sensory-motor development
RELATIONSHIP BETWEEN EARLY S-E-N-S-O-R-Y M-O-T-O-R DEVELOP
(hd)

and early language acquisition.
AND EARLY LANGUAGE ACQUISITION

Sentence 3

If you look at the work of someone like Steve Krashen, even in
S-T-E-V-E K-R-A-S-H-E-N IN RESEARCH WE HAVE-TO T-O J-U-S-T
(his-right)

second language research, his notion of, that we have to be at or just
LANGUAGE MUST SLIGHTLY-ABOVE RECEPTIVE LANGUAGE

above the language receptive capacities of the language learner, that if
TOO-FAR-ABOVE LANGUAGE LEVEL MUST LEARN MAKE U-S-E
(neg)   *(point-right)*

we are too fabove it then the capacity for the learner to actually
LANGUAGE ACQUISITION LITTLE-BIT DIFFICULT

make use of language input is certainly diminished.

SUBJECT 3

Sentence 1

And what they did was contrast the acquisition of these features with
WHAT THEY D-I-D LOOK DIFFERENT HOW THEY ACQUIRE
(point-right)

the acquisition of the same types of grammatical features in
FACIAL-EXPRESSION -F- ENGLISH OCCUR FROM STUDY LOOK
(point-left)   *(point-right)*   *(point-right)*

English, and came up with, as a result of this study, with what
LIKE CONSISTENT VARY P-A-T-T-E-R-N G-R-A-M- M-A-R ACQUIRE+ IN

seemed to be some quite consistent patterns of grammatical acquisition across the two languages.
(ENGLISH) ALL LANGUAGES

Sentence 2
Any of you who are aware of the work in this area, the work of
    THEY KNOW WORK IN THIS AREA (VERY) MAKE VERY STRONG
    (point-right)   *(point-right)*   *(point-right)*

people like Jean Piaget, who made a very very strong case for a
EXPLAIN C-A-S-E FOR LIKE CONNECT RELATIONSHIP EARLY GROW

binding relationship between early sensory-motor development and
CONNECT PLUS LANGUAGE ACQUIRE

early language acquisition.

Sentence 3
If you look at the work of someone like Steve Krashen, even in
    IDEA HAVE-TO B-E THERE O-R LITTLE-BIT SLIGHLTY-ABOVE
    (point-right)   *(point-middle)*   *(their-middle)*

second language research, his notion of, that we have to be at or
ABILITY T-O ACQUIRE I-F TOO-MUCH HIGH-ABOVE* (CAN'T)
                  (point-right-middle)

just above the language receptive capacities of the language learner,
ABILITY FOR THEM UNDERSTAND ACQUIRE.. HAVE LIMIT(1) LIMIT(2)
    (point-middle)

that if we are too far above it then the capacity for the learner to
actually make use of language input is certainly diminished.

SUBJECT 4

Sentence 1
And what they did was contrast the acquisition of these features with
    THEIR WORK WHAT COMPARE HOW ACQUIRE THOSE DIFFERENT
    (their-left) *(q)*   *(point-right)*

the acquisition of the same types of grammatical features in English,
G-R-A-M-M-A-T-I-C-A-L STRUCTURE INCLUDE+ COMPARE WITH SAME

and came up with, as a result of this study, with what seemed to be
IN ENGLISH OR NOT.. S-O WHEN COMPARE UNTIL HAVE
       (q)

some quite consistent patterns of grammatical acquisition across the
SAME+ SIGN AND ENGLISH A-S-L
       (hd) (their-right)

two languages.

Sentence 2

Any of you who are aware of the work in this area, the work of
      IF YOU INTEREST CHILDREN EDUCATION MAYBE YOU INTEREST
                         (q)

people like Jean Piaget, who made a very very strong case for a
PEOPLE LIKE P-I-A-G-E-T MAKE STRONG-FIGHT* TALK OVER

binding relationship between early sensory-motor development and
RELATIONSHIP BETWEEN (QUOTATION MARKS) S-E-N-S-O-R-Y
                 (point-right)

early language acquisition.
MOTOR M-O-T-O-R IMPROVE AND EARLY LANGUAGE ACQUISITION
   (right)   *(left)*

Sentence 3

If you look at the work of someone like Steve Krashen, even in
   LOOK A-T S-T-E-V-E K-R-A-S-H OVER SECOND LANGUAGE RESEARCH

second language research, his notion of, that we have to be at or just
FOUND.. HAVE WE CAN MUST MATCH LANGUAGE LEVEL WHEN DISCUSS
  (point-right)   *(their-right)*

above the language receptive capacities of the language learner, that if
I-F TOO-MUCH HIGH-ABOVE CAN'T (ACQUIRE) NOT FULL UNDERSTAND
        (point-right) (neg)   *(neg)*

of, that we have to be at or just above the language receptive capacities

LIMIT THEIR .. FULL COMMUNICATION
(their-right)

of the language learner, that if of, that we have to be at or just above
the language receptive capacities of the language learner, that if we
are too far above it then the capacity for the learner to actually make
use of language input is certainly diminished.

SUBJECT 5

Sentence 1
And what they did was contrast the acquisition of these features with
PEOPLE WHAT COMPARE ACQUISITION LIST WITH COMPARE
(point-arc) (q)

the acquisition of the same types of grammatical features in English,
SAME* TYPE G-R-A-M-M-A-T-I-C-A-L LIST IN ENGLISH FOUND WHAT
(q)

and came up with, as a result of this study, with what seemed to be
FOR STUDY HAPPEN WHAT LOOK LIKE VERY CONSISTENT
(q)

some quite consistent patterns of grammatical acquisition across the
P-A-T-T-E-R-N-S G-R-A-M-M-A-T-I-C-A-L ACQUISITION OVER TWO

two languages.
LANGUAGE LANGUAGE
(left) (right) (their-left-right)

Sentence 2
Any of you who are aware of the work in this area, the work of
YOU KNOW WORK WRITE LIKE J-E-A-N P-I-A-G-E-T VERY+ STRONG*
(point-right) (hd)   (point-left)

people like Jean Piaget, who made a very very strong case for a
FAVOR OVER B-I-N-D-I-N-G RELATIONSHIP WITH

binding relationship between early sensory-motor development and
EARLY S-E-N-S-O-R-Y MO-T-E-R M-O-T-O-R DEVELOP AND EARLY

early language acquisition.
LANGUAGE ACQUISITION

Sentence 3

If you look at the work of someone like Steve Krashen, even in
LIKE LOOK-AT S-T-E-V-E C-R-A-S-H-E-N IN HIS SECOND LANGUAGE
(his-right)

second language research, his notion of, that we have to be at or just
RESEARCH HIS IDEA WE HAVE-TO LITTLE-BIT SLIGHTLY-ABOVE
(his-right)

above the language receptive capacities of the language learner, that if
LANGUAGE ACQUIRE ABILITY O-F LANGUAGE LEARNER

we are too far above it then the capacity for the learner to actually
I-F TOO-MUCH HIGH-ABOVE* CAN -T- FOR LEARNER T-O MAKE

make use of language input is certainly diminished.
USE O-F LANGUAGE INPUT WILL REDUCE-DRASTICALLY

SUBJECT 6
Sentence 1

And what they did was contrast the acquisition of these features with
WELL ACTUALLY COMPARE HOW PEOPLE LEARN F-E-A-T-U-R-E-S
(point-left)

the acquisition of the same types of grammatical features in English,
WITH HOW PEOPLE LEARN SAME G-R-A-M-M-A-R F-E-A-T-U-R-E-S

and came up with, as a result of this study, with what seemed to be
ENGLISH.. FROM.. FOUND SAME SAME HOW PEOPLE LEARN OR
    (point-left-right)(left, (right)   (point-left)

some quite consistent patterns of grammatical acquisition across the
LEARN DOESN'T-MATTER WHICH LANGUAGE
(point-right)   (point both)

two languages.

Sentence 2

Any of you who are aware of the work in this area, the work of
MAYBE YOU.. EXPERIENCE WITH WORK O-F J-E-A-N P-I-A-G-E-T
        (point-arc)

people like Jean Piaget, who made a very very strong case for a

HIMSELF REALLY BELIEVE.. VERY STRONG RELATIONSHIP B-I-N-D-I-N-G

binding relationship between early sensory-motor development and
RELATIONSHIP BETWEEN EARLY S-E-N-S-O-R-Y

early language acquisition.
M-O-T-O-R DEVELOP AND EARLY LANGUAGE ACQUISITION

Sentence 3
If you look at the work of someone like Steve Krashen, even in
    I-F LOOK-AT WORK O-F S-T-E-V-E SOMEONE RESEARCH.. ANOTHER
                          (their-right) *(hd)*

second language research, his notion of, that we have to be at or just
PERSON HAVE-TO EQUAL-TO SIMILAR T-O LANGUAGE LEARN I-F

above the language receptive capacities of the language learner, that if
. HIGH-ABOVE* SOPHISTICATED VERY DIFFICULT CAN'T-UNDERSTAND
          (point-left)   *(neg)*

we are too far above it then the capacity for the learner to actually
WHAT PERSON SAY
      (point-right)

make use of language input is certainly diminished.

Subject 7

Sentence 1
And what they did was contrast the acquisition of these features with
    REALLY COMPARE HAVE ACQUIRE+ LIST F-E-A-T-U-R-E-S AND OTHER
    (their-left)

the acquisition of the same types of grammatical features in English,
HAVE G-R-A-M-M-A-R ENGLISH PUT+ COMPARE.. LOOK-AT.. HAPPEN

and came up with, as a result of this study, with what seemed to be
FOUND HAVE ALMOST SAME+ PARALLEL P-A-T-T-E-R-N F-O-R

some quite consistent patterns of grammatical acquisition across the
two languages.
ACQUIRE ACQUIRE LANGUAGE BOTH+
(left)   *(right)*

Sentence 2

Any of you who are aware of the work in this area, the work of
WHO J-O-H-N P-I-A-R-G-E.. STRONG SUPPORT+ (receptive difficulty)
(q)   (point-arc) (hd)

people like Jean Piaget, who made a very very strong case for a
EARLY THINK+ M-O-T-O-R PROCESS COMPARE WITH EARLY

binding relationship between early sensory-motor development and
LANGUAGE ACQUISITION

early language acquisition.

Sentence 3

If you look at the work of someone like Steve Krashen, even in
SOMEONE RESEARCH S-T-E-V-E K-R-A-S-H-I-N-G SECOND LANGUAGE
         (their-right)   (their-right)

second language research, his notion
RESEARCH MUST..WHAT ABILITY ACQUIRE-FROM-ME LITTLE-BIT
                   (their-left)

of, that we have to be at or just above the language receptive
SLIGHTLY-ABOVE THAN WHAT THINK CAN TOO-MUCH HIGH-ABOVE

capacities of the language learner, that if we are too far above

it then the capacity for the learner to actually make use of language
CAN'T ACQUIRE
 (neg)

input is certainly diminished.

SUBJECT 8

Sentence 1

And what they did was contrast the acquisition of these features with
SO HOW THEY COMPARE ACQUISITION F-E-A-T-U-R-E-S ACQUISITION
         (point-left)   (point-left)

the acquisition of the same types of grammatical features in English,
SAME K-I-N-D F-E-A-T-U-R-E-S IN ENGLISH WELL.. FINISH STUDY

and came up with, as a result of this study, with what seemed to be
RESEARCH FOUND SAME P-A-T-T-E-R-N-S G-R-A-M-M-A-T-I-C-A-L

some quite consistent patterns of grammatical acquisition across the
ACQUISITION BOTH LANGUAGE SAME

two languages.

Sentence 2
Any of you who are aware of the work in this area, the work of
    YOU SHOULD KNOW OVER P-I-A-G-E.. P-I-A-G-E-T MAKE STRONG*
                     (hd) (point-middle)
people like Jean Piaget, who made a very very strong case for a
SUPPORT THEORY BELIEVE STRONG RELATIONSHIP S-E-N-S-O-R-Y M-O-T-O-R
   (his-middle)   *(hd)*

binding relationship between early sensory-motor development and
MOVEMENT-OF-ARMS-AND- BODY WALK EVERYTHING AND

early language acquisition.
LANGUAGE ACQUISITION

Sentence 3

If you look at the work of someone like Steve Krashen, even in
    SOMEONE LIKE S-T-E-V-E K-R-A-S-H-E-N HE SAY (IDEA) SECOND*
                 (point-middle) (point-middle)

second language research, his notion of, that we have to be at or
LANGUAGE RESEARCH BUT MUST TALK SLIGHTLY-ABOVE MY TALK

just above the language receptive capacities of the language learner,
HIGH LEARNER LOWER TOO-FAR- ABOVE ACQUIRE-FROM-ME
   (their-middle) (point-middle) (neg)

that if we are too far above it then the capacity for the learner to
CAN'T SLIGHTLY-ABOVE SAME-LEVEL LEARN NOTHING
(neg)

actually make use of language input is certainly diminished.
SLIGHTLY-ABOVE NEED THAT PHILOSOPHY
    (hd)

SUBJECT 9

Sentence 1

And what they did was contrast the acquisition of these features with
    WELL THREE WRITE NOTE-DOWN WHAT THEY D-O WHAT WELL
    (point-right)   *(q)*

the acquisition of the same types of grammatical features in English,
COMPARE CHILDREN ACQUIRE SIGN LANGUAGE GROW-UP ACQUIRE
               (left)   *(right)*

and came up with, as a result of this study, with what seemed to be
ENGLISH (STRUCTURE) G-R-A-M-M-A-R COMPARE+ FIND
                                  (hd)

some quite consistent patterns of grammatical acquisition across the
THEIR RESEARCH SHOW HAVE+ SAME COMPARE+ CHILDREN ACQUIRE
(their-right)

two languages.
MANY SAME HOW

Sentence 2

Any of you who are aware of the work in this area, the work of
    YOU AWARE KNOW WHAT J-O-H-N P-I-A-G-E-T WORK.. PERSON WRITE
    (point-middle)   *(q)*   *(his-middle) (point-middle)*

people like Jean Piaget, who made a very very strong case for a
A-LOT-OF-TEXT STRONG* TALK OVER WELL.. RELATIONSHIP

binding relationship between early sensory-motor development and
WITH WHAT WHEN BABY CHILDREN GROW-UP THEIR HANDS EYES
       (q)   *(their-right)*

early language acquisition.
ARMS-MOVE EARLY MOVE RELATE-TO EARLY ACQUIRE LANGUAGE

Sentence 3

If you look at the work of someone like Steve Krashen, even in
                     DOESN'T-MATTER SECOND LANGUAGE RESEARCH

second language research, his notion of, that we have to be at or just

S-T-E-V-E K-R-A-S-H-E-N SECOND LANGUAGE RESEARCH AREA WELL
(point-right) (his-right)   *(point-right)*

above the language receptive capacities of the language learner, that if
THEIR LANGUAGE MUST ALMOST AHEAD ME ACQUIRE+ THEIR
(their-right) (point-right)   *(their-right)*

we are too far above it then the capacity for the learner to actually
SPEAK+ T-O ME ME-UNDERSTAND LITTLE-BIT AHEAD WHAT MY

make use of language input is certainly diminished.
UNDERSTAND ME CAN AHEAD
     (neg/hd)
IMPROVE WELL I-F FAR-AHEAD ME CAN'T ACQUIRE DAMAGE MY
     (point-right)   *(neg)*
ACQUIRE T-O LEARN SECOND LANGUAGE

SUBJECT 10

Sentence 1

And what they did was contrast the acquisition of these features with
WHAT WHAT RESEARCH WHAT COMPARE WITH G-R-A-M-M-A-R LIST IN
(point arc)   *(q)*

the acquisition of the same types of grammatical features in English,
ENGLISH COMPARE WITH SIGN LANGUAGE HOW LIST COMPARE..

and came up with, as a result of this study, with what seemed to be
RESEARCH FOUND LIST ALMOST SAME LANGUAGE ACQUISITION
        (left)

some quite consistent patterns of grammatical acquisition across the
BOTH LANGUAGE ALMOST SAME
  (their right) (their left) (hd)

two languages.

Sentence 2

Any of you who are aware of the work in this area, the work of
        SHOULD WORK AREA SOME PEOPLE STRONG EXPLAIN*
            (point-left)   *(point+ left)*
people like Jean Piaget, who made a very very strong case for a

binding relationship between early sensory-motor development
ACQUIRE+ PLUS LANGUAGE ACQUISITION.. HOW CONNECT
(point-left-right-left)

and early language acquisition.

Sentence 3

If you look at the work of someone like Steve Krashen, even in
ANOTHER S-T-E-V-E K-R-A-S-H-E-N-E-W.. SAY (who) WHAT PERSON
(point-left)

second language research, his notion of, that we have to be at or
CAN ACQUIRE I-F SPEAK*+ HIGH-ABOVE WILL GO-OVER-HEAD

just above the language receptive capacities of the language learner,
MAKE LITTLE-BIT SLIGHTLY-ABOVE WATCH WILL LEARN MORE
(point-left)

that if we are too far above it then the capacity for the learner to
actually make use of language input is certainly diminished.

Appendix C

Omission Types on Key Lines of Text

	Line Number						
Subject	59	90	104	116	117	139	169
1	CS	CI	CS	U	–	U	CS
2	CI	CR	U	U	U	CS	CI
3	CI	CI	CU	CR	U	U	CS
4	CU	U	CS	U	U	CS	CS
5	CI	–	CS	U	U	–	CS
6	CS	–	U	–	–	–	CS
7	CI	U	CS	U	U	CS	CS
8	CI	–	U	–	CU	U	CR & CS
9	CI	U	U	CR	–	CR	U
10	CI	CR	U	–	U	CS	CS
Total	10	7	10	7	7	8	11

Note. CS = Conscious strategic omissions; CI = Conscious intentional omissions; CU = Conscious unintentional omissions; CR = Conscious receptive omissions; U = Unconscious omissions.

188

References

Altman, H. J. (1989). Error analysis in the teaching of simultaneous interpretation: A pilot study. *Fremdsprachen, 33*(3), 177–183.

Anderson, B. (1978). Interpreter roles and interpretation situations: Cross-cutting typologies. In D. Gerver, & H. W. Sinaiko (Eds.), *Language interpretation and communication* (pp. 217–230). New York, NY: Plenum Press.

Aquiline, C. (2000, July). *World Federation of the Deaf: Towards a policy on Deaf education.* Paper presented at the International Congress of Educators of the Deaf, Sydney, Australia.

Astington, J., Harris, P. L., & Olsen, D. R. (Eds.). (1988). *Developing theories of mind.* Cambridge, United Kingdom: Cambridge University Press.

Atwood, A. (1985). Environmental distractions in interpreting. *Journal of Interpretation, 2,* 94–98.

Atwood, A., & Gray, D. (1986). Interpreting: The culture of artful mediation. In M. McIntire (Ed.), *Interpreting: The art of cross-cultural mediation* (pp. 80–85). Silver Spring, MD: RID Publications.

Baetens Beardsmore, H. (1986). *Bilingualism: Basic principles* (2nd ed.). Clevedon, United Kingdom: Multilingual Matters Ltd.

Baker, C., & Cokely, D. (1980). *American Sign Language: A teacher's resource text on grammar and culture.* Silver Spring, MD: T. J. Publishers.

Baker, M. (1992). *In other words: A coursebook on translation.* London, United Kingdom: Routledge.

Baker-Shenk, C. (1986). Characteristics of oppressed and oppressor peoples. In M. McIntire (Ed.), *Interpreting: The art of cross-cultural mediation* (pp. 43–53). Silver Spring, MD: RID.

Barik, H. A. (1975). Simultaneous interpretation: Qualitative and linguistic data. *Language and Speech, 18,* 272–297.

Beaman, K. (1984). Co-ordination and subordination revisited: Syntactic complexity in spoken and written narrative discourse. In D. Tannen (Ed.), *Coherence in spoken and written discourse* (pp. 45–80). Norwood, NJ: Ablex.

Beylard-Ozeroff, A., Králová, J., & Moser-Mercer, B. (Eds.). (1998). *Translators' strategies and creativity: Selected papers from the 9th International Conference on Translating and Interpreting. Prague, September 1995.* Philadelphia, PA: John Benjamins.

Bialystok, E., & Ryan, E. B. (1985a). Toward a definition of metalinguistic skill. *Merrill-Palmer Quarterly, 31,* 229–251.

Bialystok, E., & Ryan, E. B. (1985b). The metacognitive framework for the development of first and second language skills. In D. L. Forrest-Pressley, G. E. Mackinnon, & T. G. Waller (Eds.), *Metacognition, cognition and human performance*, (pp. 207–252). New York, NY: Academic Press.

Bialystok, E. (1991a). Metalinguistic dimensions of bilingual proficiency. In E. Bialystok (Ed.), *Language processing in bilingual children* (pp. 113–140). Cambridge, United Kingdom: Cambridge University Press.

Bialystok, E. (Ed.). (1991b). *Language processing in bilingual children.* Cambridge, United Kingdom: Cambridge University Press.

Bialystok, E. (1993). Metalinguistic awareness: The development of children's representations of language. In C. Pratt, & A. F. Garton (Eds.), *Systems of representation in children: Development and use* (pp. 211–233). Chichester, United Kingdom: Wiley.

Bienvenu, M. J. (1987). Third culture: Working together. *Journal of Interpretation, 4*, 1–12.

Blewett, J. (1985). *Problem solving in interpreting.* Milperra, Australia: Macarthur Institute of Higher Education.

Bowen, M. (1980). Bilingualism as a factor in the training of interpreters. In J. E. Alatis (Ed.), *Georgetown University round table on languages and linguistics, 1980: Current issues in bilingual education* (pp. 201–207). Washington, DC: Georgetown University Press.

Bowman, J., & Hyde, M. (1993). Manual communication as support for deaf students in the regular classroom. *Australian Teacher of the Deaf, 33*, 32–46.

Brasel, B. (1975). The effects of fatigue on the competence of interpreters for the deaf. In H. J. Murphy (Ed.), *Selected readings in the integration of deaf students at CSUN* (pp. 19–22). Northridge, CA: California State University.

Bremner, A., & Housden, T. (1996). *Issues in educational settings for deaf students and interpreters.* Retrieved from http://www.signs-of-development. org/SG/ETSG/Issues.pdf

Brennan, M. (1992). The visual world of BSL: An introduction. In D. Brien (Ed.), *Dictionary of British Sign Language/English* (pp. 1–133). London, United Kingdom: Faber & Faber.

Brennan, M. (2001). Making borrowings work in British Sign Language. In D. Brentari (Ed.), *Foreign vocabulary in sign languages* (pp. 49–86). Mahwah, NJ: Lawrence Erlbaum.

Brennan, M., & Brown, R. (1997). *Equality before the law: Deaf people's access to justice.* Durham, United Kingdom: Deaf Studies Research Unit, University of Durham.

Brien, D. (Ed.). (1992). *Dictionary of British Sign Language/English.* London, United Kingdom: Faber & Faber.

Brislin, R. (Ed.). (1976). *Translation· Applications and research*. New York, NY: Gardner Press.

Brown, P., & Fraser, C. (1979). Speech as a marker of situation. In K. Scherer, & H. Giles (Eds.), *Social markers in speech* (pp. 33–62). Cambridge, United Kingdom: Cambridge University Press.

Brown, L. (1993). *The new shorter Oxford English dictionary*. Oxford, United Kingdom: Clarendon Press.

Burns, R. B. (1997). *Introduction to research methods*. Melbourne, Australia: Addison Wesley Longman.

Burns, S., Matthews, P., & Nolan-Conroy, E. (2001). Language attitudes. In C. Lucas (Ed.), *The sociolinguistics of sign languages* (pp. 181–216). Cambridge, United Kingdom: Cambridge University Press.

CACDP. (1997). *Directory 1997/98*. Durham, United Kingdom: Council for the Advancement of Communication with Deaf People.

Carter, S. M., & Lauritsen, R. R. (1974). Interpreter recruitment, selection and training. *Journal of Rehabilitation of the Deaf, 7*(3), 52–62.

Cavell, J. L., & Wells, M. (1986). The interpreter as cross-cultural mediator: How does a student learn to do it? In M. McIntire (Ed.), *Interpreting: The art of cross-cultural mediation* (pp. 95–110). Silver Spring, MD: RID Publications.

Cerney, B. (2000). The ten c's of effective target texts. *Journal of Interpretation*, 131–150.

Chafe, W. (1980). *The pear stories: Cognitive, cultural and linguistic aspects of narrative production*. Norwood, NJ: Ablex.

Chafin Seal, B. (1998). *Best practices in educational interpreting*. Needham Heights, MA: Allyn & Bacon.

Christie, K., Wilkins, D. M., Hicks McDonald, B., & Neuroth-Gimbrone, C. (1999). GET-TO-THE-POINT: Academic bilingualism and discourse in American Sign Language and written English. In E. Winston (Ed.), *Storytelling and conversation: Discourse in Deaf communities* (pp. 162–189). Washington, DC: Gallaudet University Press.

CIT at 21: Celebrating excellence, celebrating partnership. Proceedings of the 13th National Convention of the Conference of Interpreter Trainers (2000). Silver Spring, MD: RID Publications.

Clark, E. V. (1978). Awareness of language: Some evidence from what children say and do. In A. Sinclair, R. J. Jarvella, & W. J. M. Levelt (Eds.), *The child's conception of language,* (pp. 17–43). Berlin, Germany: Springer-Verlag.

Cokely, D. (1981). Sign language interpreters: A demographic survey. *Sign Language Studies, 32*, 261–286.

Cokely, D. (1983a). Metanotative qualities: How accurately are they conveyed by interpreters? *The Reflector, 5*, 15–22.

Cokely, D. (1983b). When is pidgin not a pidgin? An alternate analysis on the ASL-English contact situation. *Sign Language Studies, 38*, 1–24.

Cokely, D. (1985). *Towards a sociolinguistic model of the interpreting process: Focus on ASL and English* (Unpublished doctoral dissertation). Georgetown University, Washington, DC.

Cokely, D. (1992a). *Interpretation: A sociolinguistic model*. Burtonsville, MD: Linstok Press.

Cokely, D. (1992b). Effects of lag time on interpreter errors. In D. Cokely (Ed.), *Sign language interpreters and interpreting* (pp. 39–69). Burtonsville, MD: Linstok Press.

Cokely, D. (Ed.). (1992c). *Sign language interpreters and interpreting*. Burtonsville, MD: Linstok Press.

Cokely, D. (1995, September). *When worlds collide: Reflections on interpreting differing cultural realities*. Keynote paper presented at the Issues in Interpreting 2 conference, University of Durham, United Kingdom.

Cokely, D. (2001). Interpreting culturally rich realities: Research implications for successful interpretation. *Journal of Interpretation*, 1–46.

Compton, M., & Shroyer, E. (1997). Educational interpreter preparation and liberal education. *Journal of Interpretation, 7*(1), 49–61.

Cooper, C. L., Davies, R., & Tung, R. L. (1982). Interpreting stress: Sources of job stress amongst conference interpreters. *Multilingua, 1*(2), 97–107.

Corfmat, P. (1990). *Please sign here: Insights into the world of the deaf*. Worthing, United Kingdom: Churchman.

Corker, M. (1997). Deaf people and interpreting: The struggle in language. *Deaf Worlds, 13*(3), 13–20.

Crystal, D., & Davey, D. (1969). *Investigating English style*. Bloomington, IN: Indiana University Press.

Crystal, D. (1984). *Who cares about usage?* New York, NY: Penguin.

Crystal, D. (1987). *The Cambridge encyclopedia of language*. Cambridge, United Kingdom: Cambridge University Press.

Crystal, D. (1995). *The Cambridge encyclopedia of the English language*. Cambridge, United Kingdom: Cambridge University Press.

Cummins, J. (1980). The cross-lingual dimensions of language proficiency: Implications for bilingual education and the optimal age issue. *TESOL Quarterly, 14*, 175–188.

Dahl, C., & Wilcox, S. (1990). Preparing the educational interpreter: A survey of sign language interpreter training programs. *American Annals for the Deaf, 135*(4), 275–279.

Darò, V. (1994). Non-linguistic factors influencing simultaneous interpretation. In S. Lambert, & B. Moser-Mercer (Eds.), *Bridging the gap: Empirical research in simultaneous interpretation* (pp. 249–271). Philadelphia, PA: John Benjamins.

Darò, V., Lambert, S., & Fabbro, F. (1996). Conscious monitoring of attention during simultaneous interpretation. *Interpreting, 1*(1), 101–124.

Davis, J. (1989). Distinguishing language contact phenomena in ASL. In C. Lucas (Ed.), *The sociolinguistics of the Deaf community* (pp. 85–102). San Diego, CA: Academic Press.

Davis, J. (1990a). *Interpreting in a language contact situation: The case of English-to-ASL interpretation* (Unpublished doctoral dissertation). University of New Mexico, Albuquerque.

Davis, J. (1990b). Linguistic transference and interference: Interpreting between English and ASL. In C. Lucas (Ed.), *Sign language research: Theoretical issues* (pp. 308–321). Washington, DC: Gallaudet University Press.

Davis, J. (2000). Translation techniques in interpreter education. In C. Roy (Ed.), *Innovative practices for teaching sign language interpreters* (pp. 109–131). Washington, DC: Gallaudet University Press.

Dean, R., & Pollard, R. Q. (2001). The application of demand-control theory to sign language interpreting: Implications for stress and interpreter training. *Journal of Deaf Studies and Deaf Education, 6*(1), 1–14.

Demanez, S. (1987). Secondary education for hearing and adolescent deaf people. Two years experience of interpreting in French Sign Language. In J. Alegria et al. (Eds.), *Deaf life. Today ... and tomorrow? Pedagogy and deafness* (Vol. 4, pp. 113–122). Brussels, Belgium: Mecaprint.

Deuchar, M. (1979). *Diglossia in British Sign Language* (Unpublished doctoral dissertation). Stanford University, Stanford, CA.

Deuchar, M. (1984). *British Sign Language*. London, United Kingdom: Routledge & Kegan Paul.

Dicker, L. (1976). Intensive interpreter training. *American Annals of the Deaf, 121*(3), 312–319.

Domingue, R., & Ingram, B. (1978). Sign language interpretation: The state of the art. In D. Gerver, & H. W. Sinaiko (Eds.), *Language interpretation and communication* (pp. 81–86). New York, NY: Plenum Press.

Donath, P. (1987). Interpreting for deaf people: A first stocktake. *Das Zeichen 1*(1), 62–63.

Eighinger, L. (2000, February 26). Re: Literate interpreters [IEPFAC email discussion list message—now defunct].

Emmorey, K., & Lane, H. (Eds.). (2000). *The signs of language revisited: An anthology to Ursula Bellugi and Edward Klima*. Mahwah, NJ: Erlbaum.

Enkvist, N. E. (1973). Should we count errors or measure success? In J. Svartvik (Ed.), *Errata* (pp. 16–23). Lund, Sweden: CWK Gleerup.

Erting, C., Johnson, R., Smith, D., & Snider, B. (Eds.). (1994). *The Deaf way: Perspectives from the international conference on Deaf culture.* Washington, DC: Gallaudet University Press.

Erting, C. (1994). Introduction. In C. Erting, R. Johnson, D. Smith & B. Snider (Eds.), *The Deaf way* (pp. xxiii–xxxi). Washington, DC: Gallaudet University Press.

Fenton, S. (1993). Interpreting in New Zealand: An emerging profession. *Journal of Interpretation, 6*(1), 155–166.

Finegan, E., Besnier, N., Blair, D., & Collins, P. (1992). *Language: Its structure and use.* Sydney, Australia: Harcourt Brace Jovanich.

Fischer, T. (1993). Team interpreting: The team approach. *Journal of Interpretation, 6*(1), 167–174.

Fleischer, L. (1975). *Sign language interpretation under four conditions* (Unpublished doctoral dissertation). Brigham Young University, Provo, UT.

Flores d'Arcais, G. B. (1978). The contribution of cognitive psychology to the study of interpretation. In D. Gerver, & H. W. Sinaiko (Eds.), *Language interpretation and communication* (pp. 385–402). New York, NY: Plenum Press.

Fontana, S. (1999). Italian Sign Language and spoken Italian in contact: An analysis of interactions between Deaf parents and hearing children. In E. Winston (Ed.), *Storytelling and conversation: Discourse in Deaf communities* (pp. 149–161). Washington, DC: Gallaudet University Press.

Ford, L. (1981). *The interpreter as a communication specialist.* Paper presented at the Third International Symposium on Interpretation of Sign Languages, Bristol, United Kingdom.

Forrest-Pressley, D. L., Mackinnon, G. E., & Waller, T. G. (Eds.). (1985). *Metacognition, cognition and human performance.* New York, NY: Academic Press.

Foster, S. B., & Walter, G. G. (Eds.). (1992). *Deaf students in postsecondary education.* London, United Kingdom: Routledge.

Fox, G. (Ed.). (1988). *Collins COBUILD essential English dictionary.* Glasgow, United Kingdom: William Collins Sons & Co.

Freedle, R. (Ed.). (1979). *Advances in Discourse Processing: Vol. 2. New Directions in Discourse Processing.* Norwood, NJ: Ablex.

Frishberg, N. (1990). *Interpreting: An introduction* (2nd ed.). Silver Spring, MD: RID Publications.

Frishberg, N. (2000). An interpreter creates the space. In K. Emmorey, & H. Lane (Eds.), *The signs of language revisited: An anthology to Ursula Bellugi and Edward Klima* (pp. 169–192). Mahwah, NJ: Erlbaum.

Frishberg, N., & Wilcox, S. (1994). Issue paper: Differentiating training from education, technical and professional. In E. Winston (Ed.), *Mapping* our course: A collaborative venture. Proceedings of the 10th National Convention of the Conference of Interpreter Trainers, March 1994 (pp.15–20). Washington, DC: CIT.

Fromkin, V., Rodman, R., Collins, P., & Blair, D. (1990). *An introduction to language* (2nd Australian ed.). Sydney, Australia: Holt, Rinehart & Winston.

Garton, A., & Pratt, C. (1998). *Learning to be literate: The development of spoken and written language.* Oxford, United Kingdom: Blackwell.

Gentile, A., Ozolins, U., & Vasilakakos, M. (1996). *Liaison interpreting: A handbook.* Melbourne, Australia: Melbourne University Press.

Gerot, L., & Wignell, P. (1995). *Making sense of functional grammar.* Cammeray, Australia: Antipodean Educational Enterprises.

Gerver, D. (1969). The effects of source language presentation rate on the performance of simultaneous conference interpreters. In E. Foulke (Ed.), *Proceedings of the 2nd Louisville Conference on Rate and/or Frequency Controlled Speech* (pp. 162–184). Louisville, KY: University of Louisville.

Gerver, D. (1974). The effects of noise on the performance of simultaneous interpreters: Accuracy of performance. *Acta Psychologica, 38,* 159–167.

Gerver, D., & Sinaiko, H. W. (Eds.). (1978). *Language interpretation and communication.* New York, NY: Plenum Press.

Gile, D. (1995). *Basic concepts and models for interpreter and translator training.* Philadelphia, PA: John Benjamins.

Goffman, E. (1974). *Frame analysis.* New York, NY: Harper & Row.

Goffman, E. (1981). *Forms of talk.* Oxford, United Kingdom: Basil Blackwell.

Goldman-Gisler, F. (1978). Segmentation of input in simultaneous translation. *Journal of Psycholinguistic Research, 1*(2), 127–140.

Goldman-Gisler, F., & Cohen. M. (1974). An experimental study of interference between receptive and productive processes relating to simultaneous translation. *Language and Speech, 17*(1), 1–10.

Gran, L. (1998). Developing translation/interpretation strategies and creativity. In-training development of interpreting strategies and creativity. In A. Beylard-Ozeroff, J. Králová, & B. Moser-Mercer (Eds.), *Translators' strategies and creativity: Selected papers from the 9th International Conference on Translating and Interpreting, Prague, September 1995* (pp. 145–162). Philadelphia, PA: John Benjamins.

Greenhaw, D. (1985). Postsecondary education survey of interpreter services: A statistical study. *Journal of Interpretation, 2,* 40–57.

Gregory, S., & Hartley, G. (Eds.). (1992). *Constructing deafness.* Milton Keynes, United Kingdom: Open University Press.

Grosjean, F. (1982). *Life with two languages: An introduction to bilingualism.* Cambridge, MA: Harvard University Press.

Grosjean, F. (1997). The bilingual individual. *Interpreting, 2*(2), 163–188.

Gumperz, J. (Ed.). (1982). *Discourse strategies.* Cambridge, United Kingdom: Cambridge University Press.

Gumperz, J., & Hymes, D. (Eds.). (1972). *Directions in sociolinguistics: The ethnography of communication.* New York, NY: Holt, Rinehart & Winston.

Halliday, M. A. K. (1978). *Language as a social semiotic: The social interpretation of language and meaning.* London, United Kingdom: Edward Arnold.

Halliday, M. A. K. (1979). Differences between spoken and written language: Some implications for literacy teaching. In G. Page, J. Elkins, & B. O'Connor (Eds.), *Communication through reading: Proceedings of the 4th Australian Reading Conference* (pp. 37–52). Adelaide, Australia: Australian Reading Association.

Halliday, M. A. K. (1985). *Spoken and written language.* Burwood, Australia: Deakin University Press.

Halliday, M. A. K. (1993). *Language in a changing world.* Deakin, Australia: Applied Linguistics Association of Australia.

Halliday, M. A. K. & Hasan, R. (1985). *Language, context and text: Aspects of language in a social semiotic perspective.* Burwood, Australia: Deakin University Press.

Hansen, B. (1991). Sign language interpreting in Scandinavia. In World Federation of the Deaf (Ed.), *Equality and self-reliance. Proceedings of the XI World Congress of the World Federation of the Deaf. Tokyo, Japan, 2–11 July 1991* (pp. 887–894). Tokyo, Japan: Japanese Association of the Deaf.

Harrington, F. (2000). Sign language interpreters and access for Deaf students to university curricula: The ideal and the reality. In R. P. Roberts, S. E. Carr, D. Abraham, & A. Dufour (Eds.), *The critical link 2: Interpreters in the community. Selected papers from the 2nd International Conference on Interpreting in legal, health and social service settings, Vancouver, BC, Canada, 19–23 May 1998* (pp. 219–238). Philadelphia, PA: John Benjamins.

Harrington, F. (2001a). Deaf students and the interpreted classroom: The effect of translation on education? In F. Harrington, & G. H. Turner (Eds.), *Interpreting interpreting: Studies and reflections on sign language interpreting* (pp. 74–88). Gloucestershire, United Kingdom: Douglas McLean.

Harrington, F. (2001b). The rise, fall and re-invention of the communicator: Re-defining roles and responsibilities in educational interpreting. In F. Harrington, & G. H. Turner (Eds.), *Interpreting interpreting: Studies and reflections on sign language interpreting* (pp. 89–102). Gloucestershire, United Kingdom: Douglas McLean.

Harrington, F., & Traynor. N. (1999, July). *Second-hand learning: Experiences of Deaf students in higher education*. Paper presented at the Pathways to Policy: Deaf Nation 2 conference. University of Central Lancashire, Preston, United Kingdom.

Harrington, F., & Turner, G. H. (Eds). (2001). *Interpreting interpreting: Studies and reflections on sign language interpreting*. Gloucestershire, United Kingdom: Douglas McLean.

Hassinen, L. & Lehtomaki. E. (1986). *Interpreting services for the deaf and deaf-blind and deafened people in Finland*. Helsinki, Finland: Finnish Association of the Deaf.

Hatim, B., & Mason, I. (1990). *Discourse and the translator*. London, United Kingdom: Longman.

Hayes, L. (1992). Educational interpreters for deaf students: Their responsibilities, problems and concerns. *Journal of Interpretation, 5*(1), 5–24.

Herbert, J. (1978). How conference interpretation grew. In D. Gerver, & H. W. Sinaiko (Eds.), *Language interpretation and communication* (pp. 5–10). New York, NY: Plenum Press.

Higgins, P. (1980). *Outsiders in a hearing world: A sociology of deafness*. London, United Kingdom: Sage Publications.

Hoffman, C. (1991). *An introduction to bilingualism*. London, United Kingdom: Longman.

Hoffman, R. (1997). The cognitive psychology of expertise and the domain of interpreting. *Interpreting, 2*(2), 189–230.

Hough, J. (1981). *Court interpreting ... who are we interpreting for?* Paper presented at the 3rd International Symposium on Sign Language Interpreting, Bristol, United Kingdom.

Humphrey, J. (2000). Portfolios: One answer to the challenge of assessment and the "readiness to work" gap. In C. Roy (Ed.), *Innovative practices for teaching sign language interpreters* (pp. 153–176). Washington, DC: Gallaudet University Press.

Humphrey, J., & Alcorn, B. (1996). *So you want to be an interpreter? An introduction to sign language interpreting*. Amarillo, TX: H & H.

Hymes, D. (1967). Models of the interaction of language and social setting. *Journal of Social Issues, 23*(2), 8–28.

Hymes, D. (1972). Models of the interaction of language and social life. In J. Gumperz, & D. Hymes (Eds.), *Directions in sociolinguistics: The ethnography of communication* (pp. 35–71). New York, NY: Holt, Rinehart & Winston.

Ingram, R. (1974). A communication model of the interpreting process. *Journal of Rehabilitation of the Deaf, 7*, 3–9.

Ingram, R. (1978). Sign language interpretation and general theories of language interpretation and communication. In D. Gerver, & H. W. Sinaiko (Eds.), *Language interpretation and communication* (pp. 109–118). New York, NY: Plenum Press.

Ingram, R. (1985). Simultaneous interpretation of sign languages: Semiotic and psycholinguistic perspectives. *Multilingua, 4*(2), 91–102.

Ingram, R., (2000). Foreword. In C. Roy (Ed.), *Innovative practices for teaching sign language interpreters* (pp. ix–xvi). Washington DC: Gallaudet University Press.

Isham, W. (1986). The role of message analysis in interpretation. In M. McIntire (Ed.), *Interpreting: The art of cross-cultural mediation* (pp. 111–122). Silver Spring, MD: RID Publications.

Isham, W. (1994). Memory for sentence form after simultaneous interpretation: Evidence both for and against deverbalization. In S. Lambert, & B. Moser-Mercer (Eds.), *Bridging the gap: Empirical research in simultaneous interpretation* (pp. 191–211). Philadelphia, PA: John Benjamins.

Isham, W., & Lane, H. (1993). Simultaneous interpretation and the recall of source language sentences. *Language and Cognitive Processes, 8*(3), 241–264.

Isham, W., & Lane, H. (1994). A common conceptual code in bilinguals: Evidence from simultaneous interpretation. *Sign Language Studies, 85,* 291–317.

Ivir, V. (1998). Linguistic and communicative constraints on borrowing and literal translation. In A. Beylard-Ozeroff, J. Králová, & B. Moser-Mercer (Eds.), *Translators' strategies and creativity: Selected papers from the 9th International Conference on Translating and Interpreting, Prague, September 1995* (pp. 137–144). Philadelphia, PA: John Benjamins.

Jacobs, L. R. (1976). *The efficiency of sign language interpretation to convey lecture information to deaf students* (Unpublished doctoral dissertation). University of Arizona, Tucson, Arizona.

Johnson, K. (1991). Miscommunication in interpreted classroom interaction. *Sign Language Studies, 70,* 1–34.

Johnston, T. (1989). *Auslan dictionary: A dictionary of the sign language of the Australian Deaf community*. Maryborough, Australia: Deafness Resources Australia.

Johnston, T. (Ed.). (1998). *Signs of Australia: A new dictionary of Auslan*. North Rocks, Australia: North Rocks Press.

Jones, B. E., Clark, G., & Soltz, D. (1997). Characteristics and practices of sign language interpreters in inclusive education programs. *Exceptional Children, 63*(2), 257–268.

Jones, D. M. (Ed.). (1996). *Assessing our work: Assessing our worth. Proceedings of the 11th National Convention of the Conference of Interpreter Trainers, October 1996*. Northridge, CA: CIT.

Joos, M. (1967). *The five clocks*. New York, NY: Harbinger Books.

Kamata, K. et al. (1989). A basic study of Japanese Sign Language translation. In *Proceedings of the Japanese Society of Sign Language Studies, 10* (pp. 15–29). Tokyo, Japan: Japanese Society of Sign Language Studies.

Kannapell, B. (1989). An examination of Deaf college students' attitudes toward ASL and English. In C. Lucas (Ed.), *The sociolinguistics of the Deaf community* (pp. 191–210). San Diego, CA: Academic Press.

Karmiloff-Smith, A. (1986). From meta-processes to conscious access: Evidence from children's metalinguistic and repair data. *Cognition, 23*(2), 95–147.

Kluwin, T. (1985). The acquisition of content from a signed lecture. *Sign Language Studies, 48*, 259–286.

Kopczynski, A. (1980). *Conference interpreting: Some linguistic and communicative problems*. Poznan, Poland: Adam Mickiewicz Press.

Kopczynski, A. (1994). Quality in conference interpreting: Some pragmatic problems. In S. Lambert & B. Moser-Mercer (Eds.), *Bridging the gap: Empirical research in simultaneous interpretation* (pp. 87–99). Philadelphia, PA: John Benjamins.

Kummer, K. (Ed.). (1987). *Proceedings of the 28th Annual Conference of the American Translators Association*. Albuquerque, NM: Learned Information.

Kurz, I. (1993). Conference interpretation: Expectations of different user groups. *The Interpreters' Newsletter, 5*, 13–21.

Kyle, J., & Woll, B. (1985). *The study of deaf people and their language*. Cambridge, United Kingdom: Cambridge University Press.

Labath, J. E. (1998a). Independent study techniques: Using videotapes of American Sign Language models. In *Celebrating the vision: RID in the 21st century. Proceedings of the 15th National Convention of the Registry of Interpreters for the Deaf, August 1997* (pp. 59–69). Silver Spring, MD: RID Publications.

Ladd, P. (2002). *Understanding Deaf culture: In search of Deafhood*. Clevedon, United Kingdom: Multilingual Matters.

Lambert, S., & Moser-Mercer, B. (Eds.). (1994). *Bridging the gap: Empirical research in simultaneous interpretation*. Philadelphia, PA: John Benjamins.

Lane, H. (1993). *The mask of benevolence: Disabling the Deaf community*. New York, NY: Vintage Books.

Lane, H., Hoffmeister, R., & Bahan, B. (1996). *A journey into the DEAF-WORLD*. San Diego, CA: DawnSignPress.

Lawrence, R. (1987). Specialized preparation in educational interpreting. *Journal of Interpretation, 4*, 87–90.

Lawson, L. (1981). The role of sign in the structure of the Deaf community. In B. Woll, J.G. Kyle, & M. Deuchar (Eds.), *Perspectives on British Sign*

Language and deafness (pp. 166–177). London, United Kingdom: Croom Helm.

Le Ny, J. (1978). Psychosemantics and simultaneous interpretation. In D. Gerver, & H. W. Sinaiko (Eds.), *Language interpretation and communication* (pp. 289–298). New York, NY: Plenum Press.

Lee, D. (1982). Are there really signs of diglossia? Re-examining the situation. *Sign Language Studies, 35*, 127–152.

Lee, R. (1997). Roles, models and world views: A view from the States. *Deaf Worlds, 13*(3), 40–44.

Livingston, S., Singer, B., & Abramson, T. (1994). Effectiveness compared: ASL interpretation versus transliteration. *Sign Language Studies, 82*, 1–54.

Llewellyn Jones, P. (1981a). *Target language styles and source language processing in conference sign language interpreting.* Paper presented at the 3rd International Symposium on Sign Language Interpreting, Bristol, United Kingdom.

Llewellyn Jones, P. (1981b). Simultaneous Interpreting. In B. Woll, J. Kyle, & M. Deuchar, (Eds.), *Perspectives on British Sign Language and Deafness* (pp. 89–104). London, United Kingdom: Croom Helm.

Llewellyn Jones, P., Kyle, J., & Woll, B. (1979). *Sign language communication.* Paper presented at the International Conference on Social Psychology & Language, Bristol, United Kingdom.

Locker, R. (1990). Lexical equivalence in transliterating for deaf students in the university classroom: Two perspectives. *Issues in Applied Linguistics, 1*(2), 167–195.

Longacre, R. (1983). *The grammar of discourse.* New York, NY: Plenum Press.

Lörscher, W. (1996). A psycholinguistic analysis of translation processes. *Meta, 41*(1), 26–32.

Lucas, C. (Ed.). (1989). *The sociolinguistics of the Deaf community.* San Diego, CA: Academic Press.

Lucas, C. (Ed.). (1990). *Sign language research: theoretical issues.* Washington, DC: Gallaudet University Press.

Lucas, C. (Ed.). (2001). *The sociolinguistics of sign languages.* Cambridge, United Kingdom: Cambridge University Press.

Lucas, C., Bayley, R., Valli, C., Rose, M., & Wulf, A. (2001). Sociolinguistic variation. In C. Lucas (Ed.), *The sociolinguistics of sign languages* (pp. 61–111). Cambridge, United Kingdom: Cambridge University Press.

Lucas, C., & Valli, C. (1989). Language contact in the American Deaf community. In C. Lucas (Ed.), *The sociolinguistics of the Deaf community* (pp. 11–40). San Diego, CA: Academic Press.

Lucas, C., & Valli, C. (1990). ASL, English, and contact signing. In C. Lucas (Ed.), *Sign language research: Theoretical issues* (pp. 288–307). Washington, DC: Gallaudet University Press.

Lucas, C., & Valli, C. (1992). *Language contact in the American deaf community.* San Diego, CA: Academic Press.

Mackenzie, R. (1998). Creative problem solving and translator training. In A. Beylard-Ozeroff, J. Králová, & B. Moser-Mercer (Eds.), *Translators' strategies and creativity: Selected papers from the 9th International Conference on Translating and Interpreting, Prague, September 1995* (pp. 201–206). Philadelphia, PA: John Benjamins.

Madden, M. (2001). *The incidence and impact of occupational overuse syndrome on sign language interpreters in Australia* (Unpublished doctoral dissertation). Griffith University, Queensland, Australia.

Malakoff, M., & Hakuta, K. (1991). Translation skill and metalinguistic awareness in bilinguals. In E. Bialystok (Ed.), *Language processing in bilingual children* (pp. 141–165). Cambridge, United Kingdom: Cambridge University Press.

Maroney, E., & Singer, B. (1996). Educational interpreter assessment: The development of a tool. In D. M. Jones (Ed.), *Assessing our work: Assessing our worth. Proceedings of the 11th National Convention of the Conference of Interpreter Trainers, October 1996* (pp. 93–148). Northridge, CA: CIT.

Massaro, D. W. (1978). An information processing model of understanding speech. In D. Gerver, & H. W. Sinaiko (Eds.), *Language interpretation and communication* (pp. 299–314). New York, NY: Plenum Press.

McDade, R. (1995, September). *What can interpreters learn from professional footballers?* Paper presented at the Issues in Interpreting 2 conference, University of Durham, United Kingdom.

McIntire, M. (Ed.). (1986). *Interpreting: The art of cross cultural mediation. Proceedings of the 9th National Convention of the Registry of Interpreters for the Deaf, July 1985.* Silver Spring, MD: RID Publications.

McIntire, M. (Ed.). (1987). *New dimensions in interpreter education: Curriculum and instruction. Proceedings of the 6th National Convention of the Conference of Interpreter Trainers.* Silver Spring, MD: RID Publications.

McIntire, M. (1990). The work and education of sign language interpreters. In S. Prillwitz, & T. Vollhaber (Eds.), *Sign language research and application* (pp. 263–273). Hamburg, Germany: Signum Press.

McIntire, M., & Sanderson, G. (1993). Bye-Bye! Bi-Bi! Questions of empowerment and role. In *A confluence of diverse relationships: Proceedings of the 13th National Convention of the Registry of Interpreters for the Deaf* (pp. 94–118). Silver Spring, MD: RID Publications.

McKee, R. L. (1996). Identifying difficulty factors in interpreting assignments. *Deaf Worlds, 12*(2), 16–24.

Meadow, K. (1977). Name signs as identity symbols in the deaf community. *Sign Language Studies, 16,* 237–246.

Meadow-Orlans, K. P. (1990). Research on developmental aspects of deafness. In D. F. Moores, & K. P. Meadow-Orlans (Eds.), *Educational and developmental aspects of deafness* (pp. 283–298). Washington, DC: Gallaudet University Press.

Messina, A. (1998). The reading aloud of English language texts in simultaneously interpreted conferences. *Interpreting, 3*(2), 147–161.

Metzger, M. (1995). *The paradox of neutrality: A comparison of interpreters' goals with the reality of interactive discourse* (Unpublished doctoral dissertation). Georgetown University, Washington, DC.

Metzger, M. (1999). *Sign language interpreting: Deconstructing the myth of neutrality.* Washington, DC: Gallaudet University Press.

Metzger, M. (2000). Interactive role-plays as a teaching strategy. In C. Roy (Ed.), *Innovative practices for teaching sign language interpreters* (pp. 83–108). Washington, DC: Gallaudet University Press.

Mindess, A. (1990). What name signs can tell us about deaf culture. *Sign Language Studies, 66,* 1–24.

Moser, B. (1978). Simultaneous interpretation: A hypothetical model and its practical application. In D. Gerver, & H. W. Sinaiko (Eds.), *Language interpretation and communication* (pp. 353–368). New York, NY: Plenum Press.

Moser, P. (1996). Expectations of users of conference interpretation. *Interpreting, 1*(2), 145–178.

Moser-Mercer, B—(1997). Methodological issues in interpreting research: An introduction to the Ascona workshops. *Interpreting, 2*(1), 1–12.

Moser-Mercer, B., Kunzli, A., & Korac, M. (1998). Prolonged turns in interpreting: Effects on quality, physiological and psychological stress (Pilot study). *Interpreting, 3*(1), 47–64.

Murphy, H. J. (Ed.). (1975). *Selected readings in the integration of deaf students at CSUN.* Northridge, CA: California State University.

Murphy, H. (1978). Research in sign language interpreting at California State University, Northridge. In D. Gerver, & H. W. Sinaiko (Eds.), *Language interpretation and communication* (pp. 87–98). New York, NY: Plenum Press.

NAATI. (1999). *Directory of accredited and recognized practitioners of interpreting and translation.* [Database]: National Accreditation Authority of Translators and Interpreters. Retrieved from: https://www.naati.com.au/publications.html.

Napier, J. (1996). Interpreter support: An ambiguous concept? *CACDP Standard*. Durham, United Kingdom: Council for the Advancement of Communication with Deaf People.

Napier, J. (1998a, November). *What makes an ideal interpreter?* Paper presented at the inaugural conference of the Australian Sign Language Interpreters Association (Victoria), Melbourne, Australia.

Napier, J. (1998b). *An analytical study of free interpretation and its use by British Sign Language interpreters* (Unpublished master's dissertation). University of Durham, United Kingdom.

Napier, J. (1998c). Free your mind—The rest will follow. *Deaf Worlds, 14*(3), 15–22.

Napier, J. (2000). Free interpretation: What is it and does it translate into training? In A. Schembri, J. Napier, R. Beattie, & G. Leigh (Eds.), *Deaf studies, Sydney 1998: Selected papers from the Australasian Deaf studies research symposium, Renwick College, Sydney, August 22–23 1998, Renwick College Monograph No. 4* (pp. 21–33). North Rocks, Australia: North Rocks Press.

Napier, J. (2001). *Linguistic coping strategies of sign language interpreters* (Unpublished doctoral dissertation). Macquarie University, Sydney, Australia.

Napier, J. (2002). The D/deaf–H/hearing debate. *Sign Language Studies, 2*(2), 141–149.

Napier, J. (2006). Comparing language contact phenomena between Auslan/ English interpreters and deaf Australians: A preliminary study. In C. Lucas (Ed.), *Multilingualism and sign languages: From the Great Plains to Australia* (pp. 39–78). Washington, DC: Gallaudet University Press.

Napier, J., & Adam, R. (2002). A comparative linguistics analysis of BSL and Auslan interpreting. *Deaf Worlds, 18*(1), 22–28.

Neumann Solow, S. (1981). *Sign language interpreting: A basic resource book.* Silver Spring, MD: National Association of the Deaf.

Neumann Solow, S. (2000). *Sign language interpreting: A basic resource book* (Rev. ed.). Burtonsville, MD: Linstok Press.

Nida, E. (1998). Translators' creativity versus sociolinguistic constraints. In A. Beylard-Ozeroff, J. Králová, & B. Moser-Mercer (Eds.), *Translators' strategies and creativity: Selected papers from the 9th International Conference on Translating and Interpreting, Prague, September 1995* (pp. 127–136). Philadelphia, PA: John Benjamins.

Nord, C. (2000, January). *Translating as a text-production.* Paper given as part of the online Innovation in Translator and Interpreter Training Symposium, 17–25 January 2000. No longer available.

Nowell, R. C., & Stuckless, E. R. (1974). An interpreter training program. *Journal of Rehabilitation of the Deaf, 7*(3), 69–75.

O'Loughlin, K. (1995). Lexical density in candidate output and semi-direct versions of an oral proficiency test. *Language Testing, 12*(2), 217–237.

Ozolins, U., & Bridge, M. (1999). *Sign language interpreting in Australia.* Melbourne, Australia: Language Australia.

Padden, C. (1980). The Deaf community and the culture of Deaf people. In S. Gregory, & G. Hartley (Eds.), *Constructing deafness* (pp. 40–45). Milton Keynes, United Kingdom: Open University Press.

Page, G., Elkins, J., & O' Connor, B. (Eds.). (1979). *Communication through reading: Proceedings of the 4th Australian Reading Conference.* Adelaide, Australia: Australian Reading Association.

Page, J. (1993). In the sandwich or on the side? Cultural variability and the interpreter's role. *Journal of Interpretation, 6,* 107–126.

Paneth, E. (1957). *An investigation into conference interpreting, with special reference to training interpreters* (Unpublished master's dissertation). London University, United Kingdom.

Patrie, C. (1993). A confluence of diverse relationships: Interpreter education and educational interpreting. In *A confluence of diverse relationships: Proceedings of the 13th National Convention of the Registry of Interpreters for the Deaf* (pp. 3–18). Silver Spring, MD: RID Publications.

Patrie, C. (1994). Entry level to the profession. Response paper #1: The readiness-to-work-gap. In E. Winston (Ed.), *Mapping our course: A collaborative venture. Proceedings of the 10th National Convention of the Conference of Interpreter Trainers, March 1994* (pp. 53–56). Washington, DC: CIT.

Paul, P. V., & Quigley, S. P. (1990). *Education and deafness.* London, United Kingdom: Longman.

Pergnier, M. (1978). Language meaning and message meaning: Towards a sociolinguistic approach to translation. In D. Gerver, & H. W. Sinaiko (Eds.), *Language interpretation and communication* (pp. 199–204). New York, NY: Plenum Press.

Perner, J. (1988). Developing semantics for theories of mind: From propositional attitudes to mental representations. In J. Astington, P. L. Harris, & D. R. Olsen (Eds.), *Developing theories of mind* (pp. 141–172). Cambridge, United Kingdom: Cambridge University Press.

Perren, G. E., & Trim, J. L. M. (Eds.). (1971). *Applications of linguistics: Selected papers of the 2nd International Congress of Applied Linguistics, 1969.* Cambridge, United Kingdom: Cambridge University Press.

Peterson, R. (2000). Metacognition and recall protocols in the interpreting classroom. In C. Roy (Ed.), *Innovative practices for teaching sign language interpreters* (pp. 132–152). Washington, DC: Gallaudet University Press.

Phillip, M. J. (1994, April). *Professionalism: From which cultural perspective?* Paper presented at the Issues in Interpreting Conference, University of Durham, United Kingdom.

Plant-Moeller, J. (Ed.). (1992). *Expanding horizons.* Silver Spring, MD: RID Publications.

Pollitt, K. (1997). The state we're in: Some thoughts on professionalization, professionalism and practice among the UK's sign language interpreters. *Deaf Worlds, 13*(3), 21–26.

Pollitt, K. (2000a). Critical linguistic and cultural awareness: Essential tools in the interpreter's kit bag. In C. Roy (Ed.), *Innovative practices for teaching sign language interpreters* (pp. 67–82). Washington, DC: Gallaudet University Press.

Pollitt, K. (2000b). On babies, bathwater and approaches to interpreting. *Deaf Worlds, 16*(2), 60–64.

Pratt, C., & Garton, A. F. (Eds.). (1993). *Metalinguistic awareness: The development of children's representations of language.* Chichester, United Kingdom: Wiley.

Prillwitz, S., & Vollhaber, T. (Eds.). (1990). *Sign language research and application: Proceedings of the International Congress on Sign Language Research and Application, March 1990.* Hamburg, Germany: Signum Press.

Qian, H. (1994). Looking at interpretation from a communicative perspective. *Babel: International Journal of Translation, 40*(4), 214–221.

Quigley, S. (1965). *Interpreting for deaf people: A report of a workshop on interpreting.* Washington, DC: US Department of Health, Education and Welfare.

Riccardi, A. (1998). Interpreting strategies and creativity. In A. Beylard-Ozeroff, J. Králová, & B. Moser-Mercer (Eds.), *Translators' strategies and creativity: Selected papers from the 9th International Conference on Translating and Interpreting, Prague, September 1995* (pp. 171–179). Philadelphia, PA: John Benjamins.

Richards, J., Platt, J., & Platt, H. (1992). *Dictionary of language teaching and applied linguistics.* Singapore, Singapore: Longman.

Roberts, R. (1987). Spoken language interpreting versus sign language interpreting. In K. Kummer (Ed.), *Proceedings of the 28th Annual Conference of the American Translators Association* (pp. 293–307). Albuquerque, NM: Learned Information.

Roberts, R. P., Carr, S. E., Abraham, D., & Dufour, A. (Eds.). (2000). *The critical link 2: Interpreters in the community. Selected papers from the 2nd International Conference on Interpreting in Legal, Health and Social Service Settings, Vancouver, BC, Canada, 19-23 May 1998.* Philadelphia, PA: John Benjamins.

Romaine, S. (1995). *Bilingualism* (2nd ed.). Oxford, United Kingdom: Blackwell.

Roy, C. (1987). Evaluating performance: An interpreted lecture. In M. McIntire (Ed.), *New dimensions in interpreter education: Curriculum and instruction. Proceedings of the 6th National Convention of the Conference of Interpreter Trainers, November 6–10, 1986* (pp. 139–147). Silver Spring, MD: RID Publications.

Roy, C. (1989a). *A sociolinguistic analysis of the interpreter's role in the turn exchanges of an interpreted event* (Unpublished doctoral dissertation) Georgetown University, Washington, DC.

Roy, C. (1989b). Features of discourse in an American Sign Language Lecture. In C. Lucas (Ed.), *The sociolinguistics of the Deaf community* (pp. 231–252). San Diego, CA: Academic Press.

Roy, C. (1992). A sociolinguistic analysis of the interpreter's role in simultaneous talk in a face-to-face interpreted dialogue. *Sign Language Studies, 74*, 21–61.

Roy, C. (1993). The problem with definitions, descriptions and the role metaphors of interpreters. *Journal of Interpretation, 6*, 127–154.

Roy, C. (1996). An interactional sociolinguistic analysis of turntaking in an interpreted event. *Interpreting, 1*(1), 39–68.

Roy, C. (2000a). *Interpreting as a discourse process.* Oxford, United Kingdom: Oxford University Press.

Roy, C. (2000b). Re: More words of advice, anyone? [IEPFAC email discussion list message—now defunct].

Roy, C. (Ed.). (2000c). *Innovative practices for teaching sign language interpreters.* Washington, DC: Gallaudet University Press.

Roy, C. (2000d). Training interpreters—Past, present and future. In C. Roy (Ed.), *Innovative practices for teaching sign language interpreters* (pp. 1–14). Washington, DC: Gallaudet University Press.

Russell, D. (2000, October). *If you'll pause a moment, I'll interpret that: Courtroom interpreting.* Paper presented at the 13th National Convention of the Conference of Interpreter Trainers, Portland, OR.

Ryan, E. B., & Giles, H. (1982). *Attitudes towards language variation: Social and applied contexts.* London, United Kingdom: Edward Arnold.

Sacks, H. (1974). An analysis of the course of a joke's telling in conversation. In R. Bauman & J. Sherzer (Eds.), *The ethnography of speaking* (pp. 337–353). Cambridge, United Kingdom: Cambridge University Press.

Sanderson, G., Siple, L., & Lyons, B. (1999). *Interpreting for postsecondary deaf students: A report of the National Task Force on Quality of Services in the Postsecondary Education of Deaf and Hard of Hearing Students.* Northeast Technical Assistance Center: Rochester Institute of Technology, Rochester, NY.

Saur, R. E. (1992). Resources for deaf students in the mainstreamed classroom. In S. B. Foster, & G. G. Walter (Eds.), *Deaf students in postsecondary education* (pp. 96–113). London, United Kingdom: Routledge.

Schank, R., & Abelson, R. (1977). *Scripts, plans, goals and understanding: An inquiry into human knowledge and structures.* Hillsdale, NJ: Erlbaum.

Schegloff, E. (1972). Sequencing in conversational openings. In J. Gumperz, & D. Hymes (Eds.), *Directions in sociolinguistics: The ethnography of communication* (pp. 346–380). New York, NY: Holt, Rinehart & Winston.

Scheibe, K. (1986). Creative problem solving. In M. McIntire (Ed.), *New dimensions in interpreter education: Task analysis, theory and application* (pp. 152–173). Silver Spring, MD: RID Publications.

Scheibe, K., & Hoza, J. (1986). Throw it out the window! (The code of ethics? We don't use that here): Guidelines for educational interpreters. In M. McIntire (Ed.), *Interpreting: The art of cross cultural mediation* (pp. 128–134). Silver Spring, MD: RID Publications.

Schein, J. D., & Delk, M. R. (1974). *The Deaf population of the United States.* Silver Spring, MD: National Association of the Deaf.

Schembri, A. (1996). *The structure and formation of signs in Auslan (Australian Sign Language). Renwick College Monograph, No. 2.* North Rocks, Australia: North Rocks Press

Schembri, A., Napier, J., Beattie, R., & Leigh, G. (Eds.). (2000). *Deaf studies Sydney, 1998: Selected papers from the Australasian Deaf studies research symposium, Renwick College, Sydney, 22–23 August 1998. Renwick College Monograph, No. 4.* North Rocks, Australia: North Rocks Press.

Scherer, K., & Giles, H. (Eds.). (1979). *Social markers in speech.* Cambridge, United Kingdom: Cambridge University Press.

Schiavetti, N. E., & Metz, D. E. (1997). *Evaluating research in communication disorders.* Needham Heights, MA: Allyn & Bacon.

Schick, B., Williams, K., & Bolster, L. (1999). Skill levels of educational interpreters working in public schools. *Journal of Deaf Studies and Deaf Education, 4*(2), 144–155.

Schiffrin, D. (1993). "Speaking for another" in sociolinguistic interviews. In D. Tannen (Ed.), *Framing in discourse* (pp. 231–263). New York, NY: Oxford University Press.

Scott Gibson, L. (1992). Sign language interpreting: An emerging profession. In S. Gregory, & G. Hartley (Eds.), *Constructing deafness* (pp. 253–258). Milton Keynes, United Kingdom: Open University Press.

Scott Gibson, L. (1994, April). *Open to interpretation: The cult of professionalism.* Paper presented at the Issues in Interpreting conference, University of Durham, United Kingdom.

Seleskovitch, D. (1976). Interpretation: A psychological approach to translating. In R. Brislin (Ed.), *Translation: Applications and research* (pp. 92–116). New York, NY: Gardner Press.

Seleskovitch, D. (1978). *Interpreting for international conferences.* Washington, DC: Pen and Booth.

Seleskovitch, D. (1992). Fundamentals of the interpretive theory of translation. In J. Plant-Moeller (Ed.), *Expanding Horizons: Proceedings of the 12th National Convention of the Registry of Interpreters for the Deaf August 6–11, 1991* (pp. 1–13). Silver Spring, MD: RID Publications.

Shaw, R. (1997). Many stones to form an arch: Co-operation and consideration as the cornerstones of successful interpretation. *Journal of Interpretation, 7*(1), 23–38.

Sherwood, B. (1987). Third culture: Making it work. *Journal of Interpretation, 4,* 13–24.

Simon, J. H. (1994). *An ethnographic study of sign language interpreter education* (Unpublished doctoral dissertation). University of Arizona, Tucson, Arizona.

Sinclair, J., & Coulthard, R. (1975). *Towards an analysis of discourse: The English used by teachers and pupils.* London, United Kingdom: Oxford University Press.

Sinclair, A., Jarvella, R. J., & Levelt, W. J. M. (Eds.). (1978). *The child's conception of language.* Berlin, Germany: Springer-Verlag.

Siple, L. (1993). Working with the sign language interpreter in your classroom. *College Teaching, 41*(4), 139–142.

Siple, L. (1995). *The use of additions in sign language transliteration* (Unpublished doctoral dissertation). State University of New York, Buffalo.

Siple, L. (1996). The use of additions in sign language transliteration. In D. M. Jones (Ed.), *Assessing our work: Assessing our worth. Proceedings of the 11th National Convention of the Conference of Interpreter Trainers, October 1996* (pp. 29–45). Northridge, CA: CIT.

Siple, L. (2000, July). *Working with the sign language interpreter in your classroom.* Paper presented at the International Congress of Educators of the Deaf, Sydney, Australia.

Smith, M. (2000). Enhancing self-regulation in ASL/English interpreting: Promoting excellence in interpreter education. In *CIT at 21: Celebrating excellence, celebrating partnership. Proceedings of the 13th National Convention of the Conference of Interpreter Trainers* (pp. 89–102). Silver Spring, MD: RID Publications.

Stauffer, L. (1994). Entry level to the profession. Response paper #2: A response to the readiness-to-work-gap. In E. Winston (Ed.), *Mapping our course:*

A collaborative venture. *Proceedings of the 10th National Convention of the Conference of Interpreter Trainers, March 1994* (pp. 57–59). Washington, DC: CIT.

Steiner, B. (1998). Signs from the void: The comprehension and production of sign language on television. *Interpreting, 3*(2), 99–146.

Sternberg, M. L. A., Tipton, C. C., & Schein, J. D. (1973). *Curriculum guide for interpreter training.* Unpublished manuscript, Deafness Research & Training Center, New York University, New York, NY.

Stewart, D., Schein, J., & Cartwright, B. E. (1998). *Sign language interpreting: Exploring its art and science.* Boston, MA: Allyn & Bacon.

Stokoe, W. (1969). Sign language diglossia. *Studies in Linguistics, 20,* 27–41.

Stokoe, W., & Kuschel, R. (1979). *A field guide for sign language research.* Silver Spring, MD: Linstok Press.

Strong, M., & Rudser, S. F. (1992). The subjective assessment of sign language interpreters. In D. Cokely (Ed.), *Sign language interpreters and interpreting* (pp. 1–14). Burtonsville, MD: Linstok Press.

Stuckless, E. R., Avery, J. C., & Hurwitz, T. A. (Eds.). (1989). *Educational interpreting for deaf students: Report of the National Task Force on Educational Interpreting.* Rochester, New York: Rochester Institute of Technology.

Sunnari, M. (1995). Processing strategies in simultaneous interpreting: "Saying it all" versus synthesis. In J. Tommola (Ed.), *Topics in Interpreting* (pp. 109–119). Turku, Finland: University of Turku, Center for Translation & Interpreting.

Sutcliffe, T. H. (1975). Interpreting at higher levels of thought. In R. M. Ingram & B. L. Ingram (Eds.), *Hands across the sea: Proceedings of the 1st International Conference on Interpreting* (pp. 205–211). Silver Spring, MD: RID Publications.

Sutton-Spence, R., & Woll, B. (1998). *The linguistics of British Sign Language.* Cambridge, United Kingdom: Cambridge University Press.

Svartvik, J. (Ed.). (1973). *Errata.* Lund, Sweden: CWK Gleerup.

Swabey, L. (1992). Interpreting in community settings: A comparison of sign language and spoken language interpreters. In J. Plant-Moeller (Ed.), *Expanding horizons: Proceedings of the 12th National Convention of the Registry of Interpreters for the Deaf, August 1991* (pp. 106–119). Silver Spring, MD: RID Publications.

Tannen, D. (1979). What's in a frame? Surface evidence for underlying expectations. In R. Freedle (Ed.), *Advances in Discourse Processing: Vol. 2. New directions in discourse processing* (pp. 137–181). Norwood, NJ: Ablex.

Tannen, D. (Ed.). (1984a). *Coherence in spoken and written discourse.* Norwood, NJ: Ablex.

Tannen, D. (1984b). *Conversational style.* Norwood, NJ: Ablex.

Tannen, D. (1993). *Framing in discourse.* Oxford, United Kingdom: Oxford University Press.

Taylor, M. (1993). *Interpretation skills: English to American Sign Language.* Edmonton, Canada: Interpreting Consolidated.

Taylor, M. (2002). *Interpretation skills: American Sign Language to English.* Edmonton, Canada: Interpreting Consolidated.

Tommola, J. (Ed.). (1995). *Topics in interpreting.* Turku, Finland: University of Turku, Center for Translation & Interpreting.

Tunmer, W. E., & Bowey, J. A. (1984). Metalinguistic awareness and reading acquisition. In W. E. Tunmer, C. Pratt, & M. L. Herriman (Eds.), *Metalinguistic awareness in children: Theory, research and implications* (pp. 144–168). Berlin, Germany: Springer-Verlag.

Tunmer, W. E., & Herriman, M. L. (1984). The development of metalinguistic awareness: A conceptual overview. In W. E. Tunmer, C. Pratt, & M. L. Herriman (Eds.), *Metalinguistic awareness in children: Theory, research and implications* (pp. 12–35). Berlin, Germany: Springer-Verlag.

Tunmer, W. E., Pratt, C., & Herriman, M. L. (Eds.). (1984). *Metalinguistic awareness in children: Theory, research and implications.* Berlin, Germany: Springer-Verlag.

Turner, G. H. (2001). Interpreting assignments: Should I or shouldn't I? In F. J. Harrington, & G. H. Turner (Eds.), *Interpreting interpreting: Studies and reflections on sign language interpreting* (pp. 67–73). Gloucestershire, United Kingdom: Douglas McLean.

Tweney, R. (1978). Sign language and psycholinguistic process: Fact, hypothesis and implications of interpretation. In D. Gerver & H. W. Sinaiko (Eds.), *Language interpretation and communication* (pp. 99–108). New York, NY: Plenum Press.

Ure, J. (1971). Lexical density and register differentiation. In G. E. Perren, & J. L. M. Trim (Eds.), *Applications of linguistics: Selected papers of the 2nd International Congress of Applied Linguistics* (pp. 443–452). Cambridge, United Kingdom: Cambridge University Press.

Viera, J. A., & Stauffer, L. K. (2000). Transliteration: The consumer's perspective. *Journal of Interpretation,* 83–100.

Wadensjö, C. (1998). *Interpreting as interaction.* London, United Kingdom: Longman.

Wardhaugh, R. (1992). *An introduction to sociolinguistics.* Oxford, United Kingdom: Blackwell.

Wells, J. (1996). Educational interpreting: Consumer awareness, rights and responsibilities project. In D. M. Jones (Ed.), *Assessing our work: Assessing* our worth. *Proceedings of the 11th National Convention of the Conference of Interpreter Trainers, October 1996* (pp. 149–178). Northridge, CA: CIT.

West, E. A. (1994). Dialogue videojournals: Connecting teacher and student through interactive communication. In E. Winston (Ed.), *Mapping our course: A collaborative venture. Proceedings of the 10th National Convention of the Conference of Interpreter Trainers, March 1994* (pp. 217–225). Washington, DC: CIT.

Wilcox, S., & Wilcox, P. (1985). Schema theory and language interpretation. *Journal of Interpretation, 2*, 84–93.

Winston, E. (1989). Transliteration: What's the message? In C. Lucas (Ed.), *The sociolinguistics of the Deaf community* (pp. 147–164). San Diego, CA: Gallaudet University Press.

Winston, E. (Ed.). (1994). *Mapping our course: A collaborative venture. Proceedings of the 10th National Convention of the Conference of Interpreter Trainers, March 1994*. Washington, DC: CIT.

Winston, E. (Ed.). (1999). *Storytelling and conversation: Discourse in Deaf communities*. Washington, DC: Gallaudet University Press.

Winston, E. A., & Monikowski, C. (2000). Discourse mapping—Developing textual coherence skills in interpreters. In C. Roy (Ed.), *Innovative practices for teaching sign language interpreters* (pp. 15–66). Washington, DC: Gallaudet University Press.

Witter-Merithew, A. (1982). The function of assessing as part of the interpreting process. *Professional Interpreting. Journal of the Registry of Interpreters for the Deaf, 1*(2), 8–15.

Witter-Merithew, A. (1986). Claiming our destiny, Part I. *RID Views*, October, 12.

Witter-Merithew, A. (1986). Claiming our destiny, Part 2. *RID Views*, November, 3–4.

Woodward, J. (1972). Implications for sociolinguistics research among the Deaf. *Sign Language Studies, 1*, 1–7.

Woodward, J. (1973). Some characteristics of Pidgin Sign English. *Sign Language Studies, 3*, 39–46.

Wray, A., Trott, K., & Bloomer, A. (1998). *Projects in linguistics: A practical guide to researching language*. London, United Kingdom: Hodder Headline Group.

Wurm, S. (2014). Deconstructing translation and interpreting prototypes: A case of written-to-signed-language translation. *Translation Studies*. DOI: 10.1080/14781700.2013.819293

Zimmer, J. (1989). Toward a description of register variation in American Sign Language. In C. Lucas (Ed.), *The sociolinguistics of the Deaf community* (pp. 253–272). San Diego, CA: Academic Press.

Index

Figures and tables are indicated by "f" and "t" following page numbers.

sociolinguistic factors within, 43,
149, 166
translation styles and, 12, 105
distinct bilinguals, x
dynamic equivalence, 3

education. *See* Deaf education;
training for interpreters
educational interpreting, 75–83.
See also university lecture
interpreting
additions in, 81–82
competencies required for, 77–79
demand for, 75
free vs. literal, 79–81, 82–83
intelligibility of language in,
69–70
interpreter qualifications for,
156–60, 163–65
omissions in, 79–80, 81
roles and responsibilities in, 75,
76–77
educational strategy of language
production, 151–52
Eighinger, L., 84
empowerment strategy of language
production, 151, 152
enculturation, 10, 15, 17
English, Signed, 14, 14n1, 27–28, 70,
71
Enkvist, N. E., 61
equivalence
cultural, 11, 26, 56, 60, 119–20
dynamic, 3
in free interpretation, 10, 119–20
lexical, 90
linguistic, 11, 26, 56, 119–20
errors, omissions as, 58–61, 66, 154
error taxonomy, 58, 59
ethnographic transliteration, 80
expanded renditions, 62
expository monologues, 32
extralinguistic interference, 43, 44
eye contact, 18

Fabbro, F., 46
facial expressions, 19
facilitator of communication model, 3
familiarity, omission patterns and,
126–32, 127f, 131t, 153
feedback, 43, 46, 99n2
field of discourse, 21
Finegan, E., 23, 24
fingerspelling
in ASL, 30–31, 112
in Auslan, 31, 112, 169
in BSL, 112, 169
code-mixing and, 55–56
in free interpretation, 113, 114,
114t, 115, 116
lexically dense text and, 39
in literal interpretation, 113–14,
114t, 116, 141
in manual representation of English,
14n1
situational variation and, 70
translation styles and, 112–16, 114t
in university lecture interpreting
study, 112–16, 114t, 149
Fischer, T., 44
Fleischer, L., 90
Fontana, S., 30
foreigner talk, 30, 30n2
formal register, 24, 25, 26, 28, 70
frame theory, 7–8, 50, 52, 53, 124
free interpretation
benefits of using, 8, 11, 148–49
blending with literal interpretation,
xviii, 147–48, 149–50
of BSL, 51–53
of culturally sensitive information,
52n2, 147
defined, 10, 12, 103, 173
in educational settings, 79–80
equivalence in, 10, 119–20, 148
examples of, 103–4, 173–74
fingerspelling in, 113, 114, 114t,
115, 116
interpreter training on, 164–65

Kluwin, T., 34
knowledge. *See* cultural knowledge; linguistic knowledge
knowledge-based coping strategies, 45, 47–51, 63
knowledge elicitation, 101
knowledge-lean skills, 77
knowledge-rich skills, 77
Kopczynski, A., 58–60

lag time
defined, xii
metalinguistic awareness and, 61
omissions and, xx, 59, 60–61
Lakoff, G., 32, 36
Lambert, S., 46
Lane, H., 13
language
context of situation and use of. 20–23
pidgin, 29, 30
signed. *See* signed languages
situational variation in. *See* situational language variation
source, xi, 2
target, xi, 2
worldwide variations of, ix
written vs. spoken, 35–38
language contact, xviii, 29, 54–56
Lawrence, R., 83–84
Lawson, L., 28
lectures. *See also* university lecture interpreting
defined, 32
discourse markers in, 34–35
lexical density of, 33, 35, 36, 37, 38
modes of speech production in, 32–33
register used in, 33, 35
Lee, R., 3
lexical density
interpreting for, 37–40
of lectures, 33, 35, 36, 37, 38, 155

omission patterns and, 132–35, 134–35*t*
in written vs. spoken language, 35–38
lexical equivalence, 90
lexical omissions, xx, 60, 61
lexical words, 36–37, 98, 115
linguistic coping strategies
defined, xv, 147
linguistic and cultural knowledge as, 47–51, 63
metalinguistic awareness and, 45–47, 48, 65, 136
omissions as. *See* omissions
transference skills as, 56, 115, 116
translation styles as. *See* translation styles
for university lecture interpreting, 40
linguistic equivalence, 11, 26, 56, 119–20
linguistic interference, 43, 44, 54–55, 56, 116
linguistic knowledge
in conference interpreting, 69
as coping strategy, 47–51, 63
metacognitive strategies and, 123
linguistic repertoire, 23, 24
linguistic transference, 54–56, 112–16, 147, 149–50, 152
linguistic transliteration, 80
lipreading, 14, 52
literal interpretation
blending with free interpretation, xviii, 147–48, 149–50
of bsl, 52–53
defined, 10, 104, 174
in educational settings, 79–81, 82–83
environmental considerations for, 12
examples of, 104, 174
fingerspelling in, 113–14, 114*t*, 116, 141
interpreter training on, 164–65
linguistic markers of, 174

conscious unintentional. *See* conscious unintentional omissions
defined, 57
delay, xx, 58
educational background and, 118–19, 119–20t, 120, 125, 160
in educational interpreting, 79–80, 81
as errors, 58–61, 66, 154
familiarity and patterns of, 126–32, 127f, 131t, 153
interpreter training on, 165
lag time and, xx, 59, 60–61
in lecture interpretations, 117–20t, 117–26, 122–25t, 129–30, 131t, 153, 188
lexical, xx, 60, 61
lexical density and patterns of, 132–35, 134–35t, 153–55
in linguistic decision-making process, 40, 135
metalinguistic awareness of, 46–47, 63, 66, 136–37, 148, 156
as mistakes, 58, 60
morphological, xx, 60, 61
obligatory, 59
optional, 59, 60
rendition categories and, xxi, 62–63
skipping, xx, 58
strategic, xix, xxi, 57, 61–63
taxonomies for, xx, 58–60, 64–65, 66, 117
translation styles and, 119–20, 120t, 121, 125
types of, xx, 57, 58, 64–65
unconscious. *See* unconscious omissions
open-ended problems, 44
oppression of Deaf community, 5, 13, 14, 15
optional omissions, 59, 60
oralism, 14
Ozolins, U., 85

Padden, C., xiv–xvn2, 13, 15
paradox of neutrality, 49–50
paternalism, 15
Patrie, C., 85, 163
Paul, P. V., 76
performance errors, 58, 59
Perner, J., 46
perseveration technique, 28
Peterson, R., 122–23, 165–66
Phillip, M. J., 16
pidgin languages, 29, 30
Pöchhacker, Franz, xix
Pollitt, K., 16, 149, 150
pragmatic transliteration, 80
Pratt, C., 45
preparatory coping strategies, 42–43, 160–61
problem solving
    creative, 41, 44–45
    spontaneous, 43–45, 65
professionalization of interpreters, xiii–xiv, 15–16, 52
psycholinguistic model, xii, 2
purist strategy of language production, 151
Pym, A., xxi

Qian, H., 49
Quigley, S. P., 76

Rawlings, B. W., 13
reading aloud, as mode of speech production, 32–33
reduced renditions, xxi, 62–63
reduplication additions, 82
reflective journaling, 43
reflective practice, xxi
register
    consultative, 24, 25–26
    discourse environment and, 86
    formal, 24, 25, 26, 28, 70
    frozen, 24, 25
    informal, 24, 26
    intimate, 24, 26

dominant, xviii
educational background and,
    111–12, 111*t,* 160
fingerspelling and, 112–16, 114*t*
free. *See* free interpretation
language contact phenomena and,
    54–56
in lecture interpretations, 103–5,
    107–16, 148–50, 174–87
linguistic transference and, 112–16,
    147
literal. *See* literal interpretation
metalinguistic awareness and, 56
moving between, xix
omissions and, 119–20, 120*t,* 121,
    125
sociolinguistic considerations and,
    166
transliteration, xviii*n*1, 10, 79–82, 90.
    See also literal interpretation
Traynor, N., 157
Turner, G. H., 42
turn-taking sequences, impact of
    interpreters on, 47–49

unconscious omissions
    defined, 64–65
    example of, 57
    hypotheses regarding, 96
    in lecture interpretations, 117–18,
        124–26, 125*t,* 129–30, 131,
        153
university lecture interpreting, 83–92.
    See also educational
    interpreting; university lecture
    interpreting study
    access issues in, 89–90
    adaptations necessary for, 20, 39
    areas of analysis in, xvii–xxii
    competencies required for, 84–85,
        87, 91–92
    efficiency of, 86–87
    familiarity and preparation for,
        83–84, 160–61

free, 39–40, 107–11, 111*t*
intelligibility of language in, 69–70
interpreter qualifications for, 156,
    158, 159–60, 163–65
linguistic coping strategies for, 40
literal, 39–40, 90, 107, 110,
    111–12, 111*t*
miscommunication in, 88
overview, xiv
register in, 25, 28
roles and responsibilities in, 84
sociolinguistic/sociocultural
    considerations in, 39
subject matter considerations in,
    83–84, 85, 91, 143–44, 156,
    159
user expectations of, 74–75, 140
university lecture interpreting study,
    94–146
conclusions regarding, 161–63
data analysis, 102–6
educational background as factor
    in, 137–39, 156, 158, 159–60
fingerspelling in, 112–16, 114*t,* 149
future research needs arising from,
    167–70
implications of, 163–66
interpreters selected for, 96–97
limitations of, 166–67
metalinguistic awareness in, 136–37
methodology, 98–102
omission patterns in, 126–35, 127*f,*
    131*t,* 134–35*t*
omission types in, 117–26, 117–20*t,*
    122–25*t,* 129–30, 131*t,* 153,
    188
reliability checks in, 105–6
research questions and hypotheses,
    94–96
sociolinguistic and sociocultural
    influences in, 137–39
source text for, 97–98
transcription conventions in,
    171–72

translation styles in, 103–5, 107–16,
148–50, 174–87
user expectations in, 139–46
Ure, J., 36, 37, 98, 133

Valli, C., 29, 30, 31
Viera, J. A., 82, 83, 140

Wadensjö, C., xx–xxi, 6, 62, 63
Wardhaugh, R., 23
Wells, J., 76–77

Wilcox, P., 7
Wilcox, S., 7
Williams, K., 78
Wilson, D., xix$n$2
Winston, E., 80–81
Woodward, J., xiv–xv$n$2, 27, 29
World Federation of the Deaf,
157

zero renditions, xxi, 62
Zimmer, J., 23, 27, 28–29, 34